The Theory and Practice
of Vocal Psychotherapy

The Theory and Practice of Vocal Psychotherapy

Songs of the Self

Diane Austin

Jessica Kingsley Publishers
London and Philadelphia

First published in 2008
by Jessica Kingsley Publishers
116 Pentonville Road
London N1 9JB, UK
and
400 Market Street, Suite 400
Philadelphia, PA 19106, USA

www.jkp.com

Library of Congress Cataloging in Publication Data
Austin, Diane (Diane S.)
  The theory and practice of vocal psychotherapy : songs of the self / Diane Austin.
    p. cm.
  ISBN 978-1-84310-878-8 (pb : alk. paper) 1. Singing--Therapeutic use. 2. Voice--Therapeutic use. 3. Psychotherapy and music. I. Title.
  ML3920.A97 2009
  615.8'5154--dc22
                                                    2008048909

British Library Cataloguing in Publication Data
A CIP catalogue record for this book is available from the British Library

ISBN 978 1 84310 878 8

To Robby for being there.
To Robin for being.
And to my clients, without whom
there would be no book.

Contents

Introduction   11

Part I: Theoretical Foundations
of Vocal Psychotherapy   15

1. The Voice   17
   The vocal connection between mother and child   21
   The lost voice   23
   Reconnection: The breath   24
   Natural sounds   27
   Toning   29
   Case example: Suzy   31
   The music in the speaking voice   32

2. Contributions from Jungian Psychology   38
   The wounded healer   40
   Parts of the self, complexes and archetypes   41
   Case example: Terry   44
   Case example: Susan   47

3. Contributions from Object Relations Theory   52
   Case example: Donna   56

4. Contributions from Trauma Theory   60

5. Contributions from Intersubjectivity   79
   Therapist's self-disclosure   86

6. The Primacy of Countertransference 88
The wise wound 92
Diving deep and surfacing 96
The therapist's hook 101
The musical hook 104
Sharing countertransference 105

Part II: Clinical Practice
of Vocal Psychotherapy *111*

7. Beginning a Practice 113
Setting the stage 113
Assessment 114
Warm-up 117
Music and words 118
Layers of listening 119

8. Resistance in Vocal Psychotherapy 123
Resistance to singing 124
Resistance in the music 126
Working through resistance 127
Therapists' resistance 129

9. Vocal Interventions 131
Breathing 132
Case example: Karen 132
Natural sounds and toning 133
Chanting 135
Vocal improvisation 136
Case example: Liz 142

10. Vocal Holding Techniques 146
Case example: Vicky 153

11. Free Associative Singing — 158
    Case example: Michelle — 162
    Adaptations of free associative singing — 164
    Resourcing — 165
    Free associative singing in supervision — 170
    Case example: Brenda — 171
    Psychodramatic singing — 173
    The empty chair — 175

12. Songs — 178
    Listening to songs — 181
    Case example: Leslie — 184
    Your inner soundtrack — 184
    Case example: Liz — 186
    Songs from the therapist — 188
    Songs from the client — 190
    Case example: Sue — 190

13. The Therapeutic Process: Connection — 193
    The therapist's need to connect — 194
    The client's need to connect to the therapist — 196
    Making connections: The therapist's inner process — 198
    Making connections: Client's insight — 200
    Disconnection and connection: Feelings — 204
    Disconnection and connection: Parts of the self — 206
    Spiritual connection — 210

Final thoughts — 213
    REFERENCES — 214
    SUBJECT INDEX — 218
    AUTHOR INDEX — 224

Introduction

She sits at the piano and tells her story
A child in a grown-up body.
'I feel like a little girl learning how to walk,' she says
'So vulnerable – what if I slip?'
Her tears fall on the keys and she skips a beat.
'Please don't stop singing,' she says
So I sing and I sing
And we sing till the storm passes over.
'Why is it so powerful?' she asks
'Why does it feel so sad to hear someone sing
"Welcome"?'

One of my first memories is sleeping beneath a piano. My father was playing that night with his jazz trio and my mother couldn't get a babysitter. I awoke in a cocoon of rhythm, melody and harmony, and I must have felt held by the music because throughout my life I have turned to music whenever I have felt lonely or unsafe.

When I was ten or eleven, I made my debut at a jam session. I can still remember the song I sang – 'Where Is Your Heart?' My father accompanied me that day on the piano, as he often would throughout the years at parties, Girl Scout functions and school shows. I loved to sing. I felt so alive when I sang. Sometimes I would lose myself for hours up in the attic, making up songs and pretending I had my own television show. I could block out everything unpleasant when I sang. I could be happy.

I also loved to make sounds, all kinds of sounds. I would imitate animal sounds: monkeys, dolphins, cats and dogs. I liked to scream and hear the sound of my own voice echoing back to me. To me these primal sounds were the music of life and they gave me a way to express things I had no words for.

I acted in my first musical in high school and I thought I had found my calling. After graduating, I attended Emerson College in Boston where I majored in Theatre Arts. The characters I played allowed me to explore unacceptable and unknown parts of myself. The opportunity to express my feelings in song, dance and dialogue provided me with a much needed emotional outlet. Although I did not realize it at the time, performing was very therapeutic for me and would prove to be a valuable resource in the career I would ultimately choose to pursue.

After college I moved to New York and worked in musical theatre but I soon grew disillusioned. I was tired of playing roles. I became aware of a deep longing to know myself. I entered Jungian analysis and my world was turned upside down. Plumbing the depths was terrifying yet worthwhile. I learned that change was slow and painful, but possible, and for me, inevitable.

I formed my own band and began writing songs that reflected the person I was becoming.

> Now I sing out of joy
> And I sing out of pain
> For the battles I've fought
> And the insights I've gained
> For I know deep inside
> That I've got to be free
> And I just can't sing songs
> That mean nothing to me.

It was hard to make a living. Both jobs and salary were unpredictable. I started teaching voice to augment my income. One day after a particularly emotional lesson, I began to think that many of the people who came to me for singing lessons were really looking for permission to feel. Some students associated singing with a time in childhood when they were free to express themselves vocally and take pleasure from it. Others who were emotionally blocked and shut down found singing was a safe way to gain access to their feelings. Because of the safe, non-judgemental structure of the voice lesson and the containing quality of songs, my students were often able to tap into emotions evoked by the deep breathing necessary to sustain tones as well as the emotional associations triggered by the music and the lyrics. Additionally, singing is more widely accepted as a form of expression than screaming, crying, or other displays of strong emotion. The majority of the students I worked with were not looking to become singing stars. They were looking for themselves.

It wasn't long before a box of Kleenex tissues appeared on the piano. I remember the day I told my therapist that when I taught voice I felt like I was doing therapy. He asked me if I had ever heard of music therapy. Could it be true? The two subjects I loved the most – combined!

In 1986 I graduated from New York University with a Master of Arts in Music Therapy. By the time I graduated I had experience working with a wide variety of people with various clinical needs: blind, autistic and developmentally delayed children, psychiatric adults, women in prison, and battered women and children. The voice was my primary instrument and singing proved effective with every population.

Throughout my studies, I also continued teaching voice to adults but my approach evolved into therapeutic singing lessons with a focus as much on self-expression and self-exploration as vocal technique. It soon became apparent to me that my 'students' were becoming 'clients' and therapeutic singing lessons were becoming vocal music therapy.

I gradually realized I wanted to work in more depth, to be qualified to practise the kind of psychotherapy I was benefiting from, to integrate the ideas and theories of depth psychology with the practice of music therapy, using the voice in particular. I knew that my personal therapy and supervision would not be enough to take me where I wanted to go, so I pursued Institute training and later a Doctorate in Music Therapy.

This book is the culmination of more than 20 years' experience as a music psychotherapist in private practice with adolescents and adults, during which I have been practising and refining my own model: Vocal Psychotherapy. Vocal Psychotherapy is the use of the breath, sounds, vocal improvisation, songs and dialogue within a client–therapist relationship to promote intrapsychic and interpersonal growth and change.

I will discuss the theoretical underpinnings that integrate the physical, psychological and spiritual benefits of singing, with theories from the fields of psychology, traumatology, addiction treatment and psychodrama. Case examples from my work in private practice will illustrate how vocal psychotherapy can be used with clients who suffer from a variety of symptoms resulting from unmet childhood needs, as well as clients with histories of emotional, physical and sexual abuse, addiction, or developmental arrests associated with being children of alcoholics or dysfunctional families. All names have been changed to protect the clients' identities. The examples will illuminate the ways in which a combination of singing, vocal improvisation and talking can be used in different stages of the healing process to retrieve, experience and integrate feelings, images and memories from the unconscious while providing a powerful reparative experience.

This book will also provide practical information, illustrating breathing, toning, and vocal improvisation exercises, along with a variety of ways to work therapeutically with songs. Vocal improvisation techniques I created and codified, such as 'Vocal Holding', 'Free Associative Singing' and 'Psychodramatic Singing', will be described in detail with examples of the ways in which these techniques work to help clients recover split-off, dissociated aspects of themselves. These parts of the personality can then be related to and gradually integrated through singing and verbal processing, resulting in a more complete, cohesive sense of self and identity.

Part I

Theoretical Foundations
of Vocal Psychotherapy

CHAPTER I

The Voice

'Hi Diane,' Cindy greets me with a smile as she enters the room. She puts her bags on the floor, comes over to the piano and sits on the bench next to my chair. She makes eye contact with me while asking if she can have a glass of water. I say 'sure' and get one from the kitchen for her.

She seems to have thought about what she needs from today's session. She says, 'I have a sense that there is a huge scream stuck in my throat.' She had a dream about this stifled scream and believes the way to access it is through vocal improvisation therapy.

She tells me the scream feels related to her history of early sexual abuse by her uncle. She also talks about feeling angry toward her mother and disappointed with her father. She feels her parents emotionally abandoned her and tells me she feels ready to 'get the scream out and deal with the pain'.

As she talks, I notice that she speaks slowly and sighs occasionally. Her voice lacks energy and the melody of her sentences often descends at the end. She sounds slightly depressed to me.

We have spent several sessions taking her history. I feel it is important for her to tell her story slowly with time for us to interact and relate to the material and each other. I have learned through experience that very wounded people can become traumatized when they have to condense a lifetime of painful and intense memories into an hour-long therapy session. Going slowly helps them to digest the feelings that emerge.

I ask Cindy if she feels like singing. I want to get a sense of her music and her singing voice. I also sense that her words are disconnected from her feelings. I think singing can offer her a way to access and express some of the emotions contained in the memories and incidents she has been describing.

Cindy has many strengths and both inner and outer resources, but I am wary of her enthusiasm to 'get the scream out'. It seems too soon in the process to work deeply. I offer her choices: 'We could tone, sing a song or improvise over chords.' She says, 'I'm a little afraid of improvising…but…yeah, let's try it.'

I ask her what she is afraid of and she says she's not sure, 'probably just the unknown of it…maybe the closeness'. She repeats, 'let's try it'. I ask her what chords she would like. She says, 'I like the key of D flat.' I begin playing D flat to G flat/B flat, medium tempo and dynamics. Cindy likes this combination. I suggest that we begin by breathing together several times and that whenever she feels ready she can begin singing sounds or words.

I feel curious. What will it be like to sing together? She sighs; we sing 'ah' in unison on an F then we move to a B flat. I sing in unison to support her vocally and emotionally. I am also 'feeling out' her response to the unison to get a sense of what she needs and what she feels comfortable with. (Is unison comforting, supportive or too merged? Does she need more tension, more distance, more differentiation?)

She begins to sing softly, 'm-m-m', then starts growling, increasing the dynamics, range and intensity of her sounds. I sing in unison with her then mirror (repeat) her sounds and at times hold the tonic to ground her vocalization. My intention is to accompany her on this journey so that she feels supported and met in the music.

She begins to sing long, legato phrases on 'ah'. She goes rapidly up the scale like a siren and then switches to intricate rhythmic patterns, syncopated 'da da, ba da' repetitive, drum-like sounds on E flat.

She seems to be exploring her range, different rhythms, vocal qualities and emotional states. I notice that she has a well-trained voice with a deep rich quality and a wide vocal range. At times it is difficult to follow her. I feel challenged yet determined to stay with her. I am living in the unknown of the moment with her and I don't know where we are going. I notice that she is changing dynamics, phrasing, pitch and vocal qualities rapidly. I am trying to stay with her and meet her laughter, screams, and gentle melodies. Now I change the chords slightly, adding some dissonant notes, and play the piano louder to support her screams and growls.

Cindy begins singing louder, then laughs and returns to the 'm-m-m' sound in the lower part of her range. She builds on a simple melodic line of repeated thirds and fourths and works her way up the scale ending with a loud scream on 'ah'. She then slides down the scale and is quiet for a moment. She breathes deeply and returns to 'm-m-m', now singing softly and rocking herself back and forth. I notice she is crying.

I rock back and forth with her and attune myself to her breathing, phrasing, dynamics and vocal quality. I notice how similar our voices sound. She stops singing but continues rocking back and forth and breathing deeply. I continue to sing and rock back and forth with her. I would usually stop singing when the client stops but Cindy is still crying and rocking herself and I feel like continuing to sing, probably because I sense that she needs this holding and containment. I feel I am soothing her. I sing 'ooo' to a melodic refrain built around A flat, B flat, D flat, A flat for a few minutes, then slow down the tempo and gradually bring the music to a close. Cindy has stopped crying.

I breathe deeply. I do not speak. My intention is to leave space for us to be in the silence together and to allow her to speak in her own time. After a few moments Cindy says, 'That was good... I feel more present now...more grounded... I really needed to get that out.'

The voice is a primary instrument in music therapy. It is the instrument we are born with, the body's own voice. Yet there is an obvious lack of literature addressing the physical, emotional, psychological and spiritual benefits of using the voice and singing in therapy and the effectiveness of vocal interventions in music psychotherapy. This is surprising since sounding and singing have been a way to communicate, express ourselves and create ritual and community since ancient times.

Throughout the years I have noticed that whenever I attend a music therapy conference, supervise a student or listen to a colleague's work, the most compelling clinical examples involve the client and therapist singing. In my own practice, I have also noticed that the most climactic moments occur when clients begin singing. They have powerful feelings, insights and memories, and make deep connections to themselves and to me. When I sing to or with clients, it is usually experienced as extremely moving and often melts away their defences so that blocked feelings can be released.

No matter what population a therapist works with – infants in neo-natal care, children with special needs, adolescents at risk, psychiatric adults, geriatrics or hospice patients – and no matter what the therapist's primary instrument may be, the most healing connections seem to occur through the voice.

Why is singing such a powerful therapeutic experience? When we sing, our voices and our bodies are the instruments. We are intimately connected to the source of the sound and the vibrations. We make the music, we are immersed in the music and we are the music. We breathe deeply to sustain the tones we create and our heart rate slows down and our nervous system is calmed. Our voices resonate inward to help us connect to our bodies and express our emotions and they resonate outward to help us connect to others.

The human voice is the most versatile of all instruments in that its resonances can be continuously changed by movements of the larynx, jaw, tongue and lips (Jourdain 1997). Singing is also a neuromuscular activity and muscular patterns are closely linked to psychological patterns and emotional response (Newham 1998). According to Levine (1997), the residue of unresolved, un-discharged energy gets trapped in the nervous system and creates the debilitating symptoms associated with trauma.

Children raised in families where the emphasis is on looking good and performing well learn early in life that their instinctual responses are not valued or acceptable. These feelings are chronically locked into the musculature of the body. Authentic feelings are cut off from the instincts and are not expressed or lived but remain in the unconscious where they wreak havoc by showing up as somatic symptoms or self-defeating behaviour. According to Woodman (1985), her female patients who have body issues and have never fully lived out their sexuality have energy blocks in their pelvis and thighs. When these blocks are released, sexual energy is able to flow through the entire body and women who had looked for cuddling and holding from men no longer try to turn their lovers into mothers.

When we sing we produce vibrations that nurture the body and massage our insides (Keyes 1973). Internally resonating vibrations break up and release blockages of energy, releasing feelings and allowing a natural flow of vitality and a state of equilibrium to return to the body. These benefits are particularly relevant to clients who have frozen, numbed-off areas in the body that hold traumatic experience.

Singing can provide clients with an opportunity to express the inexpressible, to give voice to the whole range of their feelings. Singing meaningful songs often produces a catharsis, an emotional release, due to the effect of the music, the lyrics and the memories and associations connected with the song.

The self is revealed through the sound and characteristics of the voice. The process of finding one's voice, one's own sound, is a metaphor for finding one's self.

From a scientific perspective, research has shown that singing improves our health. Researchers in the US, England, Canada and Germany have found that singing can improve one's mood by stimulating endorphin release. Singing is also able to relieve stress and boost the immune system. In a research study at the University of Frankfurt scientists found that after singing Mozart's Requiem for an hour, choir members' blood tests showed significantly increased concentrations of immunoglobin A (proteins in the immune system which function as antibodies) and hydrocortisone (an anti-stress hormone). A week later, when researchers asked members of the choir to listen to a recording of the Requiem without singing, the composition of choir members' blood did not change significantly (Clift and Hancox 2001). Other research conducted with choirs has also shown the positive health benefits of singing (Hunter 1982; Krutz et al. 2004; Weinberger 1996). Singing and making music have also been linked to lower heart rate and decreased blood pressure (Gaynor 1999).

Researchers at the University of Manchester have discovered a tiny organ in the ear, the sacculus, which forms part of the balance-regulating vestibular system in the inner ear and responds to musical frequencies. It is stimulated by low frequency, high intensity sounds like singing (sound levels in the larynx have been estimated to be as high as 130 decibels) and relays these sounds to parts of the brain that register pleasure. Your ear and your brain tend to find your singing pleasurable, even if others do not agree (Weinberger 1996).

On a similar note, in an experiment conducted by scientists at McGill University in Canada, listening to or singing a favourite piece of music stimulated the areas of the participant's brain that release dopamine and other euphoria-inducing opioids. The sounds produced chills of pleasure in the participants (Harkins 2005).

The vocal connection between mother and child

We enter the world and, with our first sound, announce our arrival. Our first cry proclaims our birth and the life force flowing through us. We begin as vital, spontaneous beings, curious and open, and the sounds we make express this. We laugh, we cry, we scream. We make sounds instinctively and receive pleasure from playing with our lips, tongue and vocal cords. There is a flow, a freedom to the sounds and movements we make that characterizes spontaneity and health.

We are also born listeners. The ear is the first sensory organ to develop and is functional four and a half months before we are born (Minson 1992). The voice is a primary source of connection between mother and child. 'During gestation, the human fetus receives musical and other sound stimuli from vibrations transmitted through amniotic fluid' (Taylor 1997, p.24). The sounds we hear in the womb, the rhythm of our mother's heartbeat, the flow of her breathing, and the nuances of her voice 'stimulate our brain and fire electrical charges into our cortex' (Minson 1992, p.92). These electrical charges provide nourishment that is critical to the development of the brain and the central nervous system (Minson 1992; Storr 1992; Tomatis 1991).

After birth, the bonding between mother and child occurs through touch, eye contact and sound (Miller 1981). Babies naturally tune in to the music of their mother's voice and, optimally, the mother is attuned to her child's sounds and learns to distinguish the nuances of the different sounds and the needs they convey. In a mutual, co-created dance of sounds and movements, mother and baby feel a sense of oneness. The infant feels safe and begins to trust the mother and 'the mother receives the instinctive reassurance that will help her understand and answer her child's messages' (Miller 1987, p.33).

Somewhere between the third and fourth month, infants produce sounds that resemble singing. The infant's babbling or singing as he or she settles down to sleep provides feelings of self-sufficiency and preserves the illusion of a comforting, soothing mother (Winnicott 1965). At about six months of age, babies enter the lalling period and move their lips and tongue rhythmically making sounds like 'la-la-la' (Moses 1954). During this stage babies are not trying to communicate; they are simply enjoying the pleasurable sensation of repeating simple syllables. 'Voice production in this wordless age leaves solely agreeable memories…[and] is practically unlimited. Happiness and displeasure can be expressed over endless periods, no hoarseness will interfere. The breathing capacity does not seem to have limits; it functions ideally' (Moses 1954, p.19).

During this same period, babies begin to recognize the sound of their mother's voice. The mother's voice is like a cord that connects the child to its life source and provides the positive intrauterine and post-birth experiences so essential to the child's ability to bond with others. The vocal interaction in speech and song between mother and child is critical to the child's developing sense of self. This sound connection reflects the emotional and psychological relationship between the mother and her child (Minson 1992; Moses 1954; Newham 1994, 1998).

As Moses (1954) points out, children go through periods of identification, imitation, borrowing and eventual acceptance while finding and becoming themselves. The vocal process, he says, reflects these same stages. Likewise, when emotions are blocked or inhibited by the intellect, the voice reflects this blockage. There is no longer any direct contact with emotional impulses.

As we grow and become ourselves, our voices reflect the changes we undergo. The sounds we make, the language we use and the music in our voices reveal much about who we are – the different aspects of our personalities, our feeling states, our emotional and psychological blocks and our comfort or discomfort in our bodies (Austin 1999b). Our contact with the outside world is largely a function of our voices, whether we are sighing, groaning, yawning, laughing, crying, shouting, speaking or singing.

The lost voice

As children continue to grow and develop, they are affected by the spoken and unspoken messages they receive from the significant people in their lives. One client I work with was told by her father, 'If you cry, I'll hit you even harder.' Of course, this client now has a very difficult time not only crying, but also vocally expressing herself in any form. When I began working with her, she spoke in a barely audible voice and sped through her sentences as if someone was chasing her.

Another client, Emily, had a mother who became very ill when Emily was eight years old. Emily had to be quiet in the house and could not have friends over to play because her mother was not to be disturbed. Unconsciously, Emily took in the message that she had to stifle her feelings and sounds of excitement and joy. 'Not just because I couldn't make noise, it was more than that... How could I allow myself to feel alive when everything around me felt dead?' In high school, Emily finally found a safe place to express herself. She came to life on stage singing roles in school musicals. After graduating from high school, Emily began to get jobs as a professional singer. However, when her mother died Emily stopped singing. Through vocal psychotherapy, Emily gradually began to express her grief, anger and the playful part of her personality. Eventually she allowed herself to sing publicly again, this time from a more authentic place.

Many of us lose our individual voices, sometimes subtly and gradually without even realizing it is happening and sometimes not so subtly. When our feelings and needs are judged or ignored, we learn to judge or ignore them. We shut down for self-preservation. Vital parts of the personality that represent our true voices are hidden away because it is not safe to express what we really think and feel. We fear disapproval, anger, tears, abandonment. If and when it is finally safe to come out, we no longer have the ability to voice our feelings and the authentic parts of who we are (Austin 2001, 2002; Miller 1981).

Our emotions are blocked and censored, and our voices reflect the blockage. 'As long as we are emotionally protective our breathing cannot be free...the voice will depend on compensating strength in the throat and mouth muscles' (Linklater 1976, p.12). When we do feel a spontaneous impulse, it is short-circuited by a secondary, inhibiting one. These secondary impulses become habitual and familiar and what is familiar feels safe. Natural impulses become difficult to trust because they are unfamiliar and unknown. Spontaneity is hard to access because it can become associated with the fear of loss of control and judgement. Additionally, neuromuscular patterns develop into habits that cut us off from our instinctual connection between emotion and breath (Linklater 1976). Our breathing becomes constricted and our vocal range becomes limited. That child who was once so alive playing in a free-flowing stream of sounds, movements and emotions is lost to us.

I have learned over the years that children who are raised in an atmosphere of fear, hostility, violence or neglect have been silenced. Sometimes this silence takes the form of withdrawing into a private world and choosing not to communicate because it is not safe to do so. Sometimes the silence is selective; some things are allowed to be talked about, some feelings are allowed expression and others clearly are not. Sometimes the silence is loud; words and feelings come tumbling out but fall on deaf ears or are beaten down and stifled. Needs and feelings remain unmet and the voice becomes inaudible, tight and tense, breathy and undefined, or simply untrue; perhaps lovely to listen to but not connected to the core of the person. In essence, a wounded person often survives by forfeiting his or her own voice.

Reconnection: The breath

Recovering one's true voice requires re-inhabiting the body. The first step in reconnecting to the body-self is learning to breathe deeply. It is interesting to note that the Greek word 'psyche' means both soul and to breathe. Breath is the life force that connects the mind, body and spirit. Mindfulness of the breath is so healing that it is common to all meditative and prayer traditions. Singing facilitates deep breathing. In order to sustain tones, one has to take in more air, thus expanding the belly and diaphragm, and then fully release the breath in order to continue the process.

There is reciprocity between the physiological and the psychological effects of breathing. Cutting off the breath by constricting the throat, chest or abdomen can sever the connection to feelings and dramatically affect the quality of both the speaking and singing voice (Austin 1986, 1991, 2001). Many people, including singers, have difficulty breathing freely. Some singers have been so overly or incorrectly trained that breathing is a highly arduous and self-conscious act.

Often, however, we unconsciously breathe shallowly to control our feelings. This only worsens the situation by creating oxygen deprivation and increased tension that heightens the stress response. Feelings are numbed or dissociated and remain unexpressed. Anxiety stays trapped inside, blocking the natural energy flow and triggering more physiological and psychological arousal resulting in increased anxiety and emotional shutdown leading to depression or psychosomatic illness (Braddock 1995; Gaynor 1999; Moses 1954).

The ability or inability to deeply inhale and exhale reflects our personality traits and psychological issues. Can we relax enough to fully take in what is occurring in the moment? Can we let go of the feelings we are holding? Can we trust our bodies to sustain the life force or do we push, force and constrict our bodies and our breath out of lack of trust or misconceptions of the breathing process? Can we allow our breath to come naturally from its own instinctual source with full power and resonance? As one client expressed it:

> I was surprised by how difficult it was to breathe without forcing it...as we continued with the deep breathing, I felt as if a knife were lodged in my lower chest. I began sighing deeply and as I slowly began to let the air flow in and out of my body I was filled with grief.

Few people hear their own voices because fear, blocked grief and rage keep the voice in the throat. 'In those brief moments when we do manage to free our authentic voices, the whole being resonates with that truth, and a marriage of personal and transpersonal is palpable in the environment' (Woodman 1985, p.64).

The way we breathe influences how we feel and what we feel has a direct effect on how we breathe. According to Gaynor (1999), 'breathing is much more than a mechanical reflex for oxygen exchange; it is the basis for all of our cellular functions, our energetic well being, even our emotional health' (pp.56–57). When we breathe deeply, we produce a current of energy that can be channelled to parts of the body that need soothing, tension release, and revitalization. Deep breathing slows the heart rate and calms and nurtures the nervous system. It stills the mind and body, relaxing the musculature and creating an experience of groundedness. The relaxed, centred state that results is beneficial to everyone but especially helpful to anyone in a state of panic or anxiety who may be hyperventilating or breathing in short, shallow bursts (Austin 1999a, 1999b, 2001, 2006; Braddock 1995; Gardner 1990; Newham 1998).

The free breath is a deep breath that flows effortlessly throughout our entire being. It is not a manipulated breath we may have learned from concepts taught by some teachers or described in many books, or a habitual breath we have become accustomed to. It is a natural breath that accesses our life energy and sets the rhythm for our own unique songs.

Breathing exercise

A breathing exercise that I often use, especially with clients who suffer from anxiety, is one that I learned from my yoga teacher. It is called alternate nostril breathing. I usually do the exercise with a client after I have explained and demonstrated it. We prepare by sitting opposite each other on chairs and keeping the head and spine in a straight, upright position. The feet are planted firmly on the ground. We begin by bringing the right hand to the nose and covering the right nostril with the right thumb and inhaling through the left nostril. We then cover the left nostril with the right index finger and exhale through the right nostril. We keep the index finger covering the left nostril and inhale through the right nostril. Again we cover the right nostril with the right thumb and exhale through the left nostril. We then inhale and switch sides so that we are exhaling and inhaling through one nostril then switching to the opposite nostril and continuing to exhale and inhale on that side. We continue this breathing pattern for several minutes.

When clients become comfortable with this exercise, I may suggest a more advanced version in which the exhalation is prolonged. We count to five as we inhale, then work up to ten as we exhale. The idea is to ultimately double the time given to the exhalation. Another variation is to count to five on the inhalation, hold the breath (both nostrils closed) for a count of five, and then exhale while counting (eventually) to ten.

Imagery can be useful, for example, asking clients to imagine they are inhaling their favourite colour or fragrance or something they need to take in and then imagine they are exhaling stress, stale air, or something they want to release. Encourage them to allow the whole body to feel the effects of the breath. Feel how the breath animates the body, from the top of the head to the tips of the toes.

Exhalation is the most relaxing part of the breath cycle and promotes the release of feelings that are being held on to. Deep exhalation empties the body of all stale air and makes it ready to receive fresh air. The nervous system is quieted and clients are able to sink down deep into their bodies and relax, thus making it easier to be emotionally present in the moment and reach a state of relative balance.

Natural sounds

Before we speak we cry, moan, babble and play with the sounds our own bodies create. I define natural sounds as sounds the body emits spontaneously, sounds that are instinctive expressions of what we are experiencing at any given moment, such as a gasp of surprise, a sigh of pleasure, a yawn, a sneeze, a groan, a whine, a laugh, a cry or a scream. As stated previously, just as we restrain our breathing in order to control our feelings, many of us consciously or unconsciously learn to control and repress our instinctive impulses and the sounds that accompany them out of fear of judgement, rejection or harm.

As we begin to allow our natural sounds to emerge, the result may be primal sounds of emotions long repressed (Rugenstein 1992). These sounds may cause anxiety because they reflect parts of the self we have abandoned or neglected. This occurs because significant people in our lives judged or abandoned them, leading us to believe these parts and their sounds are not acceptable. It follows that we may have difficulty recognizing and accepting these aspects of ourselves and their accompanying sounds and emotions. Accessing, relating to, and gradually integrating these parts of our personalities enlarges and strengthens our sense of who we are and opens the door to a richer, more fulfilling life. This journey toward wholeness is what Jung referred to as the individuation process (Austin 1986, 1991, 1993, 1996, 1999a, 2004; Jacobi 1965; Jung 1916).

Breathing exercises can help clients relax and settle deeper into their bodies and are a good way to prepare for working with vocal sounds. For some clients a playful approach is helpful. A game can provide an activity with a focus that is not on sounding 'good' but is geared toward having fun while entering unexplored territories. The emphasis is on vocal exploration and the attitude that we can all make sounds. It requires no training and is different from singing. This kind of focus can create a playful space that facilitates a therapeutic regression in order to promote spontaneity and creativity. The emphasis on playing with sounds can help clients stop thinking about what they are *doing* and allow them to be more fully present to what they are *experiencing*.

I find that singing and making sounds naturally can be even more challenging for vocalists and musicians who have had their spontaneity trained out of them. Many classically trained singers and musicians are perfectionists. They have difficulty playing and allowing themselves to make sounds that may not be aesthetically pleasing. Music theory and technique can sometimes get in the way of 'being with' whatever emerges. As one client experienced:

> The wild sounds we were making became more melodic. I wasn't thinking at this point, just doing. I wasn't stopping the flow of emotions by reasoning each sound. Then there was a point where I realized you were singing a fifth and I was on a major third. I slid into a minor third and toyed with that which got me thinking. The minute I started thinking, the flow of energy moving through my body went away as easily as it had come.

When I work with groups, I introduce an exercise by modelling it. I always say, 'I won't ask you to do anything I won't do.' I have found that my willingness to explore primitive or silly sounds makes it safer for others to take risks vocally and emotionally. Combining sounds with movements helps to keep people from thinking and responding from conditioning and habit while enabling them to stay grounded in the body and keep the energy flowing. As they continue to play with and transform sounds and movements, they become vocally and physically freer and more spontaneous. What began as a kinaesthetic exercise leads into more primitive expression and eventually into the entire realm of feelings. What occurs is a mobilization of feelings through breathing, movement and sound.

Name game

The following is one exercise that I use with groups and individuals. I begin by asking everyone to find a comfortable position sitting cross-legged on the floor or in a chair with both feet on the ground. I then suggest the following:

> Close your eyes and breathe deeply. Remember a time when you were young and enjoyed making sounds. Remember the freedom of yelling, screaming and laughing out loud. Move your tongue and see what sounds you can make. Use your lips and teeth and allow yourself to sound silly. Allow yourself to be a child again, to enjoy the sensations you can experience by riding on a vowel like 'eeeeeeeeeeeeee' or being a percussive instrument with consonants like 't-t-t-t-t-t' or 'k-k-k-k-k'. Indulge yourself. Taste the different vowels and consonants and delight in the sensual pleasure of making sounds. Now imagine all the different sounds in your name, all the vowels and consonants, and all the various textures and sensations you can play with. You can explore and enjoy changing the dynamics, the pitch and experimenting with different vocal qualities. Allow the sounds to move you, to rock back and forth, to bang on the floor, to reach for the sky, and most important, don't think!

I always begin by modelling the exercise. I play with the sounds in my name. For example, I might repeat the 'd-d-d-d-d-d-d' with a drum-like attitude and a syncopated rhythm and then draw out and ride on the 'i' as if I were riding a wave up and down. The 'aeh' becomes a baby's cry and increases in volume and intensity until it becomes a scream. The 'n' becomes a whine with a hint of a 'no' in it. I am having fun. We then go around the group and everyone takes turns playing with the vowels and consonants in their names.

Toning

Natural sounds can lead into or act as an effective warm-up for toning. Toning is the conscious use of sustained vowel sounds for the purpose of restoring the body's balance. Sound vibrations free blocked energy and resonate with specific areas of the body to relieve emotional and physical stress and tension (Campbell 1989; Crowe and Scovel 1996; Goldman 1992; Keyes 1973). Keyes (1973) refers to toning as 'an inner sonic massage' (p.35) and believes toning can heal illness and restore wholeness through toning for oneself or having another person or people tone for you.

Practitioners of toning vary from those who use it as a tool for meditation or release to those who believe in its mystical healing powers. Goldman (1992) explores toning using overtone chanting based on a number of ancient healing practices. Gardner (1990), Goldman (1992) and Hamel (1978) use specific toned vowel sounds to vibrate and activate what many believe are the seven chakras in the body. 'Chakra' is the term used by many Eastern spiritual schools to describe energy centres in the body (Gaynor 1999). Gaynor (1999) describes toning using single syllable Sanskrit words that correspond to the chakras. The Sufis assign divine properties to the vowels they use to activate each chakra.

Yoga teachers have suggested specific vowel sounds to open different parts of the body. For example, 'ooooo' vibrates the root, or lowest chakra, 'oh' vibrates the belly chakra, 'aw' the solar plexus, 'ah' the heart, 'eh' the throat, 'ih' the area between the eyebrows, also known as the third eye, and 'eee' vibrates the top of the head, or crown chakra.

Although there are various ways to tone and differing beliefs about what toning can achieve, 'all involve the use of pure, non-verbal sound to increase the flow of breath, balance energy flow, release emotion…and restore harmony to the body–mind system' (Gaynor 1999, p.98). We benefit from recognizing and going with the natural flow of energy in our bodies. Toning is one way to facilitate this process.

Toning can be a very intimate experience especially when toning with one other person. The exchange of energy and vibrations can feel similar to being physically touched. As one client described it:

> Being connected to my feelings and body in this way was a sensual experience. Towards the end of toning I felt very close to you. Your voice was deep, grounded, seeming to resonate from within me. It was like I could *feel* your voice on my body. It was pleasurable and soothing.

Toning can also be very effective when working with dissociated clients and clients with eating disorders to help them become more aware of and accepting of their bodies. Pam initially got chills whenever we toned together. Once I asked her to rub her hands together until they got warm and then place them on her jaw. We then toned on an 'eee' vowel. She could easily feel the vibrations and was fascinated enough to risk more toning. Again I asked her to rub her hands together and when they were warm to place them on her heart. We toned together on an 'ah' sound. Pam was surprised to feel her heart resonating. 'I'm not sure if I like it or not...I got those chills again. I guess I feel more alive and I feel closer to you and that is a little scary.' Pam was anorexic, hated her body, and often reported feeling 'dead' or 'empty'. Toning and singing became pleasurable ways for her to be in her body, if only for a short time. Toning together also created a feeling of closeness with me that she grew to enjoy and seek out more often.

The immediacy of toning can provide clients with a musical encounter in the here and now that is physical, emotional and spiritual. It is a safe way for clients to be directly involved on sensory and feeling levels with another (the therapist) or others who are also looking for ways to be fully present and in the moment.

Lori described her toning experience this way: 'That was so beautiful it made me cry. It made me realize that there is an expressive being inside all of us and trusting our bodies and our surroundings is the way to let that part of ourselves emerge.'

Toning and other kinds of repetitive chant-like singing or sounding can also induce an altered state of consciousness and mediate contents from the personal and collective unconscious to the conscious mind (Austin 1993, 1996).

Case example: Suzy

Suzy, an illustrator for children's books, had been working to become more assertive. 'It's difficult for me to connect with my aggression... I'm used to being the listener, the one who goes along with what everyone else wants to do...anything to avoid conflict.' Suzy's survival in a household fraught with tension and fighting depended on her ability to be adaptable. 'I was the good child... I tried to mediate, to keep the peace between my mother and father and my father and brother.'

At this point in her life she felt everyone took advantage of her 'need to please' and she was sick of it and sick of suppressing her own anger and turning it against herself. Vocal work was empowering for her. 'I hear myself and I know I'm alive, I exist and then I feel my body tingling and it's empowering especially recently because I can sing louder and my sounds don't have to be pretty.'

When we began working together a year ago, Suzy was anxious about making primal sounds and improvising. She was afraid of losing control and that something ugly or disgusting might come out of her mouth causing me to reject her. With time she realized she grew up fearing that her feelings and her self were bad, 'ugly'. She initially transferred her negative feelings toward her father on to me. Eventually, we were able to work through some of her anger and fear of rejection. She no longer saw me as her father but as a positive mothering figure. This development created a feeling of safety that freed up her self-expression.

We began this session by talking about her need to confront a colleague and the challenge that presented. She wanted to work with sounds and maybe toning. We started with deep breathing. I attuned my breathing to hers. Gradually she yawned, then groaned, and soon we were both moaning together. I said, 'Allow anything to come out that needs to.' Her sounds were low and gruff and then gravelly, mostly 'ah' sounds. The 'ah' became 'rah' and the notes changed and went up a third and then another half step. When we stopped she said she heard a voice calling to her. At first she thought it was a man but then realized it was a woman with a low voice.

I asked, 'What would help you to come out more – movement, other instruments?' She wanted us to play drums while we toned. She played an African drum, and I played the conga drum. She also wanted to keep her eyes closed. I noticed that this time her tones were clearer and stronger and mostly comprised minor intervals. I sang unison most of the time and occasionally harmony or dissonant tones. Gradually the tones became words, 'come closer…come here…don't be afraid'. Her eyes remained closed as she chanted 'down…ground' and then she went back to sounds and slowly came to a conclusion.

Afterwards she told me she had felt a tremendous rush of energy surging through her body. She said she saw a tall, dark-haired woman all alone in a forest. The woman looked like a warrior, fearless and strong. She told Suzy to take off her shoes and feel the ground under her feet, to keep her feet on the ground, to hold her ground. We talked about the connection between strength and anger that was grounded in the body; strength that can be used to be direct and effective. Suzy was very moved by the experience and felt she needed to hear those words. We ended the session by breathing together in the silence so that Suzy could begin to assimilate what she had experienced in the session.

The music in the speaking voice

Most psychotherapists are aware of the information they receive about clients from the affect, tone, inflections, tempo and dynamics of the voice (Knoblauch 2000; Moses 1954; Reik 1948). But as music psychotherapists we have an advantage (Priestley 1994). Listening is fundamental and unique to our work. We are trained to listen. We depend upon our abilities to listen to music and words with our whole selves and this ability is an essential aspect of being an effective vocal psychotherapist.

I usually audiotape all of my clinical sessions. I have learned through the years that I can receive quite a bit of 'self-supervision' from listening to the sound of the client's and my own speaking voice as well as his or her singing voice and my own. In order to illuminate my topic, I have repeatedly listened to and analysed sessions with three clients: Ann, Marie and Cindy.

Case examples

ANN

In the first month of working with Ann, I often heard judgement and sometimes self-contempt in the tone of her voice. The feelings I picked up from her did not always match her words.

What was somewhat surprising and difficult to look at and listen to was the judgement and impatience I sometimes heard in my own voice. I would have missed some significant countertransferential feelings if not for the fact that I listened to the audiotapes. I heard moments where I was inwardly judging Ann for being so judgemental. I also became aware that her voice quality (when it was loud) sometimes annoyed me. With more time and reflection I realized this vocal quality seemed indicative of repressed anger. Perhaps I was picking up her split-off feelings and identifying with them. Ann had great difficulty both expressing anger and experiencing anger directed towards her.

These realizations were very helpful to me in examining and working through my countertransference to Ann and her speaking voice. A note I made after session three reads:

> She's not letting my observations sink in or affect her. I wonder if I felt annoyed. I don't feel conscious of it but my voice sounds like I could be... I sound impatient here, as if I want her to get to the point.

After listening to the tape of the next session I wrote:

> She sounds stuck and unaware of what she needs. Why should this annoy me? I don't sound empathic when I question her, more like I'm impatient with her. I don't usually feel unempathic when a client is stuck.

In the early stages of our work together there were moments when I felt as if we were engaged in a power struggle. I could feel tension in my body and I could hear the dynamics play out in the tonality, rhythm, texture and phrasing of our conversation. We would frequently interrupt each other. Her voice sometimes had a harsh aggressive edge to it. My voice would take on a 'know it all' lecturing tone.

During these times our verbal music conveyed unrelatedness, competition versus 'trading fours'. At points, Ann would take a long 'solo'. At other points I would talk too much. Ann would often intellectualize and if I joined her we would end up lost in the words together.

An important shift occurred during the next month, however, when I realized we were not connecting and I needed to slow down my speaking rhythm and ground myself in my body in order to help Ann slow down and feel.

> She is not breathing. Am I? If I slow down the pace and leave more space it might help her to speak slower, breathe and feel the things she is talking about. I think some of this wordiness is due to anxiety and perhaps some is nervous excitement that finally she can talk about these things with someone and feel listened to!

Knoblauch (2000) writes of similar experiences with clients in *The Musical Edge of Therapeutic Dialogue*. His emphasis is on the musical elements of speech and how these elements are a major source of information about unconscious communication and action between client and therapist and can greatly influence the therapeutic process. He uses improvising and accompaniment in jazz as a metaphor for clinical technique in psychotherapy. He could have been describing aspects of my sessions when he wrote, 'Therapists employ the rhythmic dimension in their accompanying responses to patients, often unconsciously, as they shape the non verbal contours of their turn with a slowed down pace...or an acceleration' (p.38).

I found that whenever I started to intellectualize too much, joining or partially merging with Ann, if I focused on my breathing I would relax and sink down into my body. My listening improved. I became more present to myself and to Ann. I felt more empathy for the anxiety Ann was experiencing and realized again that intellectualization was a defence she employed and that she would need time to feel safe enough to begin to trust me and the process. Then she could gradually allow herself to express her deeper feelings and needs.

During this session (tenth), I spoke less but what I did say seemed to punctuate and support Ann's words. I found myself becoming more interested in her story as it unfolded before me. As I became more emotionally attuned we began to 'play together' with words and pauses and the process of releasing and expanding feelings and meanings resembled a soloist and accompanist when they get into a 'groove' together. At times we each provided tonal and percussive accompaniment to one another's words and there was a call and response feeling to the interchange. We laughed together, our eyes met frequently and there were moments when I felt I understood her and I think she felt understood. I could hear important themes coming through the words, themes to return to, and return to, and return to.

MARIE

Marie's voice quality was very different from Ann's. When Marie began working with me, she appeared quite dissociated. The music in Marie's words was airy, light and breathy like a wind instrument. It was slow, hesitant and contained many 'rests', many moments of silence. It felt like 'spirit music', disembodied and often detached from the everyday world of reality. I could sometimes hear her drifting off into space, as her voice got softer and softer. Where did she go? She said: 'A place it is hard to describe... soft, like a blanket or a cloud, dreamy... magical... I can't remember when I started to go there, it seems like it's always been there for me.'

We gradually reconstructed enough of her childhood to help us understand her need to 'fly away'. She could not physically leave so she left psychically. The lack of security, the constant moving from place to place and her parents' unhappy marriage were contributing factors in her need to escape to safety.

A recurring theme of Marie's music was 'a small voice'. Once while sitting and breathing together she heard it whisper 'listen to me... you really have to listen hard'. The voice told her it lived in a very quiet place and had been shut up there for a long time. It needed to be finally heard.

During sessions I sometimes found myself feeling sleepy when she talked, often a sign that the client is repressing feelings. In Marie's case, however, I think her feelings were often dissociated more than repressed. Attuning my speaking voice to hers in order to meet her seemed to make matters worse. A note from the fourth month of working together read:

We both sounded depressed or caught in some kind of trance-like drone. I decided to break out of our rhythmic and melodic pattern. I worked to engage her more. I leaned in and became more active. I allowed my own varying melodic patterns more freedom. My laughter, my faster and varied rhythms entered our verbal improvisation and she responded sometimes with laughs or smiles. I noticed her voice did not trail off as much as it used to. There was more energy in the room now and Marie seemed to be positively affected by this new music.

Alvarez (1992) makes the point that within a safe reliable relationship (environment), dissonance, change and even disruption may not always be experienced as traumatic but may bring surprise and opportunities for play and enjoyment. This seemed to be true for Marie.

CINDY

The sound of Cindy's speaking voice sometimes contrasted with the message her words conveyed. For example, during her eleventh session she said, 'I'm doing really well right now.' The music of her voice, however, sounded depressed. The tone was fairly uniform with little melodic variation and dropped in inflection at the end of the sentence. As it turned out, there was sadness buried inside that her voice conveyed. The sadness was connected to her fears of being abandoned if she succeeded.

At other times the music in her words sounded like muffled percussion. I often had the sense that she was stifling her anger, using her energy to squash intense feelings. Her singing voice in contrast was flexible and emotional. She possessed and made use of a wide vocal range. Because Cindy sang professionally, perhaps she felt more permission to release intense feelings while singing. Some singers feel this way. It can be an aesthetically pleasing experience to sing, and songs are vehicles and containers for emotion. The structure of a song or a chord progression can give one a sense of safety, of being held.

Sighs and deep breaths initially accented the music in Cindy's words, and her tempo was usually slow. Her voice conveyed the sounds of someone who had seen a lot and survived – the sound of the blues. I often sensed a disconnection between her words and her feelings, unless she was singing. There was also a noticeable difference in her speaking voice right after singing. Her voice sounded more embodied, enlivened, and more connected to her feelings.

In the initial phase of therapy, I often detected a defeated quality in her voice, like a slow, soft current running underneath her words. As the therapy progressed, and she was able to express her grief, fear and anger through the music, her speaking voice gradually took on more of the qualities of her singing voice. She became more playful and spontaneous. There was more of a connection between her words and her feelings. The more often she was able to express her feelings and needs, not just to me but to other people in her life, the more powerful and free she felt. Her speaking and her singing voice mirrored the transformation she had undergone in her inner and outer life.

CHAPTER 2

Contributions
from Jungian Psychology

I began Jungian analysis when I was 21 years old. I was an actress in New York City and struggling to survive the constant rejections that wounded an already fragile sense of self. A friend told me about Jung and said, 'creative types like him'. That was all I knew when I entered the office of the Jungian analyst I was to remain with for the next 20 some years.

Of course, I had no idea at the time of the profound implications this decision to enter analysis would have on my life. It was a good fit. I liked the emphasis on the creativity of the psyche, and the belief in the wisdom of the unconscious. I loved the world of dreams and myths. I preferred looking at unconscious wounds and conflicts in terms of complexes related to archetypal gods and goddesses rather than through the lens of the medical model with its pejorative diagnoses. The symbolic approach to life and the belief that there was meaning in the suffering were healing concepts that felt right to me. The invisible world beckoned and I followed.

It was during this time that I left acting and several years after that when I stopped singing professionally. I had been devouring Jungian psychology books, and stuffing myself on psychoanalytic conferences and lectures. I couldn't get enough. My drive had to do with an intense passion to find myself. I wanted to throw myself into the individuation process, to discover and accept my own unique nature with all my possibilities and difficulties and become autonomous. And most importantly, I didn't want to feel anxious and depressed any more.

So when I look at my influences, Jungian psychology is first on the list. Over the years I continue to explore and study other schools of thought and different methods and models. No one theorist has all the answers and my clients have taught me to keep an open mind.

Before continuing, however, it is important to define some concepts from depth psychology, that is, psychological theories such as Jungian psychology, object relations theory and intersubjectivity that deal with the contents of unconscious phenomena.

Transference is an unconscious process in which a person transfers or displaces feelings, thoughts and behaviour patterns, originally experienced in relation to significant figures from childhood, onto a person involved in a current interpersonal relationship. In the therapeutic process, this person is the therapist (Moore and Fine 1990). However, not all of the clients' feelings toward the therapist are transference. Some reactions are a result of the therapist's behaviour or personality traits.

Countertransference is often a controversial subject. Many analysts have been reluctant, until recently, to embrace countertransference as a primary instrument. According to Sedgwick (1994) this is probably due to Freud's early view that countertransference is related to the therapist's own neurosis and is something to be mastered through a thorough analysis. As psychoanalytic thinking has evolved, however, countertransference has been re-evaluated and redefined. Racker (1968) among others defines countertransference more broadly as the total emotional reaction of the therapist to the client. When viewed totalistically, countertransference can be used to facilitate understanding of clients and their dynamics as well as the effect they have on others.

I have found that even when my countertransference is related to my own unresolved issues, my feelings and reactions are intimately involved with the therapeutic relationship and can be useful in increasing my understanding of the client. Transference and countertransference frequently occur in musical interactions and both clients and therapists often transfer feelings and reactions onto the voice, the music or musical instruments (Austin 2004).

Jung (1929, 1946) rarely used the term 'countertransference' but referred to it in different ways. He viewed countertransference as the unconscious transferring of the patient's illness to the analyst. He spoke about 'psychic infection', 'induction' and 'participation mystique'. These fusion states, which he classified under the category of 'participation mystique', emphasized the mutuality of the analytical process and suggested that the analyst is as much in the analysis as the client. He believed that the analyst's psychological transformations could have a crucial transformative effect on the client (Sedgwick 1994).

The wounded healer

Carl Jung (1951) was the first psychologist to write about wounded healing and the wounded physician. In 1951, he made the point that it is not the analyst's openness, mental health or knowledge that is most important but 'it is his own hurt that gives him the measure of his power to heal' (p.116). A wounded healer himself (1961, 2000), he struggled with psychosis in midlife. For six years he confronted his own unconscious psyche and was drawn deeper and deeper into the visions, dreams and voices within. He returned from his night sea journey (a mythological initiation into death and rebirth) with new knowledge of the inner world and its wisdom.

In his biography, *Memories, Dreams, Reflections*, Jung (1961) wrote:

> It is of course ironical that I, a psychiatrist, should at almost every step of my experiment have run into the same psychic material which is the stuff of psychosis and is found in the insane. This is the fund of unconscious images which fatally confuse the mental patient. But it is also the matrix of a mythopoeic imagination which has vanished from our rational age. (p.188)

Later in his biography, he speaks of this difficult period as the most important time of his life, the time when he gathered the primal material that was the basis for his most significant contributions to psychology:

> The knowledge I was concerned with, or was seeking, still could not be found in the science of those days. I myself had to undergo the original experience and, moreover, try to plant the results of my experience in the soil of reality... It has taken me virtually forty-five years to distill within the vessel of my scientific work the things I experienced and wrote down at that time. (p.192)

Guggenbuhl-Craig (1971) suggests, 'there is no special healer archetype or patient archetype' (p.90). He stresses the Jungian viewpoint that each of us contains both poles of the archetype within us: healer and patient. He believes there is danger if the illness side is left entirely with the patient and the analyst loses awareness of the patient within him- or herself and projects it entirely onto the patient. Similarly it is unhealthy when patients continuously project their own inner healer onto the analyst. Both projections are understandable and appropriate for a time but a shift needs to occur so that the archetype does not remain split. The analyst needs to acknowledge his or her inner patient and become 'the wounded healer who confronts the ill and constellates their inner healing factor' (p.93). Patients need to take responsibility for their sickness and with the support of the analyst or doctor activate their own intrapsychic healer. Something in the patient's body and psyche must help in order for the patient to recover. Guggenbuhl-Craig supports the ideal of the Greek physician Aesculapius who taught, 'only the divine healer can help while the human doctor merely can facilitate its appearance' (p.96).

Jungian analyst Jess Groesbeck (1975) also draws on the wounded healer archetype in his therapeutic approach. He focuses particularly on countertransference and like Guggenbuhl-Craig (1971) believes that ultimately the mutual projections of 'patient' and 'doctor' need to be withdrawn. The analyst has to lead the way by experiencing the archetype in its totality, by allowing him- or herself to be infected by the patient's psychic wounds while simultaneously acting as a role model and a catalyst for the patient's inner healer. Because of the deeply personal aspect of this approach, he suggests that some analysts are 'constantly being analyzed and illuminated by their patients' (p.133).

Sedgwick's (1994) strong reactions to his patients led to his examination of the wounded healer, both the archetype and those analysts who use countertransference as a primary tool in their work. His study of his own countertransference-based work led him to conclude:

> It is not only where the patient feels troubled but where the analyst also does that transformation takes place...something of parallel depth and sometimes parallel confusion goes on in the analyst. (p.107)

Sedgwick stresses that it is essential for analysts to undergo their own analysis and work through their core complexes. He points out, however, how important it is to recognize that these complexes are never totally worked through and can sometimes be re-constellated by the patient's unconscious.

Parts of the self, complexes and archetypes

Music has the ability to mediate contents from the personal and collective unconscious to the conscious mind (Austin 1996). The collective unconscious is a concept applied by Carl Jung (1916, 1929) to refer to the inherited, universal and primal aspects of the personality that transcend personal experience. The energies contained in the collective unconscious can create images independent of conscious experience. These images appear in dreams, myths, fairy tales and creative expression and their central themes are believed to be similar in all people and all cultures. Jung clustered the images into archetypes. An archetype is a transpersonal, universal pattern of psychic experience and meaning and comprises emotion and image. It contains the most primitive form of the affect. An archetype has both a positive and a negative aspect (Austin 1996; Edinger 1972; Jung 1916, 1929).

Jung was a pioneer in observing and documenting the psyche's tendency toward dissociation. He believed it was an essential, natural process in the differentiation of the personality and that dissociation extended along a continuum from 'normal' mental functioning to 'abnormal' mental states (Jung 1959).

Jung believed that we are born in a state of unconscious unity. The ego is identified (or merged) with the self (the central archetype of wholeness). As one moves toward consciousness, there is a breaking up of the original unity. Parts of the personality that are never seen and related to withdraw from consciousness. These part-personalities get left out in the course of one's ego development and in the process of adapting to parental values and expectations and remain un-integrated. They become encapsulated and buried deep in the unconscious. Parts of the self are directly related to complexes. A complex is an emotionally charged energy centre comprising a number of associated ideas and images. At the core of the complex is an archetype (Edinger 1972; Jacobi 1942; Kast 1992).

According to Jung (1969), complexes are psychic fragments that have split off as a result of traumatic experiences or incompatible tendencies. The contents of the unconscious first present themselves to the ego in the form of complexes. If the complex is not made conscious it will surface as a projection. On the other hand, when we identify with a complex there is a noticeable change in our mood and attitude. Our emotional reactions are exaggerated and we lose our centre when we are 'caught in a complex'. The ego is thrown off balance and we are controlled by energies we cannot influence. We react not only to the present situation that triggered the fear or grief but also to all similar situations we have experienced throughout our lives (Austin 1996; Jung 1969; Kast 1992). Thus, we overreact. In Alcoholics Anonymous they say 'If it's hysteric, it's historic.'

Do particular complexes (i.e. abandonment complex, inferiority complex) have recognizable musical aspects? In other words, can the client's music help to identify the complex that is being constellated? To my knowledge, the answer to this question has not been researched.

However, I have found similar qualities in several clients' music when they are caught in a traumatizing aspect of the power complex. In several instances, clients who improvised music around issues involving extreme judgement or verbal or physical abuse produced music with similar qualities. In each case, the tempo was very fast. The rhythm, melody and harmony were repetitive and had an insistent, compulsive quality.

The effect of the music on these clients was also consistent. They each experienced their music as 'intense' and 'having a life of its own'. Each felt that they could have continued playing for hours without any change in the musical patterns.

One client described feeling as if she were 'possessed'. Another said he felt 'attacked by self-hatred'. Two of the clients, when asked to draw what they experienced during the improvisation, drew whirling patterns that looked like cyclones. These drawings are reminiscent of the circular, spiralling pattern that has been referred to as a 'trauma vortex' by Dr Peter Levine (1997).

When playing music with a client caught in an attacking aspect of the power complex, I have found that the music usually lacks feeling and contains a driven quality. When the clients associate the music to a part of their personality, they have given it names like 'the perpetrator', 'the predator' or 'the saboteur'.

To be caught in a complex is to be metaphorically captured by the gravity of another planet. I have described how music can be useful in identifying the sounds of someone so captured. Music can also be extremely effective in helping clients 'return to earth'; helping to differentiate their own voices from the state of unconscious identity with the complex. Music can enable clients to connect to authentic feelings (the feeling beneath the judgement). The clients can then separate from the attacker and find their own point of view.

An example of the relationship between parts of the self, complexes and archetypes follows.

Case example: Terry

Terry often complains about a judgemental voice or part of herself that is always making fun of her and criticizing everything she does. During this session, I asked her if she can sing as this critical part of herself. We decided to improvise vocally together using words. A litany of abusive comments made up the content of the lyrics we sang. At one climactic point, Terry sang a high, sharp, piercing tone. 'It's my mother,' she said. 'It's my mother's voice.'

We spent the rest of the hour talking about the way her mother treated her as a child and adolescent. She remembered once when she made her own dress for a party and her mother laughed at her and told her she couldn't do anything right. She felt shame telling me about this. She also remembered other similar situations and feeling wounded and incapable of succeeding at anything. These emotionally charged images and associations make up a complex, in this case a negative mother complex. At the core of the complex is the mother archetype. In its negative aspects this archetype can be felt as devouring and destructive. The emotions Terry felt were rage and terror and the image that emerged during the singing was a witch-like old woman.

I believe an archetype also contains sound (the high, sharp, piercing tone). There continued to be times during our work together when Terry became extremely critical of herself and devalued her accomplishments. Whenever that part took over, I noticed a change in her speaking voice. The pitch became higher, the volume louder and the tone quality sounded constricted and strident. Terry found my observations helpful in enabling her to dis-identify from this complex.

The energy contained in this destructive part (complex) is valuable because, although it is related in this case to the personal mother, it is also transpersonal (beyond the personal) and archetypal. Consciously relating to this energy humanizes it so that the aggression can be made available to the ego for positive use in the world. Terry gradually became able to use this aggression consciously instead of turning it against herself. She began to set boundaries and to protect herself by asserting her feelings and needs in a direct and effective way.

Healing involves connecting with lost or disowned parts of the personality and experiencing the feelings, images and memories associated with the complex while bringing them into consciousness. It is also crucial to the individuation process to differentiate feelings and dis-identify or separate from qualities that do not belong to us, for example, realizing you are living out your parents' unlived life and not your own.

Singing is invaluable in this healing process. It can give us access to the invisible world: the world of imagery, memory and association. Sound can function as a bridge for aspects of the self normally not heard from to cross over and make themselves known to us. In Jung's words: 'Music reaches the deep archetypal material that we can only sometimes reach in our analytic work with patients' (McGuire and Hull 1977, p.275). Music allows the image and the feelings associated with the complex to be channelled into a concrete form, for example, 'the needy part'. The ego can then relate to a pre-viously unknown aspect of the unconscious and begin to integrate it into one's self-image. The energy tied up in the dissociated part then becomes available for conscious use and the personality becomes more complete.

We all have un-integrated parts of the self. Our inner cast of characters have their own goals, their own emotions and their own voices. In vocal psy-chotherapy, their songs can be heard and brought into awareness. Then the life force contained in the music can be used to enlarge and enrich the conscious personality.

I wrote the following poem as a way to capture the essence of the process of relating to and ultimately integrating different part personalities.

A Song in Three Parts

Hopeful voice:	I want to be free. I want to unwrap all the feelings trapped inside of me.
Wounded voice:	But what will happen if I do? It sounds too risky and too good to be true.
Critical voice:	It's too late to change. You're too fragile. You'll break. Just stay where you are. You don't have what it takes.
Hopeful voice:	You're wrong about me and it's never too late. You try to destroy all I try to create.
Critical voice:	You're wrong about me. I'm your friend. I don't want to see you disappointed again.
Wounded voice:	It's true. I keep getting hurt. When will it end? My heart is broken and will never mend.

Hopeful voice:	But now we have someone to listen and guide us. We can stop hiding what's deep down inside us.
Wounded voice:	Why should I trust her? Why should I let her in? What makes her any different from the rest of them?
Hopeful voice:	I'm sick of pretending I'm doing OK. Your way hasn't worked, why not try it my way?
Wounded voice:	If I come out, there's no guarantee. Will I be safe? Who'll take care of me?
Critical voice:	I'll take care of you. I'll never stray. Once she gets to know you, she'll never stay.
Hopeful voice:	I won't be your captive any longer. I have a voice now and it's getting stronger.
Critical voice:	You don't even know what you feel.
Hopeful voice:	I'm learning to trust that my feelings are real.
Critical voice:	You don't even know what you need.
Hopeful voice:	I know that my spirit needs to be freed.
Critical voice:	You don't even know who you are!
Hopeful voice:	If I listen to you I won't get very far.
Wounded voice:	I'm scared that you'll leave and won't take me along, that I am a burden, I'm worthless, I'm wrong. I'm filled up with sadness and rage and despair. How could anyone love me? How could anyone care?
Hopeful voice:	It's true I've ignored you and wished you weren't here. I hated your neediness, hated your fear, but your pain is my pain, it's something we share. Come with me. Forgive me for being unfair.
Wounded voice:	I'll gladly come with you out into the light, if you will protect me when it gets too bright.
Critical voice:	I'm still in control here. It's foolish to run.
Hopeful and wounded voice:	Divided, you conquered. But now we are one.

Case example: Susan

Susan, a 33-year-old schoolteacher, grew up in a household with an extremely depressed mother and a dominating father. Her parents were Holocaust survivors but wouldn't allow Susan to ask them questions about their experiences or talk about the Holocaust. Yet it was a huge presence, the 'elephant in the room' that no one acknowledged. She said the house was 'filled with heaviness, no room for joy or laughter or any feelings'. Her mother committed suicide when Susan was ten years old, at which time she became a 'little adult' and her father's caretaker.

Susan entered therapy because a recent breakup with a man with whom she had been living for several years was triggering abandonment feelings. She felt the intensity of her feelings might be related to her mother's suicide that she never fully grieved. Susan was suffering from depression, anxiety and panic attacks. She wanted music therapy because she had a deep love for music and particularly enjoyed singing. She also felt that her previous experience in verbal psychotherapy was 'too cerebral'.

Diagnostically, Susan fit the criteria for borderline personality disorder, which is now being viewed by many trauma specialists as post-traumatic stress disorder. She employed primitive defences, such as splitting, denial, and more than the usual amount of projection. She experienced abandonment depression as well as severe separation anxiety. Her strengths included intelligence, creativity, a good sense of humour and an ability to express herself through music. She had studied voice for several years and found singing to be a source of empowerment.

In the initial phase of treatment, Susan experienced me not as a separate person but as a part of herself. In Jungian terms, I often carried the projection of the self – the central archetype of wholeness.

The session I describe here took place during Susan's second year of therapy. We met twice weekly for a one-hour session. This hour began with a discussion of Susan's fear of going deeper into her process. She had missed several sessions during the past month and had arrived late that day.

Susan informed me that she had worked with a 'wonderful dance therapist' for the past few weeks and wondered if she should see me only once a week from now on. I believed that Susan was splitting and was resisting the transference. I noticed that I felt annoyed when she praised the dance therapist and I wondered if Susan unconsciously wanted to induce feelings of envy in me, or if these feelings belonged to me.

We began to verbally explore Susan's fear of becoming too dependent on me. As she revealed more of herself she was afraid I would see how 'unloveable and bad' she was and I would reject her the way she felt her mother did. Perhaps she would grow to need me too much and I would move, change careers, or die. Susan lived in the tension that existed between the fear of engulfment and the fear of abandonment. In previous sessions, we had worked with her ambivalence regarding intimacy and her need for clear boundaries.

According to Machtiger (1992), a Jungian analyst, the transference–countertransference 'provides the arena for the resolution of the borderline state by reconstituting the transitional space of a "participation mystique" or more symbiotic way of being that will allow healing to take place' (p.124). The containment of the musical space is an effective way to replicate the original form of symbiotic relatedness. 'If the process is allowed to develop, eventually an internalization of the images can take place and there is a greater differentiation of self and object' (Machtiger 1992, p.129).

I suggested Susan and I explore our relationship by singing together. She agreed and requested the chords C major 7 and F minor 7. I played the piano and Susan sat beside me on a separate bench.

Susan and I often sang together improvising sounds or words. Today, she began by singing 'ah' and 'ooh' slowly and softly. I sang in unison with her at first and then alternated with harmony. As the improvisation progressed, she began to rock back and forth. I attuned myself to her breathing and rocking. She began to sing longer melodic phrases. I sometimes mirrored her melodies exactly and sometimes sang a variation of her melody. At moments, we came together in unison or harmony. Our melodies built like intertwining vines. The music had a symbiotic quality to it. I felt at one with Susan, maternal and nurturing. I enjoyed the sound of our voices blending together.

After a while, Susan began to sing words: 'We're connecting... I can ask for what I need... This is new.' Her melodies included many sevenths and ninths. The music took on a sense of space and timelessness. I mirrored her words and melodies but found myself leaving more space before responding to her music. There was tension created from the continuous shifting back and forth from major third to minor third.

At one point in the improvisation, Susan said, 'I need help... I can't hold it all together by myself any more...how to ask for help and how to get it...how to feel safe?'

I sang back, 'Do you feel safe now?' She responded, 'I feel safe now.' She then sang, 'It's kind of scary thinking about going deeper into my pain…scared when I remember. I don't feel any grounding… I'm falling into space and there's nothing to hold onto.'

Susan's psychic injuries went back to infancy and early childhood. In my experience, the client's early trauma will often resurface during spontaneous vocal work. Did Susan feel safe enough to begin a thera-peutic regression? Would the music take her where she needed to go developmentally or retraumatize her?

Susan sang, 'I'm falling through space… I'm in a big hole – a void.' As she descended into the void, she began to cry yet continued singing. 'There's nobody there – a big black hole – I'll just fall forever and I'll die.' Susan sounded like a young child. She stopped singing and cried.

I could feel her pain. I continued playing and sang 'ah's and 'ooh's, attuning my singing to her breathing. After a few moments, I sang, 'Can you hear me singing with you?' I feared she might be isolated and I wanted to companion her in this young place. I sensed this was what she needed and had never experienced. She responded, 'I can hear you… Your singing makes me cry.'

At this point in the session, I felt unsure of whether to continue with the music. I felt that Susan was deep within her abandonment complex. I knew from our work together that she had a tendency to retraumatize herself. Much of the early work with Susan was spent in this dark, dysphoric place, and she had a tendency to get stuck there and become isolated and hopeless. There was an addictive quality to her crying when she lingered too long in this place. There is a difference between a therapeutic regression which results in an insight, a release or a connection that is reparative, and a regression that creates an unproductive emotional flood in which the client seems to swim around, caught in the undertow and compelled to re-enact and relive her trauma. I wasn't sure what to do. I continued playing but stopped singing while I thought about my next intervention.

Susan, however, sang, 'Please keep singing,' so I began to sing, 'La, la, la,' in a lullaby fashion. I felt relieved – my feeling, yet it could also be what she was feeling at that point. We seemed to be in what Jung would call a participation mystique. My singing seemed to soothe her. We rocked back and forth and her crying became softer.

After a while, I sang, 'What's making you cry?' Susan sang about what she had been experiencing. 'I was falling through space and nobody heard me, nobody saw me. When you sang, another person was there – I felt relief.' Then the undertow of the abandonment complex com-pletely caught her again. She said, 'I don't want to fall through space any more – I'm scared.' I felt some brief indecision and fear. I sang, 'I think I'll come out.' Susan sang, 'I can't come out by myself; I need your help.'

Looking at the therapeutic process within a Jungian framework, I could see that Susan was moving from the negative side of the mother archetype (the void, the devouring black hole) to the positive side of the mother archetype. I was mediating this movement by being the 'good enough' mother – present, calm, containing – witnessing Susan's feeling states and helping her to name them. My presence and the facilitating musical environment enabled Susan to metabolize the affects that were overwhelming her. The shifting back and forth between the major and minor chords seemed to be yet another indication of the movement between the polarities that was necessary to restore balance in Susan's psyche.

My intervention at this juncture was simply to mirror Susan, to embody the receptive feminine by not trying to fix her but to companion and be with her. I sang, 'I'm here – I can hear you singing. I'm here – I can see you crying. I can see your body rocking back and forth. I hear your voice… You're not alone.' I then sang the lullaby-like 'la's again.

After several moments, Susan sang, 'Nobody ever did that before… Nobody ever saw me before, nobody ever heard me, nobody ever felt me…nobody cared.'

In the next phase of this session, Susan again started to get caught in the negative undertow of deprivation and lack. She sang, 'Nobody ever said, "Welcome home"' several times. Instead of mirroring or reflecting her words, I once again took on the positive mother transference by gratifying her imminent need. I sang, 'Welcome home' repeatedly. Susan eventually joined me and we sang, 'Welcome home' together.

As the singing continued, an important psychic shift took place in Susan. She was able to differentiate her own voice from the state of unconscious identity with the complex. She was no longer the abandoned child linked to an abandoning mother. She joined with me as I modelled a loving, nurturing connection to her wounded child.

We sang together, 'We'll be here for you. You belong here. We love you. You're wonderful.' Then Susan sang, 'You're a beautiful tree. Stars are watching you…growing. You don't have to fall any more… Welcome to the earth; we want to see you grow. You are a tree.'

At the end of the song, a healing image emerged: the tree. The tree symbolizes the archetype of the great mother (Murdock 1990). The tree is associated with the feminine principle. It represents the nurturing, supportive, protective aspect of the great good mother, rooted in the depth of the earth and in contact with the nourishing waters. The tree also symbolizes the individuation process and the emerging self: the synthesis of heaven, earth and water – the dynamic life process (Kast 1992; Neumann 1955).

Susan's positive maternal transference to me was facilitated by the music and intensified when I sang to her in a lullaby-like manner. The containment offered within the musical holding environment made it possible for Susan to participate in the illusion of symbiosis. According to Neumann (1973), this illusion of symbiosis in the transference is necessary for the release of archetypal images and the emergence of the positive mother image.

During this session, my countertransference was complementary to Susan's transference. I felt maternal and nurturing toward her; comfortable in the cocoon-like musical world we were creating together. At one point, I felt afraid that I might fail Susan by allowing her to drop into the abyss, that I would not know how to contain her terror. My countertransferential fear was reflected in the music at the point when I continued to play but stopped singing. I felt relief when I was able to maintain the role of good-enough mother-therapist. When I sang to Susan, I was able to provide her with a calm, reliable, empathetic source of support, thus enabling her to feel connected to me and more grounded in her own being.

CHAPTER 3

Contributions from Object Relations Theory

I remember one day while riding the subway, probably on my way to therapy, I noticed a young man across from me reading a book. I was intrigued by the title, *The Drama of the Gifted Child* (Miller 1981). Of course it was an appealing title. Who doesn't want to think of themselves as 'gifted'? The subtitle was something to do with narcissistic parents and how they negatively impact their children. That also spoke to me.

A few weeks later, I purchased the book. I read it slowly because it was so painful and I often cried while reading it. I felt Alice Miller was writing about me. She was telling my story. Although it was difficult to see in print things I knew intellectually but had not totally accepted emotionally, it was also reassuring that I was not alone. I felt understood and comforted knowing there were others out there who had experienced similar wounds as children and were still recovering from them.

Miller's (1981) basic premise is that infants and children have emotional needs to be seen, heard, mirrored, empathized with and understood. Parents who are themselves deprived, who did not receive this kind of attention from their parents, often unconsciously look to their own children to meet their needs and thus neglect the emotional needs of their children. Children are dependent on their parents for their physical and emotional survival and will do anything to avoid losing them. 'Gifted' children have an amazing ability to intuit the needs of the mother, or both parents, and will adopt the role assigned to them. Often they become caretakers or confidantes for their parents. Typically, they are perceived as extensions of their parents and their achievements and successes reflect positively on their mothers and fathers.

These parentified children sacrifice their own needs and feelings to meet parental expectations. They are often overachievers and perfectionists, unconsciously caught in the illusion that if they are only smart enough, pretty enough, talented enough, they will finally get the unconditional love and attention they crave. They lose touch with their real selves because there is no one present to accept and empathize with their feelings and needs, no one to mirror back to them their own sounds, movements and expressions, the unique qualities that reflect who they truly are.

These 'little adults' often exhibit a prematurely progressed (Kalsched 1996), adaptive or 'false' self (Miller 1981, Winnicott 1971) that overlays a regressed 'true self' (Miller 1997, p.61). The true self contains the repressed or dissociated feelings that these children never felt safe enough to express, the intense emotional world that belonged to their early childhood. Psychotherapy provides a safe and welcoming space where the small, lonely child that hides behind her accomplishments can finally ask: 'What would have happened if I had appeared before you sad, needy, angry, furious... Does this mean that it was not really me you loved, but only what I pretended to be?'(Miller 1997, p.14).

Giving up one's illusions is an extremely difficult task but a necessary one. It means accepting that the child you once were will never get the kind of love and attention she needed from the parents of the past. One must relinquish the defence of 'if only' and tolerate the truth that you were and are powerless over someone else's actions and emotions. The road to this truth is one filled with grieving, but grieving in the service of truth leads to recovery of the 'true self'.

The term 'adaptive self' feels more accurate to me because it sounds less pejorative than 'false self' and because not all of the false self is unreal. For example, children who work hard to become great artists may be achieving in order to win love and admiration, but in the process they develop talents that can serve them later in life. One of the goals of therapy is to help them decide what they want and how they want to use these abilities and skills, as well as replacing the drive for perfection with joy in the creative process.

Many of the 'adult children' Miller writes about are gifted with heightened capacities to be attentive to the feelings and needs of others as well as the sensitivity to discern the defences of those around them. It is as if they have antenna and can pick up frequencies not audible to everyone else. These abilities that helped them survive as children can be useful to them later in life as long as they are conscious of their tendency to take care of others; in fact, many choose a career in the helping professions.

Object relations theory is an offshoot of psychoanalytic theory that emphasizes interpersonal relations, primarily in the family and especially between mother and child. 'Object' actually means person and especially the significant person that is the object or target of another's feelings or intentions. The self-structure of the child is formed early in life from relationships with these significant others or parts of significant others that are internalized. These 'objects' and the developing child's relationship with them are incorporated into a self and become the building blocks of the self-system (Greenberg and Mitchell 1983; Winnicott 1965).

The residue of past relationships affects a person in the present so that the basic tendency is to be drawn to others (friends, partners) who reaffirm early self–object relationships. When these early relationships have not been healthy, have not met the basic needs of the child, or have been traumatic, the person's experience of self and his or her capacity to participate in an intimate relationship is damaged. The more traumatic the self–object relationship is, the harder it is to let go of and the more resistance there is to change (Greenberg and Mitchell 1983).

Object relations analyst Melanie Klein (1948) placed a new emphasis on the study of early childhood development. Her work with emotionally disturbed children led to her discovery of early primitive defence mechanisms and paved the way to the analysis of psychotics and borderline personality disorders. She coined the term 'Projective Identification' to describe a complex psychic interaction between client and therapist that has proven very useful in work with traumatized clients. It involves a strong countertransferential reaction on the part of the therapist. There are differing interpretations of this phenomenon but most definitions include at least two steps. First, the patient splits off parts of the self, emotions, and/or transference reactions and projects them onto the therapist. Second, the therapist identifies with the projected aspects and feels controlled by them and may unwittingly act out the feelings with the patient (Davies and Frawley 1994; Moore and Fine 1990; Ogden 1991).

Object relations theorists believe that it is possible to resolve early injuries to the self, heal developmental ruptures and acquire the ability to relate to self and others in an authentic manner. The early unmet needs Alice Miller writes about with such compassion can and must be met if healing is to take place: the need to be seen and accepted as one truly is, to be empathized with, to be understood and valued. In my experience as both a client and a therapist this can be accomplished through a reparative relationship with a psychotherapist or music psychotherapist who is present and emotionally available. If the parents have not been able to fulfil these needs so that the 'adult child' can finally grow up, the therapist provides a corrective emotional experience. Then as the clients grow stronger and develop more self-esteem, and trust, they can begin to reach out to others for support as well: twelve step groups, church groups, friends, husbands, wives. And ultimately, they learn to meet their own needs, to parent themselves.

Winnicott is another object relations theorist whose ideas have influenced me, probably due to the fact that his beliefs are so compatible with music and expressive arts therapy. He emphasizes play and its relationship to the creative process and the development of the true self. 'It is in playing and only in playing that the individual child or adult is able to be creative and to use the whole personality, and it is only in being creative that the individual discovers the self' (Winnicott 1971, p.54). Winnicott is referring to the creativity of everyday life and not necessarily artistic accomplishments. He also believes that therapy cannot begin until the client has learned to play, so it is up to the therapist to create a safe environment to facilitate a relaxed, non-purposive state in which the client can say anything without it always being interpreted. Of course this assumes that the therapist can play. 'If the therapist cannot play, then he is not suitable for the work' (Winnicott 1971, p.54). This statement carries great significance for creative arts therapists who are skilled in the art of play.

The children who had to be good to win their parents' approval, as well as traumatized children who lived in a state of hypervigilance in order to survive in a hostile environment, were robbed of their childhoods and often cannot play. They can fantasize and dissociate from reality, but although that may be life saving, it is not the same as playing.

Vocal improvisation is a form of play. A safe musical environment, it is much like Winnicott's 'potential space', the concept he used to describe a place of mutual play and creativity between infant and mother, where the infant, over time, develops and internalizes the capacity for symbolic play and the ability to generate it without the mother's presence (Winnicott 1965, 1971).

During clinical vocal improvisation, where the emphasis is on process not product and mistakes are just part of the flow of vocal play, spontaneity is released (Spolin 1963). Why is this so important? Many adults live in their heads, disconnected from their bodies and their natural instincts, and are unable to react spontaneously. This problem is exacerbated with traumatized clients who are often 'frozen' and disconnected from themselves and others. Many of these clients have never felt safe enough to play and have had to control their spontaneous impulses for fear of doing or saying something that might cause them pain. Like Beth who was beaten whenever she cried and Paul whose natural enthusiasm was squashed and replaced with feelings of shame from the constant messages he received to 'Keep quiet! Your father is in a bad mood.'

Play evokes spontaneity and spontaneity can become associated with the danger of saying or doing the wrong thing. The tragedy is that when we lose access to our spontaneity, we lose access to our authentic selves. Spontaneity is health.

Vocal improvisation within a safe environment can create opportunities for clients slowly to become less rigid and defended and more flexible and free. As they experiment with taking risks, they become comfortable with the unfamiliar, and experience permission to sound ugly, angry, to scream and cry, to make mistakes. They can create new responses to old situations. They can gradually allow other hidden parts of themselves to emerge in the music. Then they can take what they learn from vocal improvisation into their lives.

Case example: Donna

Donna, a 28-year-old model, had recently begun singing professionally. She entered therapy because severe performance anxiety was affecting her ability to sing publicly.

At first Donna described her childhood as happy. However, as therapy progressed, Donna said 'We all looked good and performed well...everyone thought we had the perfect family'. Later she confided that her mother had severe mood swings and could be funny and loving at times and then suddenly become verbally abusive and frightening. There was 'no way to know what would set her off... I felt powerless... no matter how hard I tried to be good, nothing worked.' Her father was 'not around much' but her only happy memories were of the times the family gathered around the piano and sang together. Her father loved music and played the piano quite well. Donna's older brother was in recovery from alcohol abuse.

Donna was intelligent and very attractive and possessed a beautiful singing voice. She presented the image of someone in control and independent. She had an aura of perfection about her that intimidated me at first. As we began to work together, I perceived her lovely image to be an outer shell that compensated for an inner emptiness.

During the first few months of our work together, Donna sang several songs from her act. She sang with little or no feeling and at times with inappropriate affect (smiling during a sad lyric). She lacked spontaneity. She reminded me of Winnicott's (1971) and Miller's (1981) description of someone with a false, adaptive self. Her transference at this point included trying to impress me and thereby win my approval. I suspected this was how she behaved with her parents (or parent). My countertransference included annoyance that she was constantly performing during therapy sessions. At other times, I felt confused as to who she was. She seemed to lack a stable sense of identity.

A turning point in therapy occurred during our sixth month together. Donna brought in a song with which she was having vocal problems. When she came to the end of the song, her throat constricted and she could not reach the high notes without straining her voice. We both knew the notes were within her vocal range; the highest note was a high C, and she had sung this note before in other songs without difficulty.

The lyric was 'I'm singing this song to you'. I asked her who she was singing to. She said she had not thought about it. I asked her to pick someone to sing the song to. She picked her boyfriend and chose a small black drum to represent him. I played the chords at the end of the song (Ab major 7th to Bb minor seventh) and asked her to sing, 'I'm singing this song to you' to her boyfriend. I then asked her to keep repeating this section of the song and improvise on the melody.

At first she was afraid to improvise. What if she made a mistake? I assured her she could not make a mistake, that this experience was about playing with the melody and not about doing it right. She started off singing softly and tentatively but as we continued her voice became stronger and then sounded insistent. At one point, she began to cry and said, 'It's my father I'm singing to... He looks so unhappy... I want to make him happy... I want him to feel proud of me.' Once her feelings surfaced, her voice opened up and she was able to hit the notes effortlessly.

Since Donna did not have much experience of improvising, I gradually introduced her to simple improvisation techniques and we began to improvise together more often. It quickly became apparent that Donna had a 'good ear' and was a gifted musician. I began to notice a reluctance on my part to sing with her, which made me feel very uncomfortable. I wondered if I felt threatened because of her talent and the fact that we were both singers, yet I had worked with several talented singers and had not experienced this kind of resistance before. I was puzzled about my countertransferential feelings. During one session while we sang in unison, I noticed that Donna was able to hold the note longer than I could. I realized I felt competitive with her. Later in the session, she was discussing her relationship with a close friend and said she thought her friend was competitive with her. I wondered if my feelings of competition were induced.

As our work together progressed, Donna developed a mixed mother transference to me, either idealizing me or critical of me. My countertransferential feelings were often in response to her transference. I felt the pressure of carrying the idealized aspect of the self. I felt I had to be perfect, particularly in musical interactions. I feared that if I did not magically know what Donna needed in vocal improvisations (unison, harmony, words, and so on), she would feel disappointed and be critical of me. I realized that these countertransferential feelings were behind my reluctance to improvise with Donna.

This kind of transference–countertransference dynamic could be labelled 'projective identification' (Klein 1948). Jung (1946) described this kind of interaction as a 'participation mystique' – the shared field between analyst and client. He points to 'mutual analyst–patient influence and transformation and how psychic contents flash back and forth mercurially between the participants' (Sedgwick 1994, p.6).

As Donna began to sing more spontaneously and talk in more depth about her childhood, it became clear to me that I was experiencing what Donna felt as a child. She felt she had to be perfect to survive her mother's physical and verbal attacks. She also blamed herself for the way she was treated. She developed sensitive 'radar' to intuit what her mother needed. She believed that if she could anticipate her mother's needs and comply with them, she would be safe. Of course, this was an impossible task, and Donna's own needs and feelings went unmet. Donna suffered from a deep narcissistic injury to her sense of self. Her psyche was divided between a highly effective, adaptive self and a very young terrified part that felt inadequate to meet the challenges of adult life.

At times my countertransferential feelings were difficult to sort out. I had to discern which feelings were being induced in me and were a result of projective identification and which ones were emerging as a result of issues the client and I had in common.

I received supervision on my work with Donna. As my countertransference became clearer, I no longer felt resistant to improvising with her. With an increased understanding of her psychology came increased empathy on my part. There were places where our wounds intersected. In other words, I had a 'hook' for her projections. For me, this meant that I had to be careful not to overidentify with Donna. On the other hand, this also meant that I could understand and deeply empathize with her experience. I could companion her into the depths of her being so that she could reclaim the true part of herself, gain access to her feelings and resources within, and become a more integrated and authentic person.

As our relationship deepened and we established more trust, more of Donna's 'young child self' entered the therapy. I felt maternal and nurturing toward her. Donna began to feel safe enough to bring more of her feelings into the music. During one session when we were playing drums and singing together, she stopped singing and said, 'I want you to harmonize with me.' I had been mirroring her sounds and singing counterpoint, but she did not like what I was singing. This was a significant moment in therapy because Donna had never expressed a need so directly to me before.

We sang again, and this time I harmonized with her. When processing the experience, Donna said, 'I wanted you to know what I needed... I didn't want to have to spell it out.' She said she felt 'disappointed and a little angry' that she had to tell me.

We talked about how important it was for Donna to take responsibility for her needs. She cried and said, 'It's scary to have needs... I'm not used to expressing them... I'm not supposed to have any... I don't usually even know what they are.'

It was unfamiliar for Donna to express a need directly and have it responded to in a positive way. This experience was a healing, reparative one for Donna. I experienced a mixture of feelings. There was a part of me that identified with the omnipotent, all-knowing mother and would have liked to have magically fulfilled Donna's needs. At the same time, I felt relieved that my 'fall from grace' had occurred and that not only did we both survive but the therapeutic process moved forward. I knew that for Donna to see my limitations and eventually accept them would help her to accept her own. An important aspect of our work together involved depotentiating the perfectionistic, critical part of Donna's personality that wielded so much power and replacing it with a realistic sense of self.

As the therapeutic process continued, Donna's ability to identify and express her needs and feelings grew. Her self-esteem improved and her anxiety decreased. Her singing reflected these positive changes. She became more playful and took more risks in the music. She seemed more present and in touch with her feelings. She allowed herself to let go and let the music carry her.

I learned a lot from my work with Donna. It was a humbling and enlightening experience. The last time I saw her was at the opening of her new act. I still receive her postcards telling me when and where she is appearing. Her stage fright has disappeared.

CHAPTER 4

Contributions from Trauma Theory

I was singing
And I didn't care what it sounded like
I was singing
And I felt alive
Like estranged lovers finding each other
After many years apart
My head and my heart
Embraced again
And long forgotten sounds rained
Softly around me
While fear danced through my body
And emerged as joy

I never wanted a body. It was a burden that I felt encumbered by. How much better to be a spirit, to live in the imaginal realm, to feed myself on dreams and fantasies, and write poetry and songs. After all, the body was the container for my feelings and the reality of my feelings soiled my beautiful illusions. Early on in therapy, my analyst told me that singing was a way for me to become embodied because it was a way to enter life that was aesthetically pleasing. I think he was right but entering reality was not first on my lists of things to do back then.

Later in life I learned that the body–mind connection is severed in people with histories of early childhood trauma. I remember reading Judith Herman's book, *Trauma and Recovery* (1992) and understanding from the inside out what she was talking about. I also remember attending a psycho-drama conference around the same time, where Bessel van der Kolk gave an inspiring keynote address on trauma and dissociation and the value of the creative arts therapies in accessing traumatic memories and feelings through a mind–body approach. I attended several workshops that had to do with trauma, post-traumatic stress disorder (PTSD) and attachment trauma. It suddenly seemed like everyone was talking about trauma.

A psychotherapist I knew invited me to a weekend workshop on somatic experiencing – a body-centred approach to working with trauma developed by Peter Levine. Levine's (1997) primary focus is on the sensate experience of the client: tracking the memories, affects and images that arise from a deep somatic source in the body. The work begins with 'resourcing' – helping participants access inner strengths and safe places – so that if during the workshop someone falls into a 'trauma vortex' (a continuous, unproductive re-experiencing of past trauma), the person can be redirected into a 'healing vortex' (an inner experience of feeling resourced and safe).

The workshop was very intense and revealing. It didn't take me long to succumb to the strong current pulling me under and deeper into dark, scary childhood places. I spun around and around caught in the grips of the trauma vortex; a little girl sobbing for a mother she never had. The workshop leader rushed over and tried to bring me back into the present. Some part of me did not want to come back and fought her, but eventually she got me to open my eyes, breathe and centre myself.

Later in life I learned that my mother suffered from PTSD. She never talked about her childhood and her symptoms and phobias seemed like eccentricities. She cried a lot and had fits of rage. I was often the target of her irrational anger so I never felt safe. I was also infected by her depression and anxiety. When I had enough therapy to put most of the pieces of the puzzle together, I realized I was affected not only by the way I was treated as a child, but also by the way my mother was treated as a child. Her unresolved trauma was both re-enacted with me and unconsciously passed on to me. I felt my own pain and hers. We were a family possessed by the ghosts of the past, ghosts that had never been confronted, and so continued to haunt us. This pattern is repeated in many families and is known as generational trauma. I was determined to stop the cycle, to open all the windows and clean house.

> In every nursery there are ghosts. They are the visitors from the unremem-bered past of the parents; the uninvited guests at the christening. Under all favorable circumstances the unfriendly and unbidden spirits are banished

from the nursery and return to their subterranean dwelling place... But [there are] another group of families who appear to be possessed by their ghosts. The intruders from the past have taken up residence in the nursery, claiming tradition and rights of ownership. They have been present at the christening for two or more generations. While no one has issued an invitation, the ghosts take up residence and conduct the rehearsal of the family tragedy from a tattered script. (Fraiberg, Adelson and Shapiro 1974, p.387)

When the student is ready the teacher will come, and in they came. I seemed to be attracting clients with histories of sexual, physical and emotional abuse, neglect, addictions, and people suffering from debilitating symptoms associated with attachment disorders, PTSD and developmental trauma. I listened, I empathized, I learned. I took more courses, continued my own psychotherapy and joined a supervision group led by the author of *The Inner World of Trauma* (Kalsched 1996).

I eventually had the opportunity to experience Levine's work in several private sessions. I felt much safer in a one-to-one situation. I could sense the therapist being very mindful of my psychic state and slowing the pace down when what I was telling her started to arouse strong emotions in me. She used the technique of 'titration' or 'pendulation' (Eldredge and Cole 2008), moving toward and away from activating traumatic material, to support my capacity for self-regulation of my affects so that I could tell my story without being caught up in the trauma vortex.

So, what really constitutes a traumatic experience? Psychiatrist Lenore Terr (1990) made a distinction between single-blow traumas and repeated traumas. Single shocking events, like natural disasters, technological disasters or criminal violence, may produce enduring traumatic reactions in some people. The most serious psychiatric disorders, however, are the result of prolonged and repeated unbearable stress and abuse, such as being a prisoner of war or a concentration camp inmate. Sexual, physical and emotional abuse may span the whole of childhood development. Any experience that causes an infant or child unbearable psychic pain and anxiety is traumatic, including the more cumulative traumas of unmet dependency needs, inadequate nurturing and interruptions of the attachment bond.

Attachment trauma has been widely researched. The growing interest in this form of trauma may be due to the fact that problems in the very beginning of life within the mother–infant bond will most likely affect the child throughout his or her life and can set the stage for vulnerability to other forms of trauma. Recovery requires restoring a sense of safety and security, and positive attachment relationships play a crucial role in healing attachment trauma (Bowlby 1969; Stern 1977; Stewart and Stewart 2002).

Common to all traumatic experiences is the rupture to the integrity of the self and the feelings of confusion, helplessness and terror this rupture evokes. When this rupture occurs before a coherent ego and its defences have been adequately formed, the intense affects are too overwhelming to be metabolized and processed normally, thus the devastating effects on the traumatized person's body, mind and spirit (Herman 1992; Kalsched 1996). The traumatic experience, as well as the meaning attached to it, critically affects an individual's experience of self and his or her ability to engage in an intimate relationship. Trusting another person is difficult, for at the root of developmental trauma, whether it involves sexual or physical abuse or lack of attunement, lie feelings of betrayal and psychic abandonment (Austin 2001; Bowlby 1969, 1973; Carnes 1997). Intimacy can feel dangerous for clients with histories of early trauma because close relationships can trigger intense fears of dependency, engulfment or abandonment.

It is important to remember, however, that if children have safe places to go and safe people to be with, such as a father, a grandparent or sibling, they may have a better chance of recovering. Inherent or developed resources, for example, creativity and courage, may also increase their resiliency in the face of traumatic events. As children grow and develop the capacity for speech and conceptualization, if a parent or other caretaker is able to talk or in other ways empathize about the traumatizing events, children are more likely to have the ability to cope with the repercussions of trauma.

Traumatized clients often alternate between a state of feeling overwhelmed and flooded by intense emotions connected to the re-experiencing of the trauma and a state of 'shut down', a psychic numbing, which can include avoidance of people, places and things that might trigger associations that bring on intolerable anxiety or panic. Primitive defences like denial and dissociation protect the fragile self from annihilation but also affect the integrity of the personality. Severely dissociated clients experience the self as enfeebled, fragmented or lacking in continuity (van der Kolk 1987).

The split-off, dissociated parts that inhabit the inner world of the traumatized client are often externalized in the client–therapist relationship and can be worked with in the transference–countertransference situation (Davies and Frawley 1994). In vocal psychotherapy, the relationship field is enlarged to include transference and countertransference to and in the music.

Clients who were unable to form a secure attachment to the primary caretaker, or lacked an emotionally available and consistent 'good-enough' mother (Winnicott 1971), have an accumulation of unmet dependency needs that pave the way for problems with identity formation. Without a mother who has the capacity to create a holding environment – a protective boundary that provides a sense of reliability for the baby – and the emotional presence and stability to contain the child's impulses, both loving and aggressive, the child is unlikely to develop object constancy (Winnicott 1971) – the ability to internalize the good-enough mother as a basis for a core sense of self and self-esteem regulation. Object constancy provides infants with a basic continuity of existence – what Winnicott refers to as 'going-on-being' (1965). I have noticed that clients who lack this rudimentary sense of who they are often have difficulty being alone and some suffer from severe abandonment issues, and experience a sense of falling through space with no one or nothing there to catch them. Without a fully developed sense of self as a basis for ego functioning, these clients are compromised in their ability to function as mature adults and often suffer from debilitating symptoms connected with trauma, such as drug or alcohol dependence and other addictions, depression, anxiety disorders, and self-destructive behaviour.

One such 'adult child', Peter, described it this way:

> I wake up every morning feeling anxious and all I want to do is hide under the covers. Sometimes I'm afraid to leave the house…that I'll fall apart or go crazy. I know I can look like a grown-up and I have an important job and everything, but I feel like a fraud and it's only a matter of time before they find out I'm faking it.

Abused or neglected children usually assume responsibility for the abuse they suffered. They blame themselves and often carry a sense that they are 'rotten', 'bad' or 'cursed'. They are frequently filled with shame and self-contempt that results in self-destructive acting out. It is psychologically easier to blame themselves because then they have an illusion of control over the situation, which acts as a defence against despair, and the terrors of abandonment feelings. As Kathy put it, 'I used to think if I tried harder, got better grades, and wasn't a burden, my mother would finally love me.'

It is also difficult to accept that the person you depend on for your very life is abusing you. Children need to preserve a good image of at least one parent in order to feel some small bit of safety. Fairbairn (1952) believes

these children internalize bad parental objects as a defence in an unconscious attempt to control them. These outer perpetrators are now internalized and retain their power in the inner world of the abused child.

Kalsched (1996) discovered the prominence of one dyadic structure that
results from a split in the ego or personality of the client. This dyad consists
of a regressed part usually 'feeling' in nature and a precociously advanced
part usually associated with mental processes. This advanced part persecutes
the regressed part in what seems like a misguided effort to protect it from
dangers of connection to the self and others. Getting close to others is
perceived as dangerous because the primary caretakers of infancy and
childhood were undependable, neglectful or abusive. Making connections
among the self-parts is threatening because psychological survival once
depended upon the ability to disconnect thoughts from feelings and to
distance oneself emotionally from experience.

I turn to my clients for vivid descriptions of the inner persecutor: the
witch, the predator, the beast, the rapist; as well as the inner victim: the
orphan, the wounded animal, the broken doll, the homeless man. These
images are personal and archetypal in nature and they emerge in dreams and
in creative expression like vocal and instrumental improvisation where they
can be worked with (Austin 1991, 1993, 1996, 1998, 1999b).

Davies and Frawley (1994) describe work with sexual abuse survivors
and how they struggle with the 'possession' of their patients 'by internalized
abusive objects to whom the patient remains tenaciously attached' (p.22).
Fairbairn (1952) accounts for the client's need to repeat and re-experience
painful situations over and over again by stressing the child's striving for
contact with the parent (the original love object).

> The emptier the real exchange the greater his devotion to the promising yet
> depriving features of his parents which he has internalized and seeks
> within…these internalized object relations are also projected onto the
> outside world…love objects are selected for or made into withholders or
> deprivers so as to personify the exciting object, promising but never ful-
> filling. (Greenberg and Mitchell 1983, p.173)

Fairbairn (1952) also points out one of the reasons it is so difficult to end this
destructive cycle. The client (unconsciously) feels that seeking out new and
fulfilling relationships will be a betrayal of his or her parents and, therefore,
change carries with it the childhood terror of abandonment. The resistance

to giving up the familiar, painful though it may be, for the unfamiliar, and therefore unknown, is great.

Trauma literature emphasizes the inevitability of unconscious re-enactments – specific repetition of traumatic relational paradigms and events (Davies and Frawley 1994; McCann and Pearlman 1990b; van der Kolk 1989). The critical wounds that are the source of these re-enactments become apparent during the therapeutic process as they repeatedly emerge in the words and the music and have to be worked through with the client time and time again. Freud addressed the client's need to re-enact traumatic events with his concept of the 'repetition compulsion' (Freud 1913, 1938). The 'repetition compulsion' relates to the repression of significant feelings and memories and the client's unconscious impulse to re-enact these painful emotional experiences repeatedly in an attempt to finally master them (Greenson 1967; Winnicott 1965).

Jung (1968, 1969) connected the repetition compulsion to the constellations of ever-returning complexes and the intense emotional reactions accompanying them. Narcissistically injured people, for example, may overreact to criticism because they are reacting not only to the current situation but to all similar situations experienced within their lifetimes (Edinger 1972; Kast 1992; Ulanov 1971).

I think clients also repeat and re-enact painful relationships and events in order to remember (re-member) the original loss or trauma; remember not just with the mind but also with the body and the whole self. Fraiberg et al. (1974) have written about the effect of the unremembered past, not only on the victims of trauma but also on their children, and the necessity of remembering if healing is to take place.

> In remembering they [clients] are saved from the blind repetition of that morbid past. Through remembering they identify with an injured child (the childhood self), while the parents who do not remember may find themselves in an unconscious alliance and identification with the fearsome figures of that past… When the parent can remember and reexperience his childhood anxiety and suffering, the ghosts depart, and the afflicted parents become the protectors of their children against the repetition of their own conflicted past. (p.412)

Deep characterological change requires working within a therapeutic framework that embraces regression in service of the self (Herman 1992; Kalsched 1996; Woodman 1982, 1985). Vocal psychotherapy provides a consistent, therapeutic relationship within a safe musical container that can also act as a catalyst for therapeutic regressions to occur.

Then clients can remember, fully experience and make sense of the feelings and sensations that were overwhelming as a child; intolerable because no one was present to help the child contain, understand and metabolize the intense affects. During a therapeutic regression, clients can turn back the clock and return to the 'scene of the crime'. They can grieve what was and what never will be, make meaning out of false beliefs and old confusions, and accept and integrate the past so that they can live more fully in the present.

Machtiger (1992) places great emphasis on regression in the transitional space of the transference–countertransference relationship with clients who have experienced chronic and repetitive parental failures during infancy and early childhood. 'In the blurring of boundaries the gulf is bridged, and the analyst can incarnate earlier parental figures' (p.128). Balint (1968) associates therapeutic regression with the opportunity for a new beginning: a chance to go back to a point before the 'basic fault' or childhood trauma occurred. This basic fault results from inadequate mothering, a lack of fit between the mother and child during the early formative periods.

A positive transference can provide the opportunity for a different kind of experience. The therapist becomes the new primary relationship and the client has the chance to discover and explore new and different ways of relating. A reparative experience is then possible in which the client's feelings and needs are acknowledged, understood, accepted and met (symbolically or literally). Mind, body and spirit can be reunited and a new relationship to self and others can be established. At that point, the client can let go of the past and live more fully in the present.

ANN

Ann, a 26-year-old Korean woman, entered therapy because she felt her shyness and low self-esteem were holding her back from succeeding in her career as a classical pianist. She didn't feel her reticence and lack of assertion were necessarily cultural since she had lived in the United States since the age of six and spoke English perfectly.

Her parents were both highly successful musicians and worked and travelled constantly so that Ann and her brother spent little time alone with them. Ann felt enormous pressure to do well and make her parents proud of her. She was extremely self-critical and had very high standards that seemed impossible to meet. The following session took place during our eighth month of working together. Ann wants to talk about the performance anxiety she experienced on Saturday night. Her eyes are glued to mine as she tells me, 'I felt like I was starting to disconnect from myself while playing the piano.' She was at a party and a friend asked her to play the piano. She said she didn't feel comfortable playing but her friend was insensitive to her feelings and insisted. Ann felt trapped. She speaks calmly, in the middle range of her voice and without much feeling as she tells me she has difficulty saying 'no' to people. She is afraid they will be disappointed with her and maybe even angry. Ann could never imagine saying 'no' to her parents. Her brother went through a rebellious period but Ann was always the good child. Ann wonders why she keeps finding herself in situations where she feels 'on the spot' and pressured to perform. As she continues to talk I hear what seems like resignation in the music of her voice.

This is not the first time she has spoken about her fears of performing or speaking publicly or about her tendency to dissociate when overtaken by extreme anxiety. Her anxiety seems related to an unconscious need to be perfect as a defence against the fear of being seen and judged. It seems clear to me she feels that who she really is isn't good enough. She often expresses shame and anger at being criticized by her family or teachers as well as fear of being misperceived and judged. Her expectations of herself are unrealistic, so she often feels deeply depressed after a performance of any kind. As she talks, I think about the 'gifted child' (Miller 1981) who feels she must be perfect to win her parents' love and acceptance. I can identify with the pain of having to hide one's true self and my empathy makes me feel closer to Ann.

Diane: Did you ever feel this kind of anxiety as a child?

Ann: When my parents had parties and wanted me to perform. Sometimes I said I was too tired or felt sick; once I even threw up but I always ended up doing what they wanted.

Diane: How did you feel when you had to play?

Ann: Like I had no choice…pressured, and I hated it. I didn't like all the focus on me. It felt like a responsibility.

Diane: Yes…

Ann: I'm remembering another time…when I was around eight, yes, eight years old. We had just moved to a new city and it was three months into the school year. I didn't even have a school uniform yet. I felt awkward and embarrassed. The teacher called me to the front of the room to give a speech about myself.

Diane: To introduce yourself?

Ann: Yes, and everyone was staring at me and I didn't know anyone. I felt odd, alien, I, umm, saw myself from a distance…sort of like what happened Saturday night.

Diane: It sounds very scary.

Ann: It was terrifying. I remember a pink dress I wore that day. I can hear my voice wanting to break into tears but I fought through it.

Diane: You had to hide your feelings?

Ann: Yes! I had to stay in control.

Ann tells me that she sometimes experiences her voice as 'disembodied' and 'unreal'. I notice I am breathing deeply. I feel tears welling up in my eyes. The tears feel connected to fear. Ann is sitting slumped on the couch. She looks sad and defeated. I wonder if I am feeling her feelings or my own. I ask her what she is feeling and she says, 'nothing – umm – kind of numb… I often feel numb.' Ann is someone who often 'disappears' during a session when what is being discussed touches on unprocessed early trauma. I want to help her stay in her body and in the room with me so I make an intervention toward the music. I suggest we return to the classroom she has just described. I offer her choices. We can play instruments or sing. I also suggest we set a time limit of ten minutes. The time limit is to provide more structure and safety as well as allowing for time at the end of the session to process the music if necessary.

Ann wants to sing. She wants to improvise over two chords using words. She wants me to sing with her. I ask Ann to choose two chords. She picks E minor 7 to A minor 7. She approaches the piano, sits down and takes a breath. She says, 'I don't know why this should feel so scary but it does… I want to do it, though.' I suggest we sing to, or as, the young part of herself. I begin playing softly and steadily and suggest we begin by breathing together.

Ann: (singing) I am looking out the window at the flowers and the trees.

Diane:	(singing) I am looking out the window at the flowers and the trees.
Ann:	at the flowers.
Diane:	at the flowers.
Ann:	I wish I was with the flowers.
Diane:	with the flowers.
Ann:	I am scared here. I am frightened.
Diane:	I am frightened.
Ann:	I don't know where I am.
Diane:	Where am I?
Ann:	I am floating somewhere up above… I can see everything from up here.

I mirror her and sing as her alter ego. I match her vocal quality, dynamics and phrasing. At times we sing in unison, or we harmonize. 'How will I get through this?' 'Everyone is looking at me.' 'What do they want from me?' I notice her singing voice is quite different from her speaking voice. It is soft and open and higher pitched. I believe she is experiencing a therapeutic regression. I notice how easy it is for me to connect with her in the music while she is singing from this young vulnerable place.

I sing, 'I don't want to open my mouth', referring to the speech in front of the classroom. She seems to take off from my phrase and sings 'I don't want to open myself…how can she do this to me? What is she thinking? I feel sick…what if I throw up?'

When she sings this phrase, I am reminded of the time her parents wanted her to perform and she threw up.

I continue to sing with her in unison and harmony. Her melodies are simple with few leaps. She sings slowly. There seems to be more feeling coming through in her singing. I feel willing to take risks, perhaps because I feel I understand her experience so well, the feeling of being exposed as inadequate. It feels familiar to me. I consciously slow down the tempo and sing 'Doesn't she understand what it's like to be new?'

| Ann: | To be eight years old! |
| Diane: | To be eight and new. Doesn't she understand…to feel so strange and so different. |

Ann: so strange and so different.

Diane: Doesn't she know how scared I feel?

Ann: Nobody ever knows… It must be me who's wrong if she could ask this of me. What's wrong with me? Why can't I just do this?

Tears fall from Ann's eyes. This is the first time she has ever cried during therapy. I feel she is beginning to trust me more; she is letting me in and letting herself 'in'. I feel touched by her courage to connect with this wounded, young part rather than to stay distanced from it. I think about the way children blame themselves when painful things happen to them. I feel it is important to help Ann realize she was not responsible for her teacher's insensitivity just as it was not her fault that her parents were insensitive to her needs and saw her as an extension of themselves. They never accurately perceived her. She clearly did not receive the empathy and understanding she needed during her childhood and adolescence and therefore she never felt good enough to receive the love she craved. If Ann isn't able to realize this, and mourn the loss of her childhood and all she was deprived of, she will keep finding herself in situations where she feels anxious and pressured to perform and please others. She will keep abandoning herself. She will keep re-enacting the trauma.

I feel protective toward her. I switch from singing as her alter ego to singing as myself – her therapist. We sing the following:

Diane: It's not you. She doesn't understand – you're just eight years old and scared.

Ann: I'm scared (still crying softly) … I'm far away.

Diane: So scared and far away…and you need someone there who can understand your fear. It's not your fault.

Ann: Far away.

Diane: Can you hear me?

Ann: Yes… Why do I have to go by myself to the front of the room by myself? What am I going to say? (Her voice becomes softer.)

Diane: Would you like me to come with you?

Ann: I don't want to go!

Diane: (singing softly) Then you don't have to go up there right now.
                Just come back to your body. Take a breath. It's OK now.
                Come back to this room. Come back to the present. That was
                then and this is now.

We breathe together while I continue playing the piano. I synchronize my
breath with hers. My playing becomes softer, slower and more arpeggiated
during the last part of the vocal improvisation. I also play in the upper
register of the piano. These musical interventions are intended to support her
singing and to meet her where she is emotionally. My lyrical interventions
are intended to offer empathy, understanding and to help Ann put words to
and make new meaning out of a painful childhood memory. I want to
alleviate her anxiety and work with her tendency to dissociate. I hope to
provide her with the beginnings of a reparative experience. I am also aware
that our time is coming to an end. I want to be sure to allow her time to
emerge from the altered state she is in (the regression) and process the
experience if she needs to. I feel it is very significant that Ann is accessing
feelings she couldn't express in the past and that she is not alone this time. I
am there to companion her.

During the breathing, Ann stops crying. I slowly bring the music to a
close and we sit in silence for a few moments. Then Ann looks at me and says,
'I was shocked that sadness and terror came up. It happened when I sang
about only being eight years old and that she didn't understand what it's like
to be eight years old… I felt like it was me who had to be strange, but the
teacher was asking such a big thing!' I look Ann in the eyes and say, 'Much
too big for an eight-year-old girl who had just come from another city and
didn't know anyone…much too big.' My tone of voice is very soft and slow,
almost as if I am talking to a child.

Ann asks me, 'Why did the teacher do that?' She sounds angry now and
genuinely perplexed. I say gently, 'She didn't understand…she didn't
understand how exposed you felt… She didn't see you.'

Healing childhood injuries requires revisiting past traumatic events in the
present. Clients need a dependable, empathic 'other' that is capable of
companioning them through the unconscious realm. Transforming patterns
of behaviour and defences that were once useful in protecting a fragile sense
of self, but now stand in the way of growth, can be a slow and difficult
process and one that requires the courage to let go of the familiar and step
out into the unknown.

Working with traumatized clients is not easy and not suited for everyone. Vicarious traumatization is at times unavoidable for any therapist working with trauma and is not always an indicator of the therapist's unresolved psychological issues but is part of the reality and process of trauma therapy. Vicarious traumatization is a process through which the therapist's inner experience is deeply affected and negatively transformed through empathic engagement with the client's trauma material (McCann and Pearlman 1990a). Personal memories, painful associations and strong emotions can easily be induced or awakened in the therapist when empathy leads to identification.

Current stressful circumstances in the therapist's life can make him or her more vulnerable to being strongly impacted by the client's stories and feelings of loss, disconnection and pain. Life stressors can also affect the therapist's ability to perceive and work with difficult transferential and countertransferential issues. The therapist may turn to a variety of defensive strategies, some of which open him or her to further traumatization (like dissociation). The therapist's defences will affect his or her ability to focus on the client's needs and could result in a traumatic re-enactment for the client, especially if the client seems continuously compelled to re-enact and relive his or her trauma. That's why it is essential for therapists to be in psychotherapy, supervision or peer support groups with people who are trained to recognize the signs of burnout and vicarious traumatization.

Many clients who suffer from trauma symptoms have difficulty accessing feelings. Intense or volatile emotional states may provide a relief from numbness and a sense of feeling alive. When working with a client who seems pulled toward the retraumatization cycle, the therapist has to work very slowly and sensitively, use interventions cautiously, and be extremely aware of the client's feelings, sensations and non-verbal communications from moment to moment to prevent emotional flooding and retraumatization. Resolution of profound injuries to one's sense of self involves a process of gradually accessing and naming the feelings that emerge and gaining insight into the origins of the injuries. Having a context helps the client understand the traumatic symptoms and make sense of them. Finding the meaning in the suffering is healing. A skilled, empathic therapist can guide and support clients through this rocky terrain of feelings, memories and associations and can provide them with a corrective emotional experience.

CINDY

In the following case example Cindy experiences a therapeutic regression in which she encounters a playful, young part of herself. She is able to connect with this young girl and undergo a corrective emotional experience. I use deep breathing, natural sounds, awareness of bodily sensations and improvised singing as vocal interventions.

Cindy tells me about her dream. All she remembers is that she was a little girl all alone in the house and couldn't find a way to get outside. She woke up feeling anxious. I ask her if she has any idea of how old she was in the dream. She says 'around five'. I ask what she remembers about being five years old, what was it like?

Cindy: I was a victim as a kid…a target… I cried all day the first day of kindergarten.

Diane: Were you scared of school?

Cindy: I was scared all the time… I had so much responsibility at five… I was alone a lot. I had to take care of myself.

She laughs when she tells me how bad things were. It doesn't sound like an authentic laugh. Her voice lacks energy as she talks. She speaks in a monotone with little affect. I ask her what makes her laugh about this subject. I say, 'What are you really feeling when you describe your childhood? What are you experiencing in your body?' She pauses for a moment, then takes a few deep breaths and says, 'a lot of anger…rage'. I ask if we can make space for her rage and 'be with it'. She says, 'maybe'. A few moments pass and she says, 'It's like the sound of fire when it's raging through the forest.'

Diane: Where is it located in your body?

Cindy: In my belly.

Diane: Let's take a deep breath and if you feel like it, try releasing some of the sound.

We breathe together several times and then Cindy lets out a long, loud 'Ahhh!' I notice that her face looks very tense and tight. I ask her what she is experiencing in her face and body.

Cindy: I am stopping the sound from fully coming out.

Diane: Can you relax your face? Take in another breath, now let's sigh out the tension.

Cindy:	Ah – mmmmm…I feel like a little girl in my backyard looking at the sunset. (Her eyes are closed.)
Diane:	mmm.
Cindy:	Yet part of me wants to burn the house down.
Diane:	What are you experiencing now?
Cindy:	Rage again… It's too much… I'm scared…
Diane:	I am with you. Would you like me to help you carry the rage?
Cindy:	Can you hold my hand?
Diane:	Yes.

Cindy wants to scream again. I yell with her. We pause in between each scream and breathe deeply together. The sound gradually changes to an 'm-m-m' and then a series of moans and groans. Cindy says, 'It's like labour – part of it feels like wonderful energy and part of it feels difficult.'

I suggest we try drumming while toning together, that we make a safe space and not push so hard. I am thinking that I don't want her to push feelings that aren't yet ready to emerge. We talk about the 'labour' metaphor and that perhaps the 'baby' is not yet ready to come out. I tell her that there is a tendency for many traumatized people to push and rush themselves in an attempt to get to the root of the trauma. It is often difficult to be patient with oneself and the process. I don't want Cindy to retraumatize herself unnecessarily.

Cindy gets teary while I'm talking. She says, 'The little girl is very scared. I usually don't listen to the little girl…my adult part wants to hurry up and get it over with.' I continue to encourage her to go slowly. I tell her we need to make it safe for the little girl to come out and get her needs met. I also think about the latent content of her words, the possible sexual reference. I ask if she would prefer to sing or play to the little girl to comfort her. Cindy likes the idea of singing together while we drum.

We each take a conga drum. Cindy begins playing a simple rhythm at a medium tempo. I play with her and she syncopates off of my basic beat. She begins singing 'ah-ah uh' and I join her in unison. We then harmonize and sing a simple descending melody line. We sing the following words in unison.

| Cindy: | Little girl. |
| Diane: | Little girl. |

Cindy:	Ah-h little girl.
Diane:	Ah-h little girl.
Cindy:	I'm here.
Diane:	I'm here.
Cindy:	I was pulling you.
Diane:	(I repeat her words and melody, mirroring her.) I was pulling you.
Cindy:	Making you run very fast.
Diane:	(mirroring) Making you run very fast.
Cindy:	Very fast.
Diane:	I need to listen to you.
Cindy:	Try to breathe and stay with you.
Diane:	(mirroring) Try to breathe and stay with you.
Cindy:	This is new for me.
Diane:	(in unison) This is new for me.
Cindy:	To open up my listening ears.
Diane:	(mirroring) To open up my listening ears.

We continue singing about taking time and listening and being patient. The melody remains simple but has more variety. I sing unison, harmonize with her and mirror her. At other points, I sing as her double (inner voice) and add feelings or thoughts she may not be aware of yet or have the words for. When I am accurate Cindy repeats what I have sung or responds directly to my words.

Diane:	We don't have to do anything we don't want to.
Cindy:	We don't have to make a happy face.
Diane:	We don't have to make a happy face.
Cindy:	We've got time to be a little girl…you didn't have that before. You had to grow up fast cause no one took care!
Diane:	Cause no one took care!
Cindy:	Of your precious feelings.
Diane:	Of your precious feelings.

Our phrases overlap in this last section of the 'song'. Cindy stops drumming and I continue. We sing for a few more minutes and then Cindy begins to cry. I keep singing but change the words to sounds (m-m-m and ah-h-h). I often sing up a third or fourth and descend to a minor third or fifth. I slow the tempo of the drumming and play more softly. When I notice Cindy has stopped crying I sing, 'Time to breathe'.

Cindy:	Time to play…play in the sandbox.
Diane:	In the sandbox.
Cindy:	Build a castle, then we knock it down.
Diane:	We knock it down.
Cindy:	Then we laugh.
Diane:	Then we laugh.
Cindy:	She's saying, 'Look at me mommy, I'm playing!'
Diane:	Look at me, look at me!
Cindy:	I'm pretty. I'm pretty when I smile.
Diane:	I'm pretty when I smile and when I cry and even if I'm angry, I'm still pretty.
Cindy:	Look what I can do. I'm skipping, la, la, la, la.

We continue to sing phrases using 'la', then we switch to 'li' and sing in unison and harmony. Cindy is singing playfully with the full range of her voice. I attempt to match her melodies and vocal quality. I use the drum and cymbal to accent and support our playful singing. We are now both in the imaginal realm singing as her little girl, allowing for a reparative experience to occur. I feel that Cindy's 'little girl' is getting a need filled that was never attended to in the past.

Cindy begins singing, 'Are you sleeping, are you sleeping?' and I recognize the lyrics and melody to 'Frère Jacques'. I play it on the piano and join in the song. Cindy sings, 'Why should I get up? There's nothing much to get up for.' I respond, 'What would you like this morning; what would you like to eat?' She laughs. We continue in this make believe musical world. We sing about playing hide and seek. We have sung *to* Cindy's child-self, *as* her child-self, and now I am singing as her 'good mother' while she continues to play out the role of her inner child; only this is a childhood Cindy never had.

After the session, I sit and write. I write about the process. I feel happy that I stopped Cindy from pushing herself and unwittingly creating a traumatic re-enactment with myself as the perpetrator. I haven't always been as conscious of this particular dynamic that is especially prevalent with sexually abused clients. I think about the progression of the session and Cindy's courage and creativity.

I recall Cindy's words when we processed the music: 'Playing took me by surprise!' She went on to say, 'I thought healing my abuse meant feeling a lot of pain every time I came to therapy. I didn't realize that playing and being a little girl was also a part of healing.'

Re-enactment or repetition of familiar patterns and behaviour as well as therapeutic regression are essential elements of depth psychology, traumatology and vocal psychotherapy. Controlled regression within a therapeutic re-enactment allows clients to return to earlier stages in their development to rework unresolved conflicts, address unmet dependency needs, and repair early injuries to the self. Music can easily penetrate the boundaries between the conscious and the unconscious layers of the psyche providing access to young, encapsulated parts of the self. Music can melt through rational defences and speak to, as, or for regressed parts of the personality. Music speaks in the language of dreams, the language of emotions, the language of the unconscious. Music travels through time effortlessly. A repetitive chord progression and the sound of lullaby-like singing can relax ego boundaries and enable an adult client to revisit childhood. Through the use of music and words within the therapeutic relationship, adult 'children' can have corrective emotional experiences, let go of the need to repeat the past, and experience the joy of finding one's true voice.

CHAPTER 5

Contributions
from Intersubjectivity

When I began my private practice I was studying at a psychoanalytically informed institute. The model of the therapist–client relationship that I was taught was one in which the therapist remained neutral. My own analyst also worked this way: not exactly a 'blank screen' – he was caring, compassionate, but non-disclosing and more or less anonymous so that he was available for my transferential projections.

I tried to follow this model. I remember that I stopped wearing my favourite long, dangly earrings in order to look more the part. After a while I missed my singing career. I felt like I was wearing a straitjacket. I realized I could not and did not want to work this way.

Over the years I studied at various institutes and eventually found a supervisor who was a Jungian analyst but also trained in object relations theory and was very interested in alternative therapies. It was during this period that I continuously wrestled with my role as a vocal psychotherapist. How neutral should and did I want to be? How possible was neutrality when working so collaboratively in the music with the client? Was it wrong to sometimes share my own experience, touch or hug someone, or cry with my clients?

Like many depth psychologists, one of my core beliefs is that the relationship between the client and the therapist is the primary healing agent in psychotherapy. In human development the self cannot develop without a relationship to another self or selves (Kohut 1977). In vocal psychotherapy, music can be a bridge to relationship. It can help create a safe, transitional space between the inner and the outer world (Winnicott 1971). It can provide an environment where two people can play together, where the client can explore and experiment with new ways of being and relating. Sounding, singing and vocally improvising can directly access the client's feelings and provide a means of expressing them so that they can be witnessed, shared and accepted within a significant relationship. The musical connection can help to build and strengthen the relationship between the client and the therapist just as a trusting client–therapist relationship can deepen the musical interaction. Pre-composed and improvised songs can also provide a container within which a therapeutic regression can be facilitated, and conscious and unconscious memories, feelings and associations can be accessed, processed and gradually integrated within the safety of the client–therapist relationship (Austin 1991, 1993, 1996, 1998, 1999, 2001).

A therapist's ability to remain present and to participate fully in the relationship with the client is essential if transformations of consciousness are to occur. Whether the therapist or client is silent or actively engaged in speaking, sounding, singing or playing music, both therapist and client are co-creating the therapy session.

Jung (1929) suggested the analyst is as much in the analysis as is the client and that 'the analyst's personality is one of the main factors in the cure' (Jung 1916, p.260). Sedgwick (1994) expanded on Jung's idea that the therapist's 'getting right with himself' (p.7) can have a significant transformative effect on a client. Many contemporary psychoanalytic perspectives refer to the reciprocal influence and the complex conscious and unconscious impact therapist and client have on one another (Ferenczi 1988; Kalsched 1996; Kohut 1977; Ogden 1994). Psychological growth of either party eventuates in growth of the other.

Natterson and Friedman (1995) refer to the contemporary perspective, in which therapist and client are both portrayed as real people who co-create the therapeutic relationship, as 'intersubjectivity'. An intersubjective approach places great importance on the interplay of the conscious and unconscious subjectivities of both people in the relationship. Psychological growth of either the client or the therapist results in growth of the other.

Early on in my career, I remember hearing and agreeing that a client could only progress as far as the therapist had progressed in his or her own process. I have had the experience of working through a difficult issue, and then observing a breakthrough in a client with a similar issue. Colleagues I have spoken with are familiar with this phenomenon. One of my first clients, a very sensitive and intuitive young woman, looked at me one day and said, 'You can help me grieve but I don't think you can help me with my anger.' Of course, this remark could be interpreted as a defence or transference, but I believe she was making an accurate assessment of the situation. At that point in my life, I was not very comfortable expressing anger or having anger directed toward me. I believe there is a direct correlation between what I can accept in myself and what I can accept in my clients (and others). Since then, I have worked hard to become comfortable feeling, expressing and receiving anger. I have observed that now many of my clients are able to identify and express their anger toward others and toward me and are willing to work toward transforming their anger and rage into creativity and self-assertion.

Maroda (1991) examines the therapist's motivation for doing treatment and suggests that just as most clients have the desire to be transformed and healed by the therapist, many therapists also have a need to be healed by the patient. This need will of course vary from therapist to therapist.

> We seek to be healed ourselves and we heal our old 'afflicted' caretakers as we heal our patients... As therapists we are allowed the control that eluded us as children. This control offers the legitimate possibility for facilitating a better outcome, yet also proffers a situation where our frustrated needs for intimacy are gratified while minimizing the interpersonal risks we must take. (p.38)

No matter how much inner work we have done as therapists to resolve our complexes and conflicts, there is always the possibility for more growth. Each client brings unique challenges. Some will require us to dive a little deeper and, in the process of facilitating their journeys, we might experience a measure of healing that has not occurred before.

Working as a therapist provides me with an opportunity and the impetus to continue on a path of self-awareness and individuation. Sometimes while accompanying someone through the inner world of the unconscious, darkened areas of my own psyche are illuminated and, in order to be of service to my client, I must face these unwanted and unfamiliar aspects of myself – what Jung (1959) would call the 'Shadow' – and work to accept them.

Intersubjectivity places great emphasis on the collaborative nature of psychotherapy. Collaboration does not mean that the client and therapist are identical or that their roles are the same. The relationship is equal but not symmetrical, equal but not the same (Natterson and Friedman 1995). The therapist's role is to be in the service of the client, to guide, witness, support, companion and oversee the therapeutic process. The therapist is capable of providing a reparative experience and can help clients recognize and express feelings and needs.

Because a collaborative approach is non-authoritarian, it frees therapists from the pressures of perfectionism and the unrealistic need to have all the answers. Therapists bring their professional expertise to the relationship but this approach allows them to take more risks, make more creative interventions and offer more open interpretations because their expertise does not entitle them to arbitrary power and the client is directly involved in sharing the responsibility for the treatment (Natterson and Friedman 1995). In addition, a non-authoritarian approach supports and encourages spontaneity and authenticity in the client.

The collaborative nature of the therapeutic relationship leads to eventual consensual agreement and empowers the client. Clients can often teach the therapist how to help them. Schafer (1983) believes the client is often an unacknowledged source of strength and stability in the therapeutic relationship.

Making music with another person is by its very nature collaborative. Client and therapist are both involved in a creative process that requires mutual participation and cooperation. Particularly when improvising, 'the music and the communication in the music come from two minds finding meaning together' (Ansdell 1995, p.13). Collaboration promotes understanding of self and other and increases the potential for the development of trust and intimacy. It necessitates humility on the part of the therapist and the capacity to relinquish the need to know and the need to be in control. Then we can truly listen and allow our clients to teach us how to help them.

The following example is taken from my session notes:

> She wanted to work with the orphan image from her dream, the part of her that feels withdrawn, 'in limbo'. I offered her choices. It felt like a collaborative process. She could play, sing or dance. She wanted to sound and dance and have me play the piano. She wanted a steady, continuous rhythm. Hearing this made her cry; hearing that the music would keep on going even if she stopped. It would ground her. Her sounds began with moans and sighs and then became reminiscent of a young child experimenting with her voice. Her movements were small and tentative. She gradually began

exploring the space with her arms and legs, uncurling herself as if she was coming out of a cocoon into the daylight. It was very moving. She said, 'I needed a witness…to be called out… If I stopped it didn't mean the piano's voice would stop…it would continue to speak to me so I wouldn't be alone… I could continue on.'

There are many aspects of a musical collaboration. As client and therapist work to create something together they explore the various elements of music. The client has the opportunity to experience the aesthetic and emotional significance of the effect of different harmonies, melodies and rhythms. Therapists must remain sensitive to their clients' musical and psychological needs and aware of their own musical biases while shaping musical interventions.

Improvising lyrics adds another dimension to the musical collaboration. The use of words can create a greater differentiation between the client and the therapist, perhaps because words are generally more concrete and specific than music is. I have found that when I sing my own words in response to the clients' words (instead of repeating their words), the transference and countertransference can become more complex. I am taking a more active role by questioning and using my countertransferential feelings to deepen the therapeutic process and help the clients understand and make meaning out of what they are experiencing (Austin 1998).

I am aware that I am learning from my clients all the time. I have noticed that when there is an authentic relationship between the client and myself, I am more likely to get an honest reaction to a question or an intervention. I agree with Maroda (1991) that the client 'will tell you everything you need to know if you will only listen to him and consult with him' (pp. 21–22). Of course, the client has to trust the therapist in order to risk the vulnerability of complete honesty. Much has been written about building trust and how important it is for the therapist to be consistent, dependable, accepting and empathic (Greenson 1967; Herman 1992; Kohut 1977; Miller 1981; Winnicott 1965; Yalom 2002). Many clients, especially those with deep trust issues, require even more. They require the therapist to endure being seen realistically as another human being, a human being who can admit to a feeling that the client has accurately identified, a human being who also makes mistakes and can acknowledge and take responsibility for them.

This situation arose recently with Sandy. We were improvising music and lyrics together at the piano. She chose the chords F, Bb, C7. She took the lead playing and singing and I supported her. I repeated her lyrics, sang unison, harmonized and added some lyrics of my own. When we finished I asked her what she experienced during the improvisation. She surprised me by saying she felt angry. She said I took up too much space with my singing. She went on to say, 'I can't believe I'm saying this... I know I've been working on my anger but I've never been able to express it in the moment when I feel it. It's definitely connected to what we were talking about before, you know, my mother taking up all the space... Are you all right? Now I'm feeling anxious.'

I assured Sandy I was fine and this was such progress for her. I said I realized I was singing too much at some point but for some reason I continued. She was right and I was glad she told me. She looked uncomfortable and as if she was starting to cry. 'That was so scary to say...you're sure we're all right?' I affirmed her courage in speaking up and again reassured her that I was not angry or hurt. She said, 'I guess I really am finding my own voice!'

Little (1981), Maroda (1991) and Searles (1979) address the significance of responding to clients who accurately perceive the therapist's state of mind. Many clients are extremely sensitive to the therapist's conscious and unconscious feelings and thoughts. These clients were often intuitive children whose feelings and perceptions were denied or went unacknowledged by their parents. They end up mistrusting their feelings and their sense of reality. As Fred put it, 'No one ever talked about feelings... I thought I was imagining how bad things were... I felt crazy.'

Many traditionally trained analysts and psychoanalytically oriented psychotherapists analyse why the client asks about their health rather than answering the question and then searching to see if there is a deeper meaning underlying the question. Or, analysts remain silent in the interest of not burdening the client (Maroda 1991). These therapists forget that although they can control their overt verbal responses, they cannot control what they are communicating in the interactive field between client and therapist. Thus, they may unwittingly harm the client by re-enacting an all too familiar scenario.

Alice Miller (1997) describes how silence can sometimes feel punishing. She recalls the abuse she suffered but says none of it 'was as threatening or destructive as my mother's silence at the time of my greatest dependence on her...as a child I had no choice but to suffer my mother's vindictive silence and assign the blame to myself' (pp.21–22). Of course there are times when silence is necessary and healing. Miller's concern and my own is when the therapist's silence or withholding of information is countertherapeutic.

An example of responding honestly when my client accurately identified my feeling state follows:

> Fred stared at me for a few moments. We had just finished playing music together. He played the guitar and I sang. It was a bluesy, melancholy improvisation – minor and slow. There was a flow to it, a nice exchange of musical ideas. 'Are you all right?' he asked. I wasn't crying or teary but I wasn't all right. I had received some bad news that morning. 'I'm feeling sad today,' I said. He kept staring then shook his head up and down sympathetically. We sat in silence for a few moments and then he said, 'me too'. I asked him how my revelation affected him. He said, 'I'm sorry – I hope it isn't anything too bad.' I assured him it wasn't. He then smiled and said, 'I thought you were going to do that therapist thing, you know, turn it back to me. That would have pissed me off. I knew I was picking up something.' 'Really,' I said. 'Yeah… Thanks for telling me.'

Because of the interactive nature of vocal psychotherapy, it is impossible for therapists to avoid bringing themselves into the relationship. Working deeply within the music requires an awareness of the complex multi-layered verbal and non-verbal communication that takes place between client and therapist. The importance of transference and countertransference to and within the music has been written about by Austin (1998, 1996, 2001), Dvorkin (1998), Priestley (1975), Scheiby (1998), Streeter (1999), Turry (1998) and others who stress the benefits and challenges of the musical encounter.

As my clients explore their feelings, perceptions and imaginings in the music, I explore mine and we affect each other. Although, as therapist, my attention is focused primarily on the client's musical, emotional and psychological world, the fact remains that together we are creating something that did not exist until we came together, such as a rhythm, a melody, a lyric, a new way of perceiving the self, each other and the world.

> Sounds – loud, soft, soothing
> Two voices travelling together
> Intimate strangers
> Out for a swim
> There is a sadness in the waves today
> We both feel the pull

Tears fall from her eyes
And I catch them in my melody
We wade together into the dream
And emerge with a new song.

Therapist's self-disclosure

Even the most conservative psychotherapists cannot help but disclose things about themselves in the way they dress, their body language, facial expressions, the sound of their voice and their interpersonal style. We are at all times revealing some aspect of ourselves even when we are not providing specific information. As previously discussed, this is especially true for music and vocal psychotherapists who are also continuously revealing themselves in their musical choices and interactions. This is an implicit and inevitable process. Not only are we revealing things about ourselves but just as we are observing our clients, they are also observing us (Stolorow, Brandchaft and Atwood 1987).

Self-disclosure, however, does not mean that therapists should reveal everything about themselves indiscriminately or provide answers to every question their clients pose without considering the client's best interest from a theoretical perspective. Pearlman and Saakvitne (1995) believe the essential considerations when making decisions about self-disclosure are the therapist's comfort sharing personal information, the length of time the client has been in treatment and the extent of the psychotherapist's experience. More experienced therapists feel less compelled to work by the rules. Increased confidence and self-knowledge and an ability to sort out countertransference issues enables them increasingly to trust their own instincts. Like experienced musicians, they first master theory and technique before improvising.

I have found that conscious self-disclosure can be very effective in building trust and intimacy with particular clients. Sharing my experience with certain clients can also be genuinely helpful and supportive to them. One factor that influences my viewpoint is my client base. Many of my clients suffer in varying degrees from symptoms related to traumatic childhood experiences. Many trauma survivors need a real relationship in order to establish any degree of trust and intimacy. They need the therapist to be more genuine in the relationship. A distant or detached therapist is unlikely to provide them with the kind of experience they require in order to heal (Herman 1992; McCann and Pearlman 1990b).

Besides sharing my state of mind with a client who has accurately identi-fied it (as when Fred questioned me, asking if I was all right and I told him I was feeling sad), I sometimes share my personal experiences with clients when it seems appropriate and in the service of the client. Of course, I have to be mindful of why I am doing this and whose need I am meeting. This issue speaks to the necessity for therapists to have a life outside of therapy. Having a family and friends and other interests enables therapists to lead a balanced life and helps to ensure that they do not use their clients to meet their own unmet needs. It is also important for music therapists to make music outside of therapy for the same reason.

I found that sharing personal experiences was sometimes connected to being a role model for my clients. Since many of my clients are creative arts therapists we have many things in common. For example, when Marie was struggling to write her thesis and became extremely self-critical because it was taking so long, I shared my difficulties writing my own thesis with her. She found my disclosure very supportive and 'normalizing'. I also shared practical information with her about approaches and attitudes that helped me to complete my thesis.

Similarly, when Jenna was questioning her ability to start a private practice in art therapy, I shared that I had gone through similar doubts during my first year of private practice. At first it was hard for her to believe this but as we talked she recognized the feelings I shared as similar to her own. She said, 'I don't feel so isolated now…it's just that I don't have any friends working in private practice so they don't understand my fears…do I really know enough, will I get any clients, but…wow, maybe I can do this!'

Sharing my personal experience illustrates the supportive, educative aspects of vocal psychotherapy. It did not, however, prevent further in-depth exploration of the underlying causes of Marie's or Jenna's fear and self-doubt.

CHAPTER 6

The Primacy
of Countertransference

In vocal psychotherapy, countertransference is used by the therapist as a primary instrument to gain understanding, information and knowledge of the client as well as to increase empathy and strengthen the therapeutic partnership. I refer to countertransference in the totalistic sense (Racker 1968), which includes all the feelings, sensations, images, thoughts, in short everything that arises in the therapist as a psychological response to the client.

This viewpoint is much broader than Freud's original description (1912) of countertransference as the therapist's unconscious reaction to the client's transference. The totalistic definition encompasses all the various kinds of countertransference and the names given to them by prominent analysts. I will mention some types most frequently referred to in the psychoanalytic literature.

Racker (1968) defines 'complementary identification' as countertransference that occurs when the client treats the therapist as a significant person or thing from the client's life. The therapist identifies with this person and may even act and feel like the person.

Racker (1968) defines 'concordant identification' as a type of countertransference that occurs when the therapist identifies and empathizes with the client. There is a union between the various experiences, impulses and defences of the subject and the object. Racker makes the point that concordant identification is usually excluded from the concept of countertransference unless the term is used in its wider sense.

The wider sense is preferred. If one considers that the analyst's concordant identification (his understandings) are a sort of reproduction of his own past processes, especially of his own infancy, and that this reproduction or re-experience is carried out as response stimuli from the patient, one will be more ready to include the concordant identification in the concept of countertransference. (p.135)

Priestley (1994) equates concordant identification with what she calls 'empathic' or 'e-countertransference' (p.87). She associates e-countertransference with the image of 'a plucked string instrument (the patient) whose music resonates on its sympathetic strings (the therapist)' (p.87). In this process the therapist resonates or feels the patient's feelings, often before these feelings are available to the patient's conscious awareness. She makes the point that e-countertransference is an 'echoing form of countertransference' (p.99) in which the patient's physical or emotional pain echoes in the body of the therapist and that some e-countertransference manifestations only appear while the music therapist is improvising.

Projective identification is a primitive defence mechanism that was given special emphasis by Melanie Klein and her followers. It involves a strong countertransferential reaction on the part of the therapist and is often seen in its most obvious form with adolescents and borderline clients. There are differing interpretations of this phenomenon but most definitions include at least two steps. First, the patient splits off parts of the self, emotions and/or transference reactions and projects them onto the therapist. When this defence mechanism works (the second step), the therapist feels unconsciously controlled by the patient, identifies with the projected aspects and may unwittingly act out the feelings with the patient, for example, expressing the patient's dissociated anger (Davies and Frawley 1994; Moore and Fine 1990; Ogden 1991).

As previously mentioned, Jung (1946) referred to countertransference in different ways. He spoke about 'psychic infection', 'induction' and 'participation mystique'. He believed it was the fate of the analyst to be psychologically affected and infected by his patients, that patient and analyst were in a mutual alchemical process and that the analyst's psychological transformations could have a healing effect on the patient. These fusion states, that he described as a 'participation mystique', have both a creative and a destructive aspect and could be synonyms for projective identification (Schwartz-Salant 1989).

Following is an example of countertransference in vocal psychotherapy:

Today's session with Cindy was interesting. I felt very critical of her. I judged her music as superficial. We improvised using piano, voice and drum. She played a major chord progression and I played the conga drum. We sang sounds together, lots of call and response and lots of short melodic phrases. I felt she was attempting to be playful but it didn't feel real to me. Afterwards, when we talked about the music, I thought she was avoiding something. Her avoidance brought up anger in me. I was surprised by my reaction; I am usually more patient and would understand that she was most likely experiencing resistance. I asked her how she was feeling with me today and she replied, 'uncomfortable'. The discomfort had to do with feeling good, with having good news and feeling awkward and embarrassed for wanting to tell me about it. She said, 'I don't want to be a show-off'. After verbally processing the origins of her fear of 'bragging', I thought I sensed some anger underneath. Anger is very difficult for Cindy to feel and express. We talked about how it felt to suppress good feelings and to keep a low profile in order to feel safe. She said, 'There's a critical part of me that tells me it's wrong to say good things about myself.' I asked her if she could play that part. She agreed and picked up the woodblock. She hit it over and over again with a lot of force. She asked me to play a grounding rhythm on the conga drum so I did. Her playing had a relentless quality to it. She sped up the tempo and made primal vocal sounds. The sounds got louder. I felt like she was beating someone up. Then she stopped abruptly and said, 'It's like my father's voice…he used to say things like, 'Who do you think you are?' whenever I felt proud of something I did or wanted something more out of life.' I asked her if she ever got angry at him or at that critical part of herself. She said, 'I never got angry at him…that part, maybe… I probably turn my anger against myself'.

After the session with Cindy I had many thoughts about what had occurred and my countertransferential reactions. While writing about it, I was struck by the similarities between complementary countertransference, projective identification and psychic infection. It seemed as if Cindy was treating me as if I were her father (a negative father transference) and I was identifying with and feeling like him (complementary countertransference). Projective identification could also be used to describe what occurred. Cindy split off a feeling or a part of herself (anger, the critic or negative father complex), projected it onto me, and I unconsciously identified with the feelings and experienced them as my own (psychic infection).

Projective identification is activated when feelings are so intolerable that clients defend themselves by keeping the feelings out of conscious awareness. Although projective identification can be a disturbing experience for the therapist, it is also a way to learn about the client's inner world on a gut level, to walk in their shoes so to speak. More than a defence, projective identification provides the client with a means to communicate important information about the self, information that is too unbearable to consciously know about and express in any other way.

There were other countertransferential feelings present during Cindy's session. I felt her playfulness was not authentic and I thought she was avoiding something. I identified with her fear of being attacked for 'showing off'. I also had a parent who could be very critical of me and I felt as if I had heard 'Who do you think you are?' many times while growing up. I felt protective of Cindy while drumming and concerned that she might be beating herself up (symbolically). So using clinical terminology, there were many moments when I experienced concordant identification or e-countertransference, many moments when I felt like a positive mother and many moments when Cindy's wounds resonated with my own and brought us closer.

I have described concepts and ideas about countertransference and how it operates. These concepts, these terms, are of value not only as an aid in understanding the client and the therapeutic process but in conveying information to other professionals. But more important than the terms used to convey what occurred during Cindy's session, was the experience she had while sounding and playing the woodblock and the insight she gained into her issues. This insight enabled her to begin to differentiate between her authentic self and the critical, persecutory part of her. Being able to identify an aspect of the self is the first step in separating from it – separating out and peeling away the 'not me' so there is more room for the 'me'.

Any music psychotherapist working in-depth is using him- or herself, as well as the music, as an 'instrument'. This human instrument needs the continued 'fine tuning' that personal psychotherapy and/or supervision provide in order to achieve the self-knowledge and self-awareness necessary to recognize and work effectively with transference, countertransference and other unconscious dynamics that emerge in a therapeutic relationship. This self-knowledge increases therapists' confidence, resulting in the ability to trust their countertransferential reactions and use them to take the work to deeper levels. According to Jung (1951), we must 'go on learning endlessly, and never forget that each new case brings new problems to light and thus gives rise to unconscious assumptions that have never before been constellated' (p.116).

The unconscious contents of both client and therapist are easily accessed through music. Singing together is especially challenging because of the increased intimacy of using the body as the primary instrument. There is less distance between the therapeutic dyad, both emotionally and often physically. As many clients and students have reported, when you sing with someone you are not only sharing sounds but also vibrations. Some clients have found this shared energy field as intimate or even more intimate than touch. The client and therapist can affect each other psychically on a level that goes far deeper than words. The music psychotherapist needs to be well acquainted with his or her own issues, feelings, strengths and vulnerabilities not only to better understand and empathize with clients but especially to be able to differentiate the client's feelings from his or her own.

The wise wound

Therapists who are extremely empathic and sensitive to their own countertransference reactions and who use their bodily sensations, their feelings, intuition, thoughts and images as an essential part of the way they practise, are sometimes referred to as 'wounded healers' (Guggenbuhl-Craig 1971; Pearlman and Saakvitne 1995; Reinhart 1989; Searles 1979; Sedgwick 1994). Alice Miller's (1997) analytical work with psychotherapists led her to conclude that many of her clients had been highly intuitive children with an amazing ability to perceive and respond unconsciously to the needs of their narcissistic parents or caretakers. Her clients' needs for understanding, empathy and mirroring, however, were not met and had to be repressed which resulted in a deep wound – the loss of the true, feeling self. Being needed became a substitute for being seen and accepted, and guaranteed the child a measure of security.

> Later, these children not only become mothers of their own mothers but also take over at least part of the responsibility for their siblings and eventually develop a special sensitivity to unconscious signals manifesting the needs of others. No wonder they often choose to become psychotherapists. (p.9)

As Miller points out, many of these 'adult children' end up in therapy and some, because of their quest for more self-knowledge coupled with their desire to help other injured people, become therapists. The ones who have succeeded in working through many of their childhood wounds and continue on the road to recovery often become gifted therapists.

There are wounded therapists who are unaware of being injured or unconscious of the extent of their psychic wounds. Guggenbuhl-Craig (1971), Miller (1981), Pearlman and Saakvitne (1995) and Sedgwick (1994) describe some of the negative repercussions that can occur when wounded therapists do not recognize or have not sufficiently worked through their own issues. These therapists may attempt to heal themselves vicariously by healing their clients; they may unconsciously use their clients to meet their own unmet needs for understanding, mirroring and idealization. They may retraumatize clients through their own 'addiction to trauma' (Austin 2002, p.245) – the need for emotional intensity and drama to compensate for the lack of connection to their own authentic feelings.

'A therapist creates safety in part by knowing, noticing and understanding what she brings into the therapeutic relationship' (Pearlman and Saakvitne 1995, p.178). When awareness of inner conflicts or traumatic events remains unconscious or dissociated, the therapy is jeopardized. Many music therapists, especially those new to the field, are unprepared for the intensity of the feelings and the intimacy that can occur within the therapeutic relationship. There is no substitute for personal experience in psychotherapy (ideally music psychotherapy) to increase self-awareness and gain first hand knowledge of what it is like to sit on the other side of the couch.

Conversely, there are therapists who have been deeply wounded and have undergone personal analysis or another healing process and are able to recognize their own wounded part as well as their healer part. 'Such an analyst recognizes time and again how the patient's difficulties constellate his own problems, and vice versa, and he therefore openly works not only on the patient but on himself' (Guggenbuhl-Craig 1971, p.130). By working through their childhood injuries, these wounded healers gain an enhanced capacity to understand and empathize with their client's struggles. Years spent exploring their own interiority also provide them with a window into their own issues so that they are more able to discern and use countertransferential reactions to the benefit of their clients (Rippere and Williams 1985). Ideally they know what it is like to feel frightened when expressing difficult feelings and ashamed when revealing parts of themselves that have been hidden and never seen the light of day. They understand the vulnerability of trusting another human being (the therapist) when their experience has taught them that people are by nature untrustworthy. Consciously or unconsciously, they often draw upon the wisdom of their wounds and the induced feelings, sensations and other experiences of their clients to make therapeutic interventions.

Such therapists often bring an unsurpassed commitment to their work and a special appreciation of the courage necessary to confront one's difficulties in order to regain a sense of self. They can also make excellent role models for their clients. Clients generally feel safer with a therapist who has 'been there'; as they say in Alcoholics Anonymous, someone who doesn't just 'talk the talk' but who 'walks the walk'.

> What happens to a broken heart?
> It can fall forever
> then shatter
> a fragile Humpty Dumpty
> never to be put back together again
>
> It can bind itself
> with tough and tender vines
> and hide behind a crusty wall
> sacrificing life for safety
>
> Or it can heal
> become holy but not quite whole
> Its wound a space where
> every song and sigh and every
> cry is welcome
> a place where no scream
> is too loud
> and no fear too fierce to
> be held
> It can heal
> and knowing all that it knows
> still love again
> Then the broken heart becomes a
> wise wound

There are times when music psychotherapists need to join with clients to lend their ego when the client is faltering on the path or to provide a more symbiotic way of relating when there are early developmental injuries blocking the way. Participating in the 'illusion of symbiosis' (Machtiger 1992, p.127) can provide clients with a reparative experience so that they can renegotiate separation–individuation and continue on their journey to selfhood. Searles (1979) has written extensively on the necessity for therapeutic symbiosis and mutual regression when working in depth with clients, especially clients with severe psychological injuries. He believes that a therapist without an 'affliction' could not work effectively in the symbiotic phase of the client's treatment but it is critical that the therapist have the capacity to function while being partially regressed.

To accomplish this, therapists need courage and strength born of familiarity with the inner world so that they can feel and face whatever emerges from the clients' and their own unconscious while remaining emotionally present. Permeable boundaries allow therapists to have a reasonably controlled regressive experience in order to share in the clients' affective states rather than simply observing them. It is, of course, a matter of degree (Maroda 1991). Therapists' boundaries also need to be strong and resilient enough to feel intense emotions without being flooded by them. If the concept of therapeutic regression is accepted as desirable, 'then the therapist's capacity for merging and separating become vitally important' (Maroda 1991, p.36).

Anne Alvarez (1992) describes the ideal therapist as someone capable of being disturbed enough to have the capacity to relate to and feel for patients but sane enough to be with them. I would add sane enough to contain and help the client digest the unprocessed affects and conscious enough to assist the client in transforming unproductive or destructive patterns and ways of being.

Wounded healers have an acute sensitivity and almost psychic ability to tune into other people's feeling states. Using their countertransference they can help clients to identify and express their feelings and perhaps understand their unconscious conflicts. The 'antenna' that helped them survive difficult childhoods now enables them to attune finely to their clients and relate to them with a greater depth and breadth of emotional responsiveness and empathy.

I have often experienced this level of enhanced empathy when singing with clients. It seems like a combination of empathy, intuition and identification that when used consciously enables me to enter the psychic space of another person and retreat if the integrity of my boundaries is threatened. Some examples follow:

> I made a leap of faith – used my intuition and sense of Ann, where she was emotionally. She had been singing about how hard she works and yet her

brother was getting on with and enjoying his life. We sang about how hard she worked as a child and I sang, 'So they would love me', and she repeated 'So they would love me', acknowledging this as truth. We had never discussed this before... I felt so sad. It seemed as if she did too.

Marie played a minor melody and gradually I added a vocal line. She was playing how it felt growing up in her home. I got chills. I felt we were going into a 'black hole'. I wasn't sure where she was except that I felt we were entering a room that had been locked for a long time. I felt young, scared and like it was hard to breathe. I forced myself to take a deep breath and played chords to hold the melody. She also took a breath and began singing with me. When the music ended she said, 'I don't know... I didn't see anything but it felt so lonely. I don't even know which house I was in but it was empty and I was alone and frightened...but then I heard your singing and I knew I wasn't alone. The music was giving sound to my experience and making it real. It sounded like how I felt.'

Marie dreamt of a sick dolphin dying in the snow. I asked her if she could sing to or as the dolphin... She regressed to seven or eight years old, a time when she felt depressed and wanted to die. She sang about stillness, not being able to reach out and feeling isolated. I sang 'I need help...does anybody see me, or hear me...does anybody care if I just fade away?' I kept breathing deeply and checking in with myself, noticing how I was being affected by Marie and the music. Marie started crying. I continued to sing what I sensed she was feeling, about being left alone and withdrawing from life: 'Where is my cousin? I miss her. Where are my grandparents?' She cried throughout my singing and afterwards she said, 'The dolphin couldn't connect to the other dolphins so she gave up – it was so good to hear you put words to my tears. I didn't have the words; I couldn't say it but you were my voice and what you sang was true.' I was singing about the abandon-ment and disconnection she felt when she left France and her cousin and grandparents. I felt on the verge of tears while singing. I went into my own 'still snowy place'. I thought of a song I wrote years ago about snow and loss...

Diving deep and surfacing

There are times when I use my countertransferential feelings in a way that Sedgwick describes as 'beyond empathy' (1994, p.109). In these moments, I feel as if I am entering the client's inner world, consciously loosening my boundaries and allowing a part of myself to merge with the client (if it is therapeutically indicated) and then emerge, affected by the experience but psychically intact (under optimal circumstances). There is an 'in and out' quality to the experience, like diving into water and surfacing, especially when vocally improvising within a fluid yet resilient musical environment.

I have noticed a difference in quality between times when I felt unconsciously overtaken by the client's feeling states and times when it seemed I consciously chose to enter into the client's experience. In the former situation I felt I had no control; tears sprang to my eyes, rage pulsed through my body, in what could be clinically described as projective identification or a participation mystique – a primitive psychological connection in which there is often no clear sense of difference between the psychic boundaries of two persons (Perera 1932).

However, the more experience I gained singing with clients, the more I realized that I often 'choose' to enter the client's inner world through a process I describe as submerging, merging and emerging. Through studying my session notes, I found a connection between physical distance and psychological/emotional closeness. Some examples of physical proximity and the relationship to psychic connection are as follows:

> I leaned in toward Marie as she was speaking. I wanted to get a sense of what she was feeling. A wave of sadness flowed through me.

> I moved my chair closer to Ann while she was singing. I closed my eyes and allowed her music to fill me so that I could experience her inner world.

> Cindy and I sat next to each other as we sang. I attuned my breathing to hers and all of my senses were focused on her. As we sang, I felt her fear and then an overwhelming sense of grief.

I also realized that every time I invite someone to the piano to vocally improvise with me, I am making a choice to open myself to the client's unconscious. There is the physical closeness of sitting next to each other combined with the emotional closeness breathing, singing and 'vibrating' together engenders.

As mentioned in Chapter 1, singing with someone is a very intimate experience. Singing is about opening: opening to oneself and the other. The internally resonating vibrations allow for a natural flow of energy, including sensations, feelings and images, to be exchanged between the client and the therapist. Improvising with another requires leaving the safety of the structured song behind and plunging into the unknown together. The playful, spontaneous nature of improvisation creates an environment where unconscious aspects of the client and the therapist can easily emerge and co-mingle. Singing together can be an intense experience for both participants.

The following excerpts are from my session notes:

> There is usually more contact when Marie and I sing together. I feel closer to her. She appears more accessible and embodied. Am I also more present and embodied when singing? Today we sang about her childhood. Her mother was not very affectionate or comfortable with feelings. Marie sang about how lonely she felt growing up. I began to feel very spacey and sleepy. The words became sounds, 'oo' mostly. I was playing in G minor. I sang unison and harmony with her. Her melodies became more varied and she utilized more of her vocal range. I began to feel sad. Afterwards, I asked her what she was experiencing when we were singing. She said, 'There is so much I don't remember…it all seems blurry whenever I think about my childhood. When we were singing the sounds, I felt like I was comforting a sad child.'

> I hesitated and then asked Cindy if she'd like to sing to, as, or about her 'little girl'. I was feeling vulnerable today and somewhat reluctant to go with her into a place that I suspected contained feelings of fear and loss.

> Ann went into a high-pitched crying sound. I joined her and sang unison and then dissonant harmonies. Her voice sounded more raw and primal than usual. Her singing grew louder and I felt a mixture of sadness and anger going through me.

The therapist's intention is an important aspect of this process. When my intention is to enter into a state of psychic connectedness, I allow my ego boundaries to relax and move from a focused to a more diffuse state of consciousness. Claremont de Castillejo (1973) refers to diffuse consciousness as a receptive attitude, 'an awareness of the unity of all life and a readiness for relationship' (p.15).

Emerging from a state of partial identification with the client is not always so easy. My notes also contain many examples of physical distancing as an aid to psychological distancing or reining in one's ego boundaries.

Then I had to pull back a bit in my chair to get clear, to maintain my own viewpoint. I pushed the chair back and the physical distance helped me tune into my own feelings.

In most of the examples, I found I used a combination of methods to dis-identify from the client. Physical distancing, body awareness and consciously moving from feeling to thinking helped me to clarify the distinction between self and other. Sometimes simply straightening my posture was helpful; other times I would feel my feet on the floor and my pelvis on my seat to ground and centre myself in my own body. Deep breathing also enabled me to focus on my own internal feelings and sensations as well as to release feelings I absorbed from my clients. Since feelings of empathy can easily move into feelings of identification, I learned the value of shifting into thinking mode when I felt I was losing my therapeutic stance. I was not always able to do this, of course, but when I could I found it most helpful. The music was also a resource for me as well as for the client. Certain instruments, like the drum, and particular rhythms and chord patterns grounded me in my own body and helped me separate from the client when I needed to.

> I forced myself to take a deep breath and continued singing. I added a simple, repetitive rhythm in the bass part of the piano. I took another deep breath and continued playing and singing.

> It felt good, the sensation of my hands hitting the drum. I felt my body moving and my throat opening… I felt more centred. I was coming back to myself. My energy was returning. It was a relief.

> I straightened up in my seat, took a deep breath and stopped crying.

> I rolled my chair back. I needed distance, space to think about where we were and where we needed to go.

> There was a hypnotic feeling to the music. I felt like we were still in it (altered state) when the music ended. It felt good to breathe. It helped to think about what I played and sang and what she sang. I needed to help her make sense of her experience and integrate it.

Working in-depth requires using myself as the primary instrument. As Yalom puts it, 'the most elegant and complex instrument of all – the Stradivarius of psychotherapy practice – the therapist's own self' (2002, p.51). It is through this instrument that I gain information and knowledge of my clients so that my empathy and understanding are increased. Like Priestley (1994) I often resonate to the client's music when it 'strikes a chord' in me. At those moments I may feel the client's feelings (especially when they are not available to the client). This phenomenon can occur while talking as well. Some metaphor, turn of phrase or description might trigger a sympathetic vibration (Nachmanovitch 1990) in me. I may respond with a feeling, sensation, have a memory or see an image that helps me gain more insight into my client.

My own wounds have contributed to the creation of an especially sensitive instrument, an instrument that picks up subtle nuances of feelings and changes in the client's ego state and emotional presence. It is easy for me to duet with a client's grief, fear or anger. It is easy to empathize with the client's songs of struggle and hope. My own woundedness and my passion to become my true self has led me to this career and is a factor in my ability to participate more deeply and personally in the client's healing process.

Instruments are sensitive. Pianos go out of tune, violin strings can wear out and drums sometimes need repairing. Being a human instrument requires commitment to self-care. Music therapy students often ask me what I do to take care of myself, to refuel. It is easy to understand why there is a high burnout rate in our profession. Our enhanced empathy and mutuality in the way we work make us susceptible to vicarious traumatization.

I discovered years ago that it is necessary for me to 'wash the day off'. The first thing I do when I get home each evening is to take a shower. I feel like I am clearing myself of my clients' energy and the feelings I may have absorbed during the day. I try to maintain a balance between work, play and rest. I have learned that I need to exercise. Yoga is especially good for me physically, psychologically and spiritually. I need to eat healthy foods and avoid skipping meals. I need to make sure I avoid isolation. I do this by being in a supervision group, taking classes and seeing my friends as often as I can. I need to pamper myself, have a massage, get a pedicure, buy myself some flowers. Listening to or making my own music is life affirming, as is being creative in any way I choose (writing, gardening). And I must have fun, connect with my inner child and invite her to come out and play with me. Give myself what I give others (which isn't always so easy!).

The therapist's hook

> Sometimes in the distance between us
> I come too close
> A door opens and I stand on a
> Slippery threshold
> Your hand beats out a cruel rhythm
> And my heart jumps
> Hungry eyes look into mine
> A child walking on the railroad tracks
> Sings of hidden rooms and lost love
> I fear, I long, to hold her
> She vanishes then reappears like a
> Recurrent dream
> Part familiar, part mystery
> Does she belong to you or me?

I define 'the therapist's hook' as the area of woundedness that allows the therapist to get caught in the client's material. Although I had been aware of this phenomenon in the past, it took on greater clarity and significance after writing about my use of countertransference.

I believe the therapist and the client co-create the therapeutic relationship and it is important when working with countertransference to avoid placing all the responsibility on the client for inducing feelings in the therapist. I found that when I could acknowledge the reciprocity of the relationship and take responsibility for the part I played in the interaction, it greatly benefited the client.

This was my experience when I apologized to Cindy for an empathic failure. I failed to pick up on the importance of what she was talking about – an upcoming dinner party. She was describing details with little affect and I thought she might be avoiding her feelings about her mother's lack of support with the party. I made an abrupt intervention toward the music and suggested she sing her feelings about the situation. She agreed to sing but looked hurt. I asked her what she was feeling and she said, 'Misunderstood'. She had never given a dinner party before and her mother didn't 'know about these things' so she really needed my help and support. We continued talking and gradually she told me she didn't think the party was a serious enough matter to merit my attention. 'It's not that important...and you didn't seem that interested.'

She also said that she felt shame for needing help. We continued exploring her feelings and she made a connection to the way she felt with her mother. 'I never asked her for help. It just wasn't an option… I had to help her all the time.' I pointed out that asking for my help this directly was new and a major step for her. I apologized for failing to understand the significance of the party. She began crying and said my apology touched her. She said:

> My mother never owned her stuff…she put it all on me… She said hurtful things and never apologized when I confronted her. When I was younger I always just assumed she was right cause she was the parent…and I was so used to feeling wrong all the time.

I realized after the session that I identified with some of the things Cindy said. I never asked my mother for help either and didn't expect any.

The following excerpt is an example of the therapist getting 'hooked' in the client's material. It illustrates the valuable information that can be obtained when the therapist is willing to look closely at his or her part in the interaction.

> Ann came to the piano and played and sang the feelings she had about her boyfriend's confession the night before. The music was in a minor key and slow in 4/4 time and seemed very structured and controlled. Her voice was barely audible and lacked feeling. I felt no impetus to join her nor did she ask me to. Afterwards, she said she didn't want to feel, especially to feel the impact of her boyfriend's behaviour. It wasn't 'convenient'. I took a deep breath. She said, 'I feel numb.' I checked in with myself. I didn't feel anything either. We both seemed to be disconnected – disconnected from each other and ourselves. When the session was over I noticed I felt mildly depressed and tired. I thought I had picked up Ann's 'numbness'. Upon further reflection I noticed some anger, but at who? Was I angry with her boyfriend or at Ann for showing no reaction to what I perceived as a betrayal? I realized I wanted Ann to get angry instead of putting up with this. I felt angry at her passivity. Images flashed before me of times when I put up with unacceptable behaviour because I was afraid of the repercussions of getting angry and taking action. I would then feel angry with myself for being passive. I eventually learned the reason for my numbing out, and developed some compassion for myself. I feared losing the person if I became angry at him or her.

This association to my previous fear of anger and the connection to loss enabled me to have more compassion for Ann and insight into her behaviour.

My frustration with her passivity was related to the anger I felt toward myself when I became passive. My ability to identify with her tendency to disconnect when feelings became unmanageable made me more sensitive to when and how she dissociated in sessions and how to work with this symptom. I gained a clearer understanding of Ann's abandonment issues and how they intensified her fear of anger. If she equated anger with loss (and I think she did) then she would experience great resistance to feeling and expressing anger at her boyfriend.

Stein (1992) makes the point that it is often 'impossible to tell with complete assurance who owns which psychic contents in the transference/countertransference process' (p.69). This implies that therapists should at least consider what their clients are suggesting about them without automatically assuming the client is projecting his or her feelings onto the therapist.

I find this to be especially true when working within the intense field of a musical encounter. The collaborative process of creating music together is especially challenging because the unconscious contents for both client and therapist are easily accessed through music. Defences and boundaries are easily bypassed and the client is often directly involved on a sensory, spiritual and feeling level with the music psychotherapist especially when singing is involved (Austin 1996).

Neutrality is a questionable concept when client and therapist are singing and making music together. Music psychotherapists cannot avoid consciously or unconsciously drawing on their personal relationship to music if they are present and participating in the creative process. The connection between their relationship to music and their emotions and inner life is an intimate and multi-layered one. It follows that therapists will at times psychically affect and 'infect' (Jung 1946) their clients as much as their clients affect them.

Therapists will not usually have a strong reaction to a client's material unless they have a psychological 'hook' – a place where the client's issues intersect with their own – and a client's projections will not hold unless there is a hook to hang them on. The therapist who knows this recognizes time and again how the patient's issues constellate his or her own.

Sedgwick (1994) believes the client unconsciously finds or even creates 'areas of parallel woundedness' (p.109) in the therapist. The purpose is to induce an intense empathic connection in the here and now so that the therapist will feel and understand the client's experience. Sedgwick finds there is 'a fundamental difference in degree and quality between a countertransference wound and empathy as usually described…the usual empathic connection seems more transient and less 'hooked' (1994, p.109). This symbiotic, merged type of empathy is essential for some severely wounded clients if any kind of healing and transformation is to take place (Maroda 1991).

The musical hook

The following example illustrates another kind of hook. The 'musical hook' refers to a moment when the music and/or lyrics intersect with the therapist's issues and trigger associations, memories and feelings for the therapist. I have found that this kind of transference to the music induces a strong reaction in the therapist.

> Marie brought in a song today, 'The Rose' (McBroom 1977). She heard it on the radio and it touched her. She had never heard it before. I knew the song well. I had a history with it. I never liked the song. I thought it was corny. Then recently, I was asked to sing it at a relative's funeral service. I have been singing all my life but never before have I lost control in public. I got to the middle section of the song and I started crying. It took me several moments to pull myself together and finish singing the song. So here I am months later singing and playing 'The Rose' with Marie. I thought I would be fine today, that I probably cried before because it was a funeral and I was feeling grief and loss. But when we got to the same section I felt the tears start. I looked at Marie. She was crying too. I straightened up in my seat, took a deep breath, and stopped crying. We finished singing. Marie was sniffling and blowing her nose. After a few moments I asked her what she was experiencing. 'Different things…aware of how dead, how asleep I have felt since moving here…sad…hovering near the earth but not landing…last week I had a waking dream, a sensation of being born in the middle of the sitting room, an image of being curled up, very intense…awe at being alive…and real.'
>
> We talked about how she identified with the lyrics, how she has felt isolated for so long in a still quiet place inside of herself, afraid to wake up, afraid to live. But now she feels hopeful like the seed that is becoming a rose.

This was a difficult session for me. I felt close to tears much of the time. The song, the lyrics but also the music reminded me of my recent loss. The middle section really affected me, especially the lyrics that spoke about the way our fear of loss can keep us from fully loving someone, from following our dreams and from engaging with life. This part of the song opened up my 'middle section' and held up a mirror to some difficult issues that were front and centre for me at that time.

Sharing countertransference

Little (1951) and Gitelson (1952) were two of the first analysts to write about and strongly advocate for countertransference disclosure. Being in the minority, they failed to have a significant impact on the analytic thinking and technique of their day.

Today, there are more advocates of countertransference disclosure on a continuum from moderate (occasional disclosure with certain clients) to radical (extensive disclosure with most clients) (Pearlman and Saakvitne 1995). Maroda (1991), part of the radical school, believes:

> The therapist must disclose whatever is necessary to facilitate the patient's awareness and acceptance of the truth… The timing, nature, and extent of the countertransference disclosure can only be determined by the therapist in consultation with the patient. This second principle addresses the long-standing problem of how to determine what will be helpful and what will be 'burdensome'. The answer to the question, 'How will you know what to say and when to say it?' is 'Ask the patient.' (p.87)

I concur with Sedgwick (1994) that ideally the level of disclosure varies with each individual client – depending on the client, the reason for the disclosure, the therapeutic alliance and the length and stage of treatment. Sedgwick takes a more conservative position on the issue of counter-transference disclosure but advises if disclosure is called for then it is important that it comes from a relatively neutral stance.

The reasons cited for disclosing the countertransference primarily have to do with establishing the therapist's honesty, developing intimacy and trust, allowing the therapist and the client to remain in an authentic relationship to one another, confirming the client's sense of reality of the actual interpersonal situation as contrasted with the transferential situation and to clarify both the fact and the nature of the client's impact on the therapist and people in general (Gitelson 1952; Gorkin 1987; Maroda 1991; Natterson and Friedman 1995; Pearlman and Saakvitne 1995).

Davies and Frawley (1994) point out that with traumatized clients who have great difficulty symbolizing and naming their experience, sharing countertransferential reactions can be extremely helpful. Many therapists come to know about aspects of their clients' experience at a visceral level. If therapists are willing to share their countertransferential feelings and reactions, to name them, then a shared language can be created and clients can learn to identify their feelings and express them instead of self-destructively acting them out. As Alvarez (1992) concludes:

> To discuss these observations with the patient and show her how these processes keep repeating themselves moment by moment in the sessions seems to be far more effective than simply resorting to elaborate detective-like reconstructions about the past causes of the patient's beliefs about herself. (p.3)

I have identified three ways that I share my countertransferential feelings in reaction to the clients and the clients' music: verbally, musically and somatically. When I verbally shared my feelings with Marie, she was able to access her own feelings and to gain insight into her relationship with her mother.

> Today's session was difficult but exciting. I took a risk with Marie. I began to notice I felt very constricted and unusually self-conscious early on in the session. I felt like I was being examined under a microscope, stifled. Yuck! We were talking about her mother and her recent visit and how formal her mother is and difficult to connect with. I wanted to make a musical intervention but I couldn't seem to break free. It was as if I was afraid of doing or saying the wrong thing – not at all my usual self. Then it hit me. I was feeling the way Marie felt around her mother – self-conscious, inhibited and shut down. She previously described feeling this way very intensely during her childhood and how she would go 'flying off' into her own world probably to escape from her mother's control and judgemental perfectionism. I decided to take a risk and tell her how I was feeling. At one point, I said, 'I am having trouble being present – I feel very self-conscious and constricted – as if I am tied up and afraid to make a wrong move... I'm wondering what you're experiencing.' Marie looked shocked. Her eyes grew wide, she opened her mouth and after a long pause she said, 'How odd...that's how I am feeling. I wondered if you were judging the way I handled things with my mother, my lack of self-assertion. I actually... I felt awful being with her, totally disconnected from her and myself – and, yes, self-conscious around her – I've always been... I always feel I can't be my real self, that she won't accept it.'

Revealing my countertransference proved to be a very effective intervention. Marie, like many of my clients, is often unaware of her feelings especially if the affects are intense or intolerable. Marie communicated with me unconsciously by projecting her feeling state. When I identified with her internal experience and openly shared my feelings with her she was able to access her feelings and together we could make connections in the present and to the past. Marie also provided me with an experience of what it was like to be her as a child so that I could understand in a profound way her early and current reality in relationships. She did this in the only way she could. She often had no words. Then she looked to me to provide them. Initially I helped her to translate her music, her gestures, her moods, and her silences into something more tangible so that she could name her experience and make it known.

Sharing my countertransference to and in the music is something I do frequently. During the music my countertransference is often expressed somatically (shedding tears, getting chills, breathing deeply) or musically through my musical choices and interventions. Sharing countertransferential reactions verbally usually occurs quite naturally as part of the processing that follows a musical interaction.

These excerpts from Ann's sessions illustrate some of the ways I shared my responses to her music both during and after the music making:

> I shed a tear during the singing. Afterwards I said the music felt sad to me. Ann said she could intellectually know it was sad but she couldn't feel it. She felt disembodied – removed.

> Ann played two drums and the cymbal and I played the drum kit. I remember getting chills at one point near the end of the improvisation. I was playing and making vocal sounds loudly and forcefully to encourage her to 'let loose'. I realized at one point that I felt angry and was expressing my feelings in the music. I shared this with her. She said she felt very angry with her aunt and how she acted when she lived with Ann and her family but it was difficult to express this anger even in the music. She said she felt afraid that her anger could be destructive and could overpower her.

> I felt moved by Ann's singing. I found myself singing in unison with her more than I had before. I wanted to support the vulnerable sound I was hearing. After we sang together and Ann processed her feelings I told her I noticed a difference between the way she speaks and the way she sings. I shared my feelings of sadness during her singing and my sense that she needs to slow down and breathe more in session when she's talking so that

she can connect to her breath and her feelings. We ended by drawing her 'hidden self'. It had no mouth. Her fear was that if she gave it a mouth all the stuff inside (yellow and orange) would come rushing out.

Sharing my musical countertransference with Cindy led to changing an intervention that could have been retraumatizing and replacing it with a safer alternative:

> Cindy and I toned together to relieve the pressure she felt on her breast-bone. Afterwards she said she felt her breath being taken from her. Her associations were to having to hold her breath during sex because she didn't want to make noise and have her parents hear. I said, 'Maybe this is too intense.' It felt intense to me. I told her we could stop or do something else like vocally improvise, sing a song or draw. She decided she wanted to continue toning but to tone into her heart. We toned together focusing on her heart area and afterwards she said it felt very calming.

In this session I shared my feelings of sadness and anger to support and validate Cindy's young feelings:

> Cindy and I sang and played together (the piano). She sang about being a little girl and how lonely and isolated she was...how helpless and vulnerable she felt. I heard myself breathing deeply several times. I was releasing some intense feelings that I was experiencing. Afterwards she said, 'It wasn't that bad – a lot of kids have it worse.' I told her I felt angry for her little girl and sad. Not only was she sexually abused but she was also emotionally abandoned by her mother.

During Marie's music, I had an image of a young part of her and I got a sense of the private world she often retreated to:

> Marie played the xylophone and I sang and played the piano. The music was soft and high pitched. The chords I played held her melody and the melodic line I sang added to the lullaby quality I felt in her music. I felt mesmerized. She said the music felt very comforting, like a blanket. I told her I had an image of a child in a cocoon at one point and then I had a sense that the music was sort of weaving a spell around us. She said it felt like the place she often goes to when she needs to comfort herself – her own special world.

When I revealed my physical sensations and my feeling of sadness, Marie was able to connect with the sad, lonely part of herself:

We sang to the toy frog. Marie said he represented the part of her that has no voice. His mouth is zipped up. He can't express himself. I felt a chill. I told her I felt sad for the frog and that the music gave me chills. She started crying. I asked her what she was feeling. She said, 'The frog is unhappy…he's very lonely.' She wanted to unzip his mouth – so we did. 'Now I feel better,' she said.

I found that sharing my countertransference to and about the music was experienced by the clients as less threatening than sharing my counter-transferential feelings in direct relationship to them. Our music making took place in a shared space, what Winnicott describes as the overlap of two play areas, where communication comes about through mutual experience (Davis and Wallbridge 1981). Talking about and sharing feelings about this 'third thing' is less direct and thus protects clients from feeling too vulnerable. When I shared somatic reactions, feelings, images and thoughts evoked by the music with Ann, Cindy and Marie, they were able to accept my responses without feeling invaded or criticized. I was usually sharing my experience of something we created together, something symbolic and real.

The clients I work with benefit most from having an authentic human encounter, a real relationship in music psychotherapy. This real relationship still allows for (as demonstrated in the case examples) important tenets of analytic theory such as transference re-enactments, countertransference reactions and projections. A real relationship between client and therapist, however, makes space for the possibility of the client getting honest reactions from the therapist – something that is not usually available in normal living (Lomas 1987; Natterson and Friedman 1995; Yalom 2002). It also provides a reparative experience for clients who have never had this kind of intimacy in relationships with their parents.

An authentic relationship offers more opportunities for the therapist to model behaviour for the clients. Some of this modelling is accomplished through therapist self-disclosure. I disclose personal information and countertransferential reactions when I think it will be helpful to the client. The degree and kind of disclosure varies from client to client. According to Yalom (2002), psychotherapy outcome literature strongly supports the view that therapist disclosure facilitates client disclosure.

For many traumatized clients, an authoritarian stance represents abuse of power. These clients feel safe and thrive when the therapeutic relationship is more mutual and reciprocal (Pearlman and Saakvitne 1995).

As Jung (1961) puts it, 'When important matters are at stake, it makes all the difference whether the doctor sees himself as part of the drama, or cloaks himself in his authority' (p.133).

I love being a part of the growth process both as an observer and a participant. It is inspiring to witness the courage exhibited by my clients as they struggle to separate from the familiar and the not-me and to connect with and integrate unfamiliar, unknown aspects of themselves. Whether we are talking, sitting in silence, singing a song, or improvising musically, the intimacy created in the mutual give and take of the therapeutic relationship offers an authentic human encounter and opportunities for healing and self-discovery for both the client and the therapist.

> This encounter, the very heart of psychotherapy, is a caring, deeply human meeting between two people, one (generally, but not always, the patient) more troubled than the other. Therapists have a dual role: they must both observe and participate in the lives of their patients. As observer, one must be sufficiently objective to provide necessary rudimentary guidance to the patient. As participant, one enters into the life of the patient and is affected and sometimes changed by the encounter. In choosing to enter fully into each patient's life, I, the therapist, not only am exposed to the same existential issues as are my patients but must be prepared to examine them with the same rules of inquiry. I must assume that knowing is better than not knowing, venturing than not venturing; and that magic and illusion, however rich, however alluring, ultimately weaken the human spirit. (Yalom 1989, p.13)

Part II

Clinical Practice
of Vocal Psychotherapy

CHAPTER 7

Beginning a Practice

When I began my practice, I had recently finished studying at an analytic institute. I sat in a comfortable chair and my clients sat on the couch. The piano was behind me and the instruments were hung on the walls or placed on a small table against the wall. During that first year, I found myself using music less and less in my work.

One day I realized the physical set up of the room was contributing to my reluctance to initiate more musical interventions. Just the effort of getting up from my comfortable seat and moving to the piano bench or to get an instrument, when I wasn't sure the music would lead to an effective intervention anyway, was increasing my resistance to play music.

Creating a facilitating environment is critical to this work not only for the client but also for the therapist. During the next week, I reorganized the room so that the instruments were now physically and psychologically easy to access. I moved my seat closer to the piano and placed the instruments in the space between the clients and myself. Soon we were making music again. Reorganizing that first office taught me about the importance of, and how to create, a vocal psychotherapy space that was aesthetically inspiring while providing clients with the feeling of a safe and comfortable container.

Setting the stage

The office in which I now work is soundproof so that clients feel comfortable singing, screaming and exploring all kinds of sounds. The door is always locked – another important aspect of creating safety. It is a large room with plenty of space to move around in and indirect lighting that is bright enough yet soft enough to encourage the free flow of imagination and feelings.

A large sofa, covered with many pillows of various sizes that clients sometimes hold when they are feeling vulnerable, is next to the wall with a long low table directly in front of it. The table is covered with instruments of all types from many different countries: slit drums, an array of shakers, bells, xylophones, metallophones, tone bars, a steel drum, umbiras and a wooden flute. There is always a box of tissues nearby. To the left of the couch are different types of large drums. A rain stick and an African walking stick rest in a corner against the wall. There are more instruments under the table including an ocean drum and a Korean gong. To the left of the couch there is a small drum kit with a cymbal and a large wooden xylophone from Africa. There are two guitars leaning against the bookcase on the opposite wall.

A large Clavinova stands against the wall to the right of the couch with a piano bench and a large rolling chair in front of it. I usually sit in this chair and purchased it because it is very comfortable and adjustable. I can sit next to someone at the piano or roll over to the end of the table to accompany someone on another instrument with little effort. The Clavinova has a full-sized piano keyboard and settings for acoustic piano, electric piano, Clavinova tone, harpsichord, vibes, strings and organ as well as different volume settings. A microphone hangs on the wall behind the piano with a picture above it.

The room is decorated with artwork, masks and objects from around the world. When a client brought her stuffed animal to a session one day, we ended up singing to it. I learned from this experience. Her dog symbolized a part of her: her young wounded self. There are now many stuffed animals, puppets and some dolls on top of the bookcase that clients often use during therapy sessions as 'actors' who stand in for significant people in their lives or for aspects of clients' personalities.

Assessment

The client assessment begins with the first contact, whether it is in person or on the phone. As I have previously addressed, much can be gleaned from the sound of a person's speaking voice. The questions asked or not asked, the information given and how it is shared are also revealing. If your first meeting is in person there is also much to be learned from body language and other non-verbal communication.

For example, a potential client called me to discuss the possibility of working with me. She had been referred by someone I knew, which is often a good sign, but the tone of her voice was almost assaultive and her attitude was demanding: 'I really need someone good… Your office is so far away… My only good day is Thursday… Could you come down on your price?' Earlier in my career, I probably would have lowered my fee and freed up an hour on Thursday to accommodate her. I would have bent over backwards as we all do when we are starting out. I needed the money. I needed a client. I would have welcomed the challenge. But I had learned through the years to trust my instincts and what I heard told me that this client would require more time and energy than I had at the moment. I referred her to a colleague who I thought would be a good therapist for her and they are still working together.

The basic question has to be asked: is this going to be a good fit – for the client and for me? Do I feel we can do productive work together? Acknowledging one's limitations is part of the assessment. So it is important when making an appointment to tell the potential client, 'We can meet and see how we work together and then decide if we want to continue.' The assessment continues during the process of taking a psychosocial history. My opening question is usually some version of, 'What brings you to therapy? Is there anything urgent that is going on right now that we need to talk about?' I then explain that it is important for me to take a complete history, from childhood to the present, and that this may take more than one session.

I also take a musical history even when the client is not a musician or a creative arts therapist. Questions might include: 'Do you enjoy music?' 'What kind of music do you listen to?' 'Do you have a favourite song or artist?' 'Do you or have you ever played an instrument or wanted to?' 'Do you enjoy singing or did you in the past?' 'What made you stop?' 'How do you feel about your voice?'

When it comes to the voice and singing, many people are very self-critical. They often compare themselves to pop icons with voices overdubbed and filled out by sound effects. Singing for the pure pleasure of self-expression is not part of everyone's experience unless it is within the safety of a choir. Yet there are many closet singers who love to sing at weddings and parties, their courage bolstered with the help of a few drinks! Many clients have told me stories about singing and being judged or laughed at by their families. I have also heard about numerous voice teachers who have traumatized their students with harsh criticisms bordering on verbal abuse. When one's voice is insulted it can feel like a rejection of one's self because of the ability of the voice to reflect the personality and the intimate connection between our voices and ourselves.

I have learned through the years how important it is to use music to break up the clients' narrative of their lives. I realized that taking a history can be overwhelming and in some cases even traumatizing for clients. Having to compress one's life into two or three hours means talking about the things that brought you into therapy: the difficulties during childhood, adolescence and adulthood; the accumulated narcissistic injuries, the losses; and for some, histories filled with physical, sexual or emotional abuse, addiction and other self-destructive behaviour. After all, we come needing help so the emphasis is on our problems. Even when the therapist makes an effort to hear clients' strengths and resources (which I do), the majority of the time is taken up with, 'What went wrong?' and 'What is wrong?'

Like everything else, the things I know best I've learned from experience. I remember seeing a psychotherapist once who seemed to be rushing to take a history of my life in one session. I remember leaving his office feeling very depressed and terrible about myself. I felt angry that my life was reduced to a series of one negative event after another. After all, there were some positive things…some victories…some acts of courage…some things and people that made me feel some hope. But there wasn't time to talk about those things.

When I take a history, at some point in the session I might ask clients to musically improvise about a subject they have been talking about, for example, their high school years. The instruments on the table in front of them are mostly percussive and easy to play. Clients don't have to be musicians to play them. I play along with clients, which helps to eliminate self-consciousness. Another way to bring music into the history-taking is to ask clients if a particular song comes to mind as we talk. If it does, I ask them if they would be willing to sing or hum the song. If not, I ask them if they can remember the lyrics and share them with me or describe the mood or feeling of the song.

Including the music serves two purposes. It gives clients a chance to pause and enter another mode of communication; one that might be experienced as fun and a relief from the intensity of the discussion, or as a safe way to express feelings evoked by the subject matter. The music also provides additional information about the subject being discussed.

Sometimes, if the verbal exchange is flowing smoothly, I will wait until the latter part of the session to suggest music. Then my suggestion will usually be more open ended, such as, 'Why don't we take some time to explore the instruments and get familiar with them? or 'You've been talking about a lot of difficult things…why don't we use the remaining time to play what you're feeling?' Ending the session with music can help clients feel more centred and grounded while familiarizing them with processes that will deepen as the therapy progresses.

Warm-up

Over the years I've noticed that clients have different ways of beginning the session. Some come in already warmed up and begin talking immediately. One client told me she started crying in the elevator while thinking of what we would talk about. Some take a few moments to centre themselves before starting to speak. Some clients prefer starting the session with music. Some prefer silence. With some of my more anxious clients we've developed a ritual of beginning each session with deep breathing. Other clients warm up with small talk. This would usually be interpreted as resistance but with one very fragile client I work with, I have found it more useful to indulge in this banter for a few moments and allow her to slowly enter the feeling places that frighten her so much.

Clients new to vocal psychotherapy, and even psychotherapy, need to be educated about the process and how it works. Even then it may be difficult for them to start a session. In these situations I usually help out by asking something like 'How was your week?' or 'What are you experiencing right now?' Mary would always look at me for a few minutes, then laugh nervously, then look away. This would continue for a while and then she'd usually say, 'I don't know what to talk about.' One day I said, 'Think about your week. Look at it like a movie, scene by scene. What stands out? Any images? Music? Conversations? Did anything make you feel sad? Or angry? Or excited?' This approach really helped her and she still uses it when she has difficulty at the beginning of a session.

Jill, who was also shy and not used to talking about herself, found it more helpful to bring in a CD each week and play it at the beginning of the session. The song was always related to something she wanted to talk about and hearing the music helped her transition into the subject. When she was feeling particularly anxious, she would ask me to keep music playing softly in the background. She was uncomfortable with silence, even the silence in between the words. The musical soundtrack supported her words and made it easier for her to talk about difficult things.

Music and words

Music and words are both integral to vocal psychotherapy. The music is doing something necessary and the words are doing something necessary. There is an organic flow between the music and the words, a partnership between equals. The words take the music to a deeper level and the music takes the words to a deeper level. For example, many of Cindy's sessions and a few of Marie's took place entirely in the music. Music and lyrics were the catalyst for therapeutic growth; they opened the doors to the unconscious and provided a container for in-depth processing to occur.

Some sessions are entirely verbal yet much is revealed about the client's emotional and psychological state through the musical elements of rhythm, melody, timbre, dynamics, tempo and phrasing in the client's speaking voice, breathing patterns, silence and body language. From this perspective, the clients themselves are music. We have 'the prototypes of rhythm, melody, harmony and form in our physiological and psychological processes' (Ansdell 1995, p.9).

The music and the words within the context of the therapeutic relationship facilitate the process. The verbal and musical interventions interweave, overlap and complement each other. The melodic element of music in particular evokes concurrences between speech and music (Nordoff and Robbins 1977). The interventions are determined by the therapist's and the client's perception of what is needed or missing in the moment and the therapist's sense of what type of intervention will best serve this particular client at this particular point in the therapeutic process. When the work comes from a spontaneous or playful place, the interventions are more likely to evolve naturally out of the process and to take on new and inventive forms.

Marie's fourth session illustrates an intervention I had never used before, that combines music and words in a different way:

> Marie seemed to be having difficulty describing what occurred over the weekend. She spoke haltingly and left half finished sentences hanging in mid-air. Without thinking, I began to play the piano, pacing the music to match the rhythm of her words. The music seemed to help her to relax and get into sync with what she was saying. I noticed she began breathing more regularly and soon she was speaking more easily. Her words began to flow naturally and there was more energy in the way she was speaking.

Playing underneath her speaking was an intuitive response on my part but in retrospect it made sense. Marie's critical voice would often short-circuit her spontaneous response preventing her from completing thoughts and sentences. The music helped Marie connect her words to her body and subsequently to her feelings in a natural flow so that she could be more fully present to herself and genuine in her responses.

Sometimes the words lead to music; sometimes the music leads to words. Words and music often occur at the same time or are interwoven into the tapestry of the session in an organic way. Sometimes my interventions are intuitive – fast, obvious to me. It is staring me in the face; some issue ripe for exploring in the music or the words – peeping up calling for attention 'here I am; look at me'. Sometimes there is a feeling of resistance that I pick up and I sense the music will help work it through. Other times the client suggests it – like 'let's start with singing today' or 'there's a song that's been going through my head all week'. I have the image of a ball of different coloured yarn and several strands that catch my eye. Some are brighter than the others, throbbing with colour, so I choose one of these. Sometimes the colour is so intense I feel cautious. Perhaps it is too soon to ask that question or suggest she play that feeling – too quick – she might unravel too fast. Then the best intervention is to wait, to listen, to sit still in the unknowing and be open to being surprised and then sometimes a strand I didn't even see falls loose and changes the shape of everything.

Layers of listening

'Layers of listening' refers to the multiple facets of the listening process. When clients talk, move, make music or are silent, I listen and gather information from what they say and don't say, the sound of their voices speaking or singing, the music they play and their body language and other non-verbal communication.

I process this information on a variety of levels: I listen to my thoughts, I listen to my feelings in response to the material as well as to feelings evoked by the clients and their music (countertransference), I listen to my body and my physical sensations and I listen to my reactions that emerge in the form of imagery and intuitive hunches. After processing what I have heard, I form a verbal or musical (or combination) intervention. The client responds to the intervention and the whole process repeats itself.

It is a circular process that is ongoing and continually deepening with each go round. Sometimes each step in the process is lengthy and sometimes it all seems to happen in one creative leap. As each client's story continues to unfold, intuitions can be verified, observations can be confirmed or corrected and patterns can be recognized and made conscious. Then emotional conflicts and psychological issues that stand in the way of change can be experienced and worked through.

Being a 'good listener' does not come naturally to everyone; some have to work hard to develop this skill. The ability to listen with the whole self is an essential aspect of being an effective music therapist. I listen with what feels like an inner ear and what Reik (1948) refers to as 'the third ear' (p.144).

> Of the many and diverse competencies required of a music therapist, listening is the most *fundamental* and unique to the discipline. It precedes, shapes and monitors how the therapist responds to the client… Because no other therapeutic modality is defined by the use of music, no other modality depends so entirely upon the therapist's listening abilities in nonverbal as well as verbal modes of expression. And for this reason, no other modality can provide clients with such opportunities to be heard so fully. (Bruscia 2001, p.7)

By listening with the whole self I mean tuning in not only with our ears, but also with our bodies, minds, feelings and intuition. I mean listening to the manifest as well as the latent content (Freud 1910), the subtext as well as the text, what is not said and played as well as what is said and played by the client, the inner as well as the outer music. I also mean listening to ourselves and the inner voices that arise from our unconscious depths, listening to the thoughts, images, associations, feelings, hunches and physical sensations we have while being with and observing the client. If we are able to listen in this way, we will hear messages which:

> if deciphered lead to psychological insights that cannot be reached by any other means. If the therapist does not get these messages – if he cannot make out what they mean…he must dig deeper and deeper into himself, until he reaches the source of all psychological understanding that is in himself (Reik 1948, p.67).

In vocal psychotherapy we listen to our client's words, silences and music, what they tell us, and what they conceal. We tune in to subtle levels of communication to hear the elusive messages that travel from the client's unconscious to our own. We receive sounds and listen to their reverberations upon our psyches in order to decode the possible meanings. We are required to listen actively and with concentration in order to catch transient impressions:

fleeting tones, turns of phrase, and rhythmic and dynamic changes that occur in the client's music and words.

Besides listening to our inner voices we also need to listen and become more attuned to our own speaking and singing voices. What are we communicating with our sounds and our music about our overall physical, emotional, mental and spiritual states (Warming 1992)?

It is important to listen in layers with the whole self – body, mind and spirit; to listen to what is being said, sung or played, what is manifest and to listen to what is beneath the surface of what you have just heard. To listen, trust, yet be curious about the unconscious messages you are receiving is a significant part of being a vocal psychotherapist.

For example, a client may tell me how well she is doing, and I hear her words. However, on a deeper level beneath the words, the tone and quality of her voice suggests that she is sad. I listen to my feelings and they tell me that I feel sad. I receive another clue. I continue to listen and I hear that she is speaking with a voice that we have both associated with her 'inner child'. I hear a part of her related to unresolved feelings and issues. She continues speaking and I hear a destructive behavioural pattern being repeated with her new boyfriend. I hear that she is not aware of this. She plays the piano and sings and I hear loud, thick harmonies with a lot of 11ths and 13ths in the chords and in the melodies she is singing. She is playing and singing with a lot of force and changing tempo frequently. I listen to our interaction and I hear distance between us. I listen to my body and I am aware of chills running down my back. I hear some sadness and anger in the music. I listen to all of the information I have heard and I listen to my thoughts about it. I hear grief and rage surfacing related to a childhood pattern that is being re-enacted in which she feels abandoned and then isolates, unable to reach out for help.

Between the Lines

She says, 'I'm very self sufficient… I hate needing anyone.'
I hear, 'Can I depend on you?'
She says, 'I like to be alone…that's when I feel the safest.'
I hear, 'Will I be safe with you?'
She analyzes everything,
She has it all figured out.
I hear a lonely little girl,

Lost somewhere on her way to feeling.
She fills every single space
And leaves no room for a reply.
I hear the emptiness, the fear,
I hear, 'tell me I'm not too much!'
I sing a song that has no words,
Our voices meet then move away,
She hears, 'I understand your pain… I'm not afraid…
I've suffered too.'
We sing a lullaby, a dream,
Our voices meet, then move, then touch.
She hears, 'I'll walk you through the dark… I will not leave…
I'll stay with you.'

CHAPTER 8

Resistance in
Vocal Psychotherapy

Resistance is present from the very beginning of therapy and is a natural part of the therapeutic process. There is a part of the client that wants to grow, change, and heal old wounds and a part that wants to keep the status quo. The part that is afraid of change may be stronger in some people than in others. For example, some clients cancel the first session or show up late.

The word 'resistance' is a psychoanalytic term. According to Moore and Fine (1990, p.168), resistance is

> a paradoxical phenomenon regularly encountered in the course of insight-oriented psychotherapy... The patient...opposes the process in a variety of ways that would serve to defeat the objective of change. Resistance may take the form of attitudes, verbalizations, and actions that prevent awareness of a perception, idea, memory, feeling, or a complex of such elements that might establish connection with earlier experiences or contribute insight into the nature of an unconscious conflict.

Resistance defends the old, the familiar and the infantile from becoming exposed and altered.

Bugental (1965) believed that the therapist needs to distinguish between resistance and a client's opposition, antagonism or hostility. Resistance, instead, 'is the name given to those ways in which a person distorts his awareness to avoid becoming conscious of insupportable threat to his being...' (p.93) One of the aspects of resistance, he pointed out, is that 'resistance is layered and sequential in organization' (Bugental 1965, p.93). He wrote, on the basis of the work of Reich, of 'peeling the onion' – that our job as therapist is to 'help the patient recognize and relinquish layer after layer of assumptions' (Bugental 1965, p.102). This can be seen as layering of defences.

Resistance has also been written about in the music therapy literature. Alvin described her 'nondirective and nonauthoritarian' style as a way to create an equality in the musical partnership. She wrote that this equality reduces the client's resistance. She also made the point that 'conflictual feelings are transferred to the instrument' and that through the 'physical resistance experienced in playing the instrument…the client can symbolically work through his own resistance to therapy' (Bruscia 1987, p.100).

Simpkins characterized resistance in music as 'unmodulated extreme hypoactivity or hyperactivity'. He worked through resistance with musical improvisation. The basic approach was 'to match his music to the client's energy level, and then, by using small increments or decrements, introduce the opposite energy level until regular modulation or balance is achieved' (Bruscia 1987, p.372). Simpkins defined resistance 'as the client's efforts to defend him- or herself against intrusion and self-disclosure by avoiding, undermining, or destroying his or her relationship with the music or the therapist' (Bruscia 1987, p.373). He sometimes bypassed the resistance by working in a medium where it is not expressed.

Priestley based her work with resistance on the classical psychoanalytic model (Bruscia 1987). She identified several levels of resistance that may be expressed either musically or verbally. Using the terms 'resistance vacuum' and 'resistance energy', Priestley described how resistances sound and can be used for diagnostic purposes.

Resistance to singing

In vocal psychotherapy, almost all clients are observed to have, at some time, a resistance to singing songs, vocally improvising, playing, listening to or talking about the music. Clients often feel reluctant to sing because experience has shown them or they suspect that vocally improvising or singing significant songs may bypass their defences and access feelings more effectively than words. This may be especially true for the highly verbal client, who may feel safe and in control when talking and fears losing control, particularly when improvising vocally. Because music, and singing in particular, can facilitate regression and call forth younger aspects of one's personality, the client experiences the threat of revealing those parts of the self that have never been accepted. Toning, playing with sounds and movements, and vocally improvising elicit spontaneity, which can feel threatening to people with rigid personality structures, those with 'false self' systems, and anyone who feels that his or her authentic feelings or aspects of him- or herself are not 'correct' (Austin and Dvorkin 1993).

Some clients resist singing because they do not like the sound of their own voices. Many of these clients were told directly or indirectly that they could not sing. I often hear their stories about being laughed at, or made fun of, by siblings, parents or friends whenever they sang. Some have had voice teachers whose attitude and criticisms bordered on the abusive. And some clients compare their voices to the recording artists they admire and feel diminished by the comparison, not realizing these singers often have voices that are technologically enhanced. This issue is exacerbated when clients are also perfectionistic and self-critical.

Dislike of one's voice can also be due to projecting a disowned aspect of oneself (Jung's shadow) onto the voice. For example, when Henry began vocal psychotherapy, he was dissatisfied with the sound of his voice. He felt it was too gentle and lacking in resonance. When he sang, the tone was forced or pushed. This forced quality was Henry's attempt to project a stronger, more masculine sound and image. Henry began to resist singing. This continued until he could examine his feelings about his own natural sounds. He realized he judged his voice as feminine, which for him carried implications of weakness and neediness. The therapeutic process involved withdrawing the projections from his voice and accepting his own needs and vulnerability. As his attitude toward his young, vulnerable self changed, Henry relaxed and stopped forcing his tones. He began to enjoy singing; singing with his own voice.

Resistance to singing in the therapy session can also result from overidentification with one's voice. When this occurs it can feel like one's whole sense of self-worth is carried by the voice and how good it sounds. The client's self may feel too exposed and vulnerable when identified with the voice. Additionally, the pressure of having to sound a certain way inhibits spontaneity and the ability to be emotionally connected to the music.

Resistance to the music becomes more intense when the instrument is the voice. The voice is particularly threatening for many people because it is not once removed but intimately connected to one's breath, body, the feelings and sensations within and one's overall sense of identity.

Meg often speaks of her isolation and the sense of 'the wall' that keeps feelings in and other people out. She has said that one of the most effective ways of 'making a hole in the wall' is by singing with me. Singing for her is such a powerful means of removing blocks to intimacy that she will often resist singing during sessions. She associates feeling close with being invaded or abandoned. The self-soothing quality of singing, which has existed since infancy, reproduces the early experiences and associations to mothering. Relating to me in this regressed way becomes threatening and produces ambivalence regarding whether to reveal infantile wishes and needs through the music.

In vocal psychotherapy sessions, I have observed another form of resistance in clients who willingly sing songs and vocally improvise but avoid verbal processing of the musical content. These clients prefer to bathe themselves in the feelings of the music without making the connections that would make the unconscious expression conscious. In this way, the clients are usually gratified that they have communicated their thoughts and feelings, which might be magically received and understood by me through the music. They therefore feel no need to repeat these experiences verbally and feel no need to process the material. This type of reaction might indicate that the clients feel merged with me and assume that minimal conscious communication is necessary. In addition, the clients' clinging to the vagueness of the musical expression and unwillingness to talk about the experience in more detail can sometimes indicate that they need to protect their fragile sense of self by hiding in the music.

Resistance in the music

As in verbal therapy, resistance can exist even though the client is singing songs, improvising vocally or using the voice in other ways. Resistance in the music is usually apparent to the therapist by the lack of affect or the contradiction between the musical affect and the client's affect. A rudimentary example is an obviously sad client who needs to express her grief but who chooses to sing a happy song or to vocally improvise to an upbeat chord progression instead. Other examples are clients who hide behind their technique or sing in a 'false-self voice' that lacks emotion and connection to what they are really experiencing in the moment (Austin and Dvorkin 1993).

Sometimes the resistance is due to the fear of intimacy with the therapist. This was apparent with Lynn one day when I suggested that we play or sing together. She said she wanted to improvise vocally on the blues and she wanted to play the piano. I could sing with her. She began playing and singing at a medium tempo but the music kept picking up speed as we went along. Her vocal lines were very busy. There was very little space in the music and I had a feeling of being crowded out. When a tape of this music was played back, Lynn said it reminded her of 'someone who talks too much and says nothing'. She could hear the lack of space and feeling in the music. When I shared my feeling of being pushed out, Lynn acknowledged this and said she wanted to get away from me but was also glad I hung in with her and didn't stop singing. This experience led to an important discussion of Lynn's ambivalent feelings about being intimate with me.

Resistance is also heard in the music when a client stops sounding, toning or singing prematurely. If therapists are sensitively attuned to their client's music, they can recognize that the music is not finished. The client may be approaching 'the point of entry' (the feared, anxiety-provoking feeling or awareness). This is sometimes accompanied by a statement such as the client 'felt finished', 'didn't really think it was going anywhere', or 'was tired'. However, further exploration of the immediate experience often leads to deeper, more profound vocalizations that can reach into the world of the unconscious and the feelings and images that lie within.

It is important to emphasize that resistance is not something to be eliminated but instead offers a way toward understanding the client. It should be seen as a form of communication and respected in the same way. Resistance is simply fear and sometimes the fear is grounded in reality. There may not yet be enough trust in the client–therapist relationship to allow the client to move deeper into the process. The client may not be ready to examine certain issues, may not have the ego strength to do so and may need more time and support.

Working through resistance

Once therapists believe clients are exhibiting resistance they can then begin to think about the most effective way to communicate this to clients. This often includes recognizing the behaviour and then sharing their observations with their clients (for example, saying, 'It seems like there's a part of you that doesn't want to be here today'). If clients can acknowledge this part, or feeling, then therapists can make room for that part to be present by encouraging the clients to sing to, as or about that part of themselves. If this seems too difficult, there may be a song that reminds clients of that part of themselves and that they would be willing to sing or play for the therapist (many of my clients now carry iPods with them that contain hundreds of songs). Clients can also sing, play or draw the resistance. Creating something that can be seen, or heard, that is outside of themselves and can be witnessed by someone else, helps clients to disidentify from the feeling and realize this is not the whole of them. It is only a part that is scared to change. There is also a part that wants to move forward in spite of the fear. Working through the resistance to music or words by further exploration in music is very effective.

At times, the taping of the music can be used to help clients hear the resistance for themselves. This was illustrated in the example found under 'Resistance in the music', above. In this case, the client, Lynn, interpreted her own resistance after hearing her singing played back on tape. She was then able to confront her ambivalent feelings concerning intimacy in regard to the therapist.

Another way to work through resistance in the music is by altering the tempo and instrumentation of the music. An example is seen in the case of a 41-year-old client who was able to defend against feelings intellectually. Phyllis often interpreted her behaviours verbally in an obsessive manner throughout the session. During one session, she chose to explore the concept of 'powerful' by playing and singing an original tune. The song was in a minor key and Phyllis played it in a fast tempo with sophisticated chord changes. I recognized the lack of affect in her voice and in the music and invited her to play the song again with a slower tempo. When Phyllis played and sang slowly, a very different song emerged. She became quiet and still for the first time during the session. She said she was experiencing 'sadness'. She was then able to talk about the sadness and helplessness she experienced as a young child growing up in an alcoholic family. I asked her to play a third time, with simpler chords and in the slow tempo, and suggested that she sing to the little girl. I chose to sing with her to support her feelings. By the end of the song, Phyllis was crying. She said she 'never realized that this song was a lullaby' and that when she wrote it as a child, she wrote it to soothe herself. Owing to the musical interventions, she was able to connect her thoughts with her feelings. Her further associations indicated that she did not need to defend against her feelings and the insights they had brought. She felt unsafe and powerless to control anything in her family when she was a child but now she could create safety for herself.

With many clients, I find that pleasure in singing and making music and joy in the creative process act as motivators toward overcoming the fear of self-expression, exposure and change. Developmentally, I can also recognize a sense of progress or regression in the therapy process through the type of resistance used by the client. There will always be some resistance. As previously stated, it is part of the process. It is hoped that by working through the resistances and establishing trust and a working alliance, the clients become increasingly observant of their resistance. This indicates that the role of the therapist has been internalized and the clients can gradually increase the amount of work they do on their own. It also indicates an increased level of self-understanding, acceptance and autonomy (Austin and Dvorkin 1993).

Therapists' resistance

There are times when singing songs, vocally improvising and playing music can demonstrate therapists' resistance to the therapeutic process. Rather than basing the choice of the therapists' level of musical interaction on clients' clinical needs, therapists sometimes use musical communication to serve their own needs. This can be because the therapists have a narcissistic need for recognition and validation that has not been worked through. Therapists therefore produce music to impress the clients and gratify personal narcissism. Recognition of this factor can often be an indication of a need for the therapists to find additional time to sing and play music for their own gratification or to work through the need for recognition in their own therapy.

Therapists can also use the music defensively as a resistance to going deeper into the therapeutic process. This can be due to their lack of knowledge and training in verbal processing. They may be defending against feelings of inadequacy by acting on the impulse to do something they do well. Not knowing what else to do and feeling an urge to offer a response, these therapists may decide to sing songs, vocally improvise or play music when the clients would be better served by talking about their problems and being listened to and supported, questioned, challenged and helped to find words for their feelings and needs.

Music psychotherapists should always be conscious of why and how they are using the music at any given moment. The therapists' own unresolved issues may be getting in the way of their objectivity or they may be having countertransferential reactions. An example from my private practice is when I suggested listening to or singing a song when I was feeling uncomfortable with a client. Later I realized I was feeling tension in the silence that persisted for several minutes. Instead of sitting with the discomfort until the client spoke or commenting or questioning her about it, I took flight into the music.

There are also times when *not* playing music demonstrates therapists' resistance to the therapeutic process. One reason for this may be that therapists lack confidence in their ability to understand and make meaning from the music being offered by the client in the session. Music psychotherapists may also avoid singing and playing because they do not feel musically competent. This defence may be triggered particularly when the client is more musically proficient than the therapist and the therapist feels threatened or, as with clients' resistance, the therapist may be afraid of criticism. This is most prominent when therapists feel identified with a particular instrument such as the voice. Singing is therefore avoided because of the danger of the therapists' revealing themselves through their voices and the fear of the loss of self-esteem because of real or perceived inadequacies in their singing (their 'self').

Sometimes therapists feel more comfortable with words because of the illusory sense of control or mastery that words can provide. Therapists, like clients, may devalue or distrust the irrational, unconscious 'feminine' world that one experiences with music and especially singing which is so intimately connected to the body and the self. Jungian theory has shown this fear of the feminine usually relates to issues with the personal or archetypal mother and one's own wounded feminine nature which includes the whole realm of feelings and sensations, a world easily accessed by the sensuality of sound and vibrations.

As with playing too much, therapists can avoid going deeper into clients' issues by not playing enough. Again, it may be for reasons previously mentioned or it may be because the therapist is colluding with the client not to address this joint issue. The therapist may not see the client's resistance because it is ego syntonic with the therapist's own. The therapist's resistance to the therapeutic process, whether by singing and playing too much or avoiding the music, needs to be addressed (Austin and Dvorkin 1993).

CHAPTER 9

Vocal Interventions

The focus of vocal psychotherapy is helping people connect with their authentic selves. They may be people whose lives are manageable and who feel they should be content and yet something is missing. They have lost access to their spirituality, their creativity or some vital part of themselves. They intuitively know there is more to life, but may not know what it is or where and how to find it.

They may be people who have trust issues and difficulty forming intimate relationships, always picking unavailable partners or going from one person to the next looking for that one special person who will complete them. Their fears of commitment may have to do with early abandonment or engulfment experiences and/or low self-esteem that restrict them from letting anyone get too close. As Rick put it, 'If someone really gets to know me, gets to see beneath the act, they will reject me so it's better for me if I take off before that happens.'

They may be people who have lived in a 'false' or adaptive persona or self, people who have fragmented, dissociated psyches or people who hide and isolate because they are isolated from who they truly are. These 'self' or identity disorders can begin in early childhood when there is a rupture or series of 'breakdowns' in the mother–infant or mother–child relationship and they result in the lack of a stable, coherent sense of self and/or a diminished sense of self-esteem and self-acceptance. So what happened externally becomes internalized (disintegration, splits in the psyche, self-destructive behaviours).

The heart of my work is about connection and integration and the ways in which voice work within a reparative relationship facilitates this process. A dependable connection with someone (the therapist) who is perceived as safe and attuned can provide a corrective emotional experience. This good-enough mother-therapist companions the client through the unconscious realm. The music strengthens the connection between the client and the therapist. Sounding and singing lead the way and help the client retrieve lost or hidden parts of the self. Singing is a catalyst for self-expression and is a powerful way to open the heart and release grief, and grieving is necessary to let go of past and present losses in order to accept the present and who you are today. Singing and sounding also provide access to feelings, memories and sensations so that splits (mind–body, thinking and feeling, conscious and unconscious) can be healed and clients can achieve a more complete sense of self.

Breathing

At the core of vocal psychotherapy is the use of the voice and singing to make clinical interventions that move the therapeutic process forward. The physical and psychological benefits of deep breathing are always a part of any vocal intervention. Sometimes, however, breathing is the intervention as illustrated in the following example.

Case example: Karen

Karen, a 30-year-old architecture student, sat beside me at the piano. I suggested we do some breathing together before singing. Singing was very risky for Karen, but she felt it would benefit her. As a child, she tried to avoid her mother's physical attacks and her father's verbal attacks by making herself as invisible as possible. She was thin, wraithlike, and spoke in a quiet, tense voice. Being seen or heard was dangerous while growing up and even though she yearned to be listened to and acknowledged, the old fears were deeply embedded in her psyche.

We began to breathe together, sipping the air in slowly as if through a straw then exhaling on an 's-s-s' sound, like a balloon slowly deflating. As we began the second round she looked at me and said, 'I'm flying off,' shaking her body as if she had chills. Karen remembered 'blanking out a lot' as a child. When her mother hit and kicked her, she would leave her body and go off into her own world. This dissociative defence that initially protected her psyche from annihilation no longer served her, but had become habitual and took over in times of stress and anxiety. I asked her what would help her feel safer and she said, 'Close to the ground feels safer…to sit on the floor.' I grabbed two pillows and we sat on the floor facing each other.

I suggested that for today we stay with the breathing and work on ways to help her stay in her body. We began the breathing exercise again, and I asked her to slow down the process and tell me everything she was experiencing. She started feeling anxious on the exhalation and felt herself starting to 'go up'. I suggested we use movement to ground her. We raised our arms on the inhalation and on the exhalation we pretended to be pulling a heavy bar down. We kept eye contact throughout. After several attempts she was able to stay present during the exhalation. She said the movement and the support she experienced through moving together and keeping eye contact was very helpful. 'I felt you wouldn't let me go off – I started to. I was very scared but I stayed with you… I felt the breath going down into my lower body – scary, very scary there. That's where the terror lives. I couldn't stay there too long but I didn't fly off! That's good. I'm getting better.'

Natural sounds and toning

Natural sounds and toning, as discussed in Chapter 1, are effective ways to increase awareness of the breath and bodily sensations while also providing an outlet for emotions and spontaneous vocal expression. For instance, before singing a song or vocally improvising, I will ask clients to inhale and exhale several times. On the last few exhalations I will suggest they allow a tone or sound to emerge. This usually increases the duration of the exhalation and grounds them more solidly in the moment. Sometimes, even in the middle of a conversation, I will notice clients are tense, anxious, talking too fast or taking a breath and holding onto it. I will ask them to stop talking, breathe in deeply and exhale allowing a moan, a groan or any sound at all to emerge. I usually join in which reduces any self-consciousness they might be experiencing. Many clients are surprised to find they enjoy making free, playful sounds. Others are amazed by the sometimes childlike or primal sounds that emerge – intuitive and instinctual sounds that have been long repressed because there was no appropriate social setting in which to make them. When they surrender to the process of spontaneously vocalizing, there is a release and often an experience of relief afterwards. When they continue talking, they are usually more embodied and present.

For a number of years now, I have taught Clinical Vocal Improvisation in the graduate music therapy programme at New York University. Each year I give the students an assignment to tone three times a week for a month and then to write about their experiences in a log. Most of the students are impressed by how deeply toning affects them.

Sue wrote:

> The more I did the toning exercise, more emotions came to the surface. Sometimes thoughts and feelings that I did not know I had entered my mind. One day I was very anxious so I lay on my bedroom floor and toned for ten minutes or more. I felt my body calming down, my heart beating slower, and I could feel parts of my body that I shut off over time (feet, hands, voice).

Deb was impressed by the vibrations she felt and how deep she was able to breathe:

> The breathing and the vibrations I felt helped me focus on a problem I am having. I was able to think about it in a different way. It was a great experience for me.

Jon also found relief from a problem:

> It got intense. I focused on oohs because they felt just right. It's been a crazy week, and I definitely felt those little oozy puddles of different thoughts-emotions-experiences jiggling as I oohed at them. Or perhaps with them? All the stress of the incident with my guitar eased its way out in the process.

Both Sandy and Lauren had positive emotional experiences through toning:

> The toning exercise brought me to a more grounded place. It allowed me to feel my body more, as I felt connected to my breathing and I could feel grief. It allowed me to express the grief that I always have hidden somewhere inside me on holidays.

> When I was finished, I realized I had been toning for over a half hour. So it had become MORE than just a class assignment – it really filled an emotional need for me – and I felt satisfied and comforted when it was over.

And So-Jin discovered her voice:

While I was continuing the Ahhhhhhhhhh sound I realized, wow, this is my voice. I have been living my whole life with my voice but I never really listened to it or felt it. I must have ignored it… Wow, this is my very own voice. I felt tears in my eyes as I met my voice.

Chanting

Chanting is an intervention that I often use with groups and sometimes with individual clients. According to the Oxford English Dictionary (OUP 2002), a chant is 'a short musical passage in two or more phrases each with a reciting note to which any number of syllables may be sung, or singing unmetrical words; a psalm, canticle, etc.' (p.379). Chants may range from a simple melody of one or two pitches with no rhythm at all, to more complex musical structures that include rhythmic speaking, singing of words or sounds. The rhythms of chant are varied 'from the pounding heartbeat of native American drums, to the polyrhythmic chants of West Africa, to the incredibly complex rhythmic patterns of the Balinese Monkey Chant' (Gass and Brehony 1999, p.11).

Chanting is an ancient art that has been connected to religious rituals throughout history. Diverse spiritual traditions use chants to focus the mind and consider chant a path to greater spiritual development. Chant is used in Hindu, Christian, Buddhist, Jewish, Islamic, African, Native American, Shamanic and Goddess or Pagan rituals and is believed to have healing effects on the body and consciousness. The repeated sequences bring together vibration, thought and breath. Only recently has the Western world begun to realize the therapeutic effects chanting can have on the body, mind and spirit (Campbell 1989; Gass and Brehony 1999).

I have found chanting to be very effective in creating group cohesion. This can happen in many ways and take many forms. For example, at a baseball game the chant of 'Let's go Mets' allows fans to feel at one with each other and their team. We come together despite our differences when we choose to give our voices, our energy and our spirits to a common song and intention. In a therapeutic setting, the sound of voices singing simple, repetitive melodies combined with significant words can foster a sense of comfort and belonging. Individual voices begin to touch each other and consciously or unconsciously search for a common vibration. Voices can become so attuned that it sometimes seems as if one voice is singing. Especially in times of crisis or disaster, chanting together can build community, create a sense of unity and safety, inspire hope and empower people to take action.

I will sometimes chant with individual clients to ground and resource them at the end of a difficult session. Sometimes we will chant during a session when they have a difficult task ahead of them and have a strong need to feel my support and encouragement. We often use drums to accompany our chanting. Drumming and chanting can be very empowering and can intensify the connection to self, other and the transpersonal or spiritual realm.

Somewhere in my travels I heard this chant, which I rewrote:

> See my garden grow,
> Return of the sun, the return of the sun
> Feel the earth beneath my feet
> Return of the sun, the return of the sun
> My heart is flying free
> Return of the sun, the return of the sun
> All will be well
> All will be well.

Hear audio example at www.dianeaustin.com.

Vocal improvisation

I regard the whole vocal psychotherapy session (and series of sessions) as an improvisation – a creative process for both participants. The 'chord structure' that I improvise over is composed of my musical knowledge and preferences and my theoretical knowledge based on theories and techniques from depth psychology, trauma theory, twelve-step philosophy, psychodrama and of course music therapy. The 'chord changes' are chosen from my knowledge of the clients I work with, their particular wounds, strengths and needs and our working relationship at that moment in time. My intention is to create a safe environment that facilitates the emergence of the client's spontaneous self.

Vocal improvisation in music psychotherapy can be viewed in three complementary ways: as a creative experience in the here and now, as a bridge to the unconscious so that repressed or dissociated psychic contents can come to consciousness through playing with sounds and words, and as a symbolic language (Austin 1996). When we are improvising vocally we are in the moment, present to ourselves, the music and our accompanying feelings and sensations. We are also moving toward the future and the creation of something that has not yet come into being and the sounds, melodies and words we improvise trigger feelings, memories and associations from the past (Austin 1996; Turry 1998).

Improvisation comes from a natural impulse and when that impulse is not blocked, but is allowed free expression through vocal and musical play, spontaneity is released (Spolin 1963). Spontaneity plays a dynamic role in most forms of psychotherapy. When clients are able to be spontaneous they can allow for the natural flow of impulses and can express themselves from an authentic centre of being. Healing can occur because clients can connect with their true voices. They can experience themselves freed from the tyranny of 'shoulds' and 'oughts' and access and release genuine feelings, thereby opening a channel to the self.

> The heart of improvisation is the free play of consciousness as it draws, writes, paints and plays the raw material emerging from the uncon- scious…the real story is about spontaneous expression and it is therefore a spiritual and psychological story rather than a story about the technique of one art form or another. (Nachmanovitch 1990, p.9)

Vocal improvisation is a creative process and 'is potentially in and of itself an agent of change, a transforming experience for both client and therapist' (Turry 2001, p.352). It requires both to become comfortable with the attitude of not knowing, which requires courage. It frees the client and the therapist from old frames of reference and ready-made responses and allows space for the creation of new ways of being to emerge from feelings and impulses we are experiencing in the moment. There is a sense of flowing with time and our evolving consciousness and a feeling of being enlivened when we can create our own form (music, sounds, words) instead of 'con-forming' – duplicating someone else's way of being or acting.

Researchers and scientists from Johns Hopkins University's Peabody Institute discovered that 'when jazz musicians improvise, their brains turn off areas linked to self-censoring and inhibition, and turn on those that let self-expression flow' (Johns Hopkins Medicine 2008). The research was motivated by the scientists' curiosity about the almost trance-like states jazz musicians enter to create their unique and personal improvisations and the connection between these states and the brain. They found that a region of the brain known as the dorsolateral prefrontal cortex slows down activity during improvisation. This area is linked to self-censoring and planned actions. At the same time, researchers saw increased activity in the medial prefrontal cortex, an area of the brain linked with self-expression and creativity. 'This type of brain activity may also be present during other types of improvisational behaviour that are integral parts of life for artists and non-artists alike…without this type of creativity, humans wouldn't have advanced as a species' (Johns Hopkins Medicine 2008).

Maslow (1976) was interested in and studied people who fulfilled their potential and led healthy and happy lives. He found that being and staying creative was one of the most important criteria these people had in common and that being creative had a motivating power that enhanced psychological and physical well-being. According to Jung, we become ourselves in multiple creative acts and creativity is essential to the healing process (Kast 1992).

I believe everybody can sing and improvise vocally as long as they have a facilitating musical environment. As Turry states, 'everyone has inherent, inborn musicality, regardless of pathology' (1998, p.161). A safe place and a trusting relationship, combined with musical forms that engage the clients' sensibilities, can enable clients to take musical risks and call forth the creativity that is essential to the individuation process. If they can face the unknown and take risks sounding and singing, the chances are they will eventually transfer this ability to the rest of their lives.

These quotes are taken directly from my session notes of clients talking about singing and vocally improvising. I have created three composite characters out of the combined experiences of many clients.

Voices on Voice

Voice one: I'm afraid of coming here and falling apart. Another voice, another me, comes out here, especially when I sing, and I'm not sure I want it to.

Voice two: I didn't want to sing. This took me by surprise because my voice is my main instrument and here it was not available. I just kept playing the piano. I concentrated on staying present. That's a major issue for me. Then I stopped and listened for a moment. My voice emerged from deep within me and went to meet you. That's how it felt.

Voice three: Initially, I was feeling sad. As my voice became more assertive and forceful, my feeling changed to more of an angry feeling. I started to sing about finding a new job, making a new start, and having a new life. When I finished singing, I felt really good.

Voice one: I'm afraid of making mistakes. I still have a voice in me that wants a perfect song with a lot of insight and musical freedom. How can I live up to that?

Voice two: The strange thing is that I couldn't really hear what you were singing. I could only feel the changing vibrations, very subtly, as you went from one tone to another: from the lower register and a big deep vibration to a higher register with a clear, sharp vibration. I played with those moving vibrations. I had to listen with my whole self rather than just my ears. I waited for the music in me to move rather than making it happen.

Voice three: This is perhaps the place I would rather be more than anywhere else on earth. It's like walking between the worlds. It's an altered state that I didn't try to induce. I'm in the middle of sounds and open to receiving them.

Voice one: When I come here and sing, I often feel the split in myself. There's an older more developed part and a more feeling part. The feeling part feels more like a baby.

Voice two: I felt connected to you. I felt energized and 'bigger' than myself, like my energy was coming out in all directions through my voice. I felt like I was expanding the amount of space I was inhabiting.

Voice three: I felt so relieved to actually sing what I had been feeling.

Voice one: My voice comes from a very deep hidden place. I'm afraid to bring it out into the world more completely. I'm afraid of my stronger emotions coming out – my pain and anger.

Voice two: When you sing with me, I feel like you're reaching inside me, past all the things I can do for people, past how I look and how smart I am – to just me. This feels very new, to be contacted in this way.

Voice three: Afterward, it took some time to fully return to a verbal state. I didn't want to return. I knew I could and would, but I would rather have stayed there for another hour or so. This world of music is where I find inspiration and healing.

Voice one: The music had a magic about it and a power that was very healing. The resistance I had felt about singing was still

	standing in front of me but now it was only a dwarf, where earlier it had been a giant!
Voice two:	I closed my eyes and felt the sound. Then I started humming. You hummed with me and I felt more secure. I began to sing: 'I don't want to cry. I want sunshine.' You sang these words with me, I felt like you took care of me, sort of like a mother. Your low tone and the piano and the harmonizing made me feel safe and secure. I wanted to keep singing forever.
Voice three:	I felt love in these sounds. It's hard to put into words. The only thing I know for certain is that this work connects me to my soul and it heals. Of this, I have no doubt whatsoever.

Vocal improvisation mediates between the conscious and unconscious worlds and accesses all the riches that are not usually available to us. Clients' feelings, experiences and situations that are discussed during the therapy session can be further explored and illuminated while vocally improvising with the therapist. The following example is from a session with Cindy who has been talking about her mother and the feelings she evokes.

> Cindy said she felt tired. She seemed depressed. She talked in a monotone without much energy. She had spent the weekend at her mother's and felt drained. 'She's so needy and clingy and yuck…she has no boundaries, she sucks up all the air.' I wondered if she was sitting on her anger. Anger was a difficult feeling for her to express and she usually turned it against herself. I asked her if she'd be willing to explore her feelings in the music. She moved over to the conga drum and I took the African drum. She beat out a powerful rhythm in 4/4 time. I played and sang with her and at times created a polyrhythm by playing eighth note triplets. She began to yell 'back off' and I gathered she was yelling at her mother. I joined her and the yelling became chanting – 'give me space' and 'I am here – here I am – this is my space'. Afterwards she said we were singing a lot of harmonies using thirds, fourths and fifths. 'I felt angry at first but it turned into energy, it was empowering – especially when we sang those harmonies.'

Sometimes the vocal improvisation comes first and gives birth to feelings, memories, images or parts of the self:

> Marie and I are playing the piano. I am playing chords in the key of C and she is playing the melody. She begins singing 'ah' up a third and back down again. I sing unison and then harmonize with her… Afterwards she tells me

she saw a small child. The child was hiding because she felt ugly and ashamed and didn't want anyone to look at her. She was not ready to come out of hiding. I told her that she didn't have to come out until she wanted to.

Free improvisation as used by music therapists has direct parallels to Freud's technique of free association. When clients improvise vocally or instrumentally with or without words, they are free-associating and creating a musical portrait of themselves or parts of themselves. These musical improvisations can reveal much about a client's strengths, vulnerabilities, conflicts and feelings. Much can also be learned about the therapeutic relationship and the transference and countertransference dynamics when client and therapist vocally improvise together (Austin 1998, 2001, 2002, 2004; Darnley-Smith and Patey 2003; Streeter 1999; Turry 1998, 2006).

Vocal improvisation can also be looked at as symbolic communication. According to Priestley (1994), 'The guided expression of the music…can reduce the patient's resistance to denied or split-off emotion as it can lower the threshold of consciousness. It allows this emotion to be experienced symbolically in sound or movement and therefore a little less painfully' (p.7).

> Phyllis and I were singing together to a simple melody and chord progression. We began in unison, and then I began to harmonize and mirror her musical phrases. When the improvisation ended, Phyllis said, 'I was distracted when you left my note. I felt anxious. I wanted you to stay with me… I lost my focus. I started to focus on what you were doing.' As we continued to discuss the music, she said she was reminded of how she felt as a child, stupid and not able to focus. I pointed out how unsafe her home was and how hyper-vigilant she had to be to survive. How could she concentrate on her work when she was so attuned to her parents' behaviour? 'Yes, she said. 'And I never knew when my mum would leave us alone with my father.'

When I vocally improvise with clients I give them choices. Sometimes we sing a cappella and, at other times, with varied instrumental accompaniment. Depending on the clients and their needs in the moment, we may sing with a drum, a xylophone, a singing bowl, a guitar or piano. At times the client and I play the same instrument. Sometimes clients might play their primary instrument (for example piano or cello), and I might accompany them on a different instrument or use only my voice. At other times I might play the piano while the two of us improvise vocally. It is essential that the music is meeting their needs and not my own.

Case example: Liz

Liz began treatment with me when she was a 28-year-old music therapy student. She had previously been in verbal psychotherapy for a year or so but did not feel she was getting to her core issues – the effect of her mother's alcoholism and abusive behaviour towards her. Liz was closer to her father who also drank heavily but 'was not a mean drunk'. She has two younger brothers that she took care of throughout her childhood.

Liz had difficulty identifying and expressing feelings and needs: 'There are no words to say what it feels like… I can't even put a description on it.' As the therapy progressed, it became apparent that the intensity of Liz's feelings terrified her. She learned early in life to 'shut down' and dissociate from her feelings. She described an early memory of her mother yelling and holding a knife. Liz began crying and her mother said: 'Stop crying or I'll shut you up.' So Liz learned to shut off her self-expression and protect her fragile self with dissociative defences. Her difficulty 'being present' to her feelings was compounded by a fear that she would end up 'crazy' and 'out of control' like her mother if she allowed herself to cry or get angry.

Fortunately, Liz's love of music gave her a creative and emotional outlet:

> Songs have been a way that I could put words on something that I otherwise probably wouldn't have found the words to say… When I'm singing songs or improvising music, I can get more in touch with what's going on inside me… It's not quite as easy when I'm just talking.

It was easier for Liz to access feelings in the music. She particularly enjoyed singing with me so we often 'toned' or improvised together. In her words, 'It's scary to get in touch with very deep feelings when I'm all alone… It's more comfortable when someone is singing or playing with me.'

I will describe a therapy session that took place during our fourth month of working together. Liz was feeling anxious when she arrived. She said that she had dreamt of her mother that morning. It was 'something about sitting at the dinner table'. Dinner time was always stressful in her home.

I asked her if she would like to explore the dream musically. She said that she felt like singing and wanted me to play A minor 7 to D minor 7 on the piano. She sat beside me on a separate chair.

We began by breathing together as I played the chords for support. Liz said she felt tightness in her chest and throat. She began to sigh and I sighed with her. She started singing long tones, mournful-sounding 'ah's. I sang in unison with her. The melody was simple and centred around the minor third interval. She stopped after a few minutes and said: 'I feel congested.' I asked her what else she was experiencing and she said: 'I feel like there's something stuck in my throat.' I asked if she felt able to continue singing and she said: 'Yes.'

My thoughts at that moment were about resistance and that people sometimes stop playing or singing when they are approaching the 'point of entry' and are about to access feelings (Austin and Dvorkin 1993). I wondered what feeling might be 'stuck in her throat'.

She began to sing, softly at first. I joined her and we sang in unison and harmonized. She sang long, held notes; the quality was somewhat breathy. We made eye contact throughout the singing this time. The eye contact seemed to add support to the vocalizations. The singing grew louder and stronger (less breathy). I matched her volume, quality and phrasing. Her voice soared higher and higher and then cracked and she began crying.

When we processed what Liz had experienced during the singing, she said: 'Seeing your mouth wide open and hearing loud, high pitched sounds while also making these sounds myself, opened something up...hurt, that's when I cried.' She had a memory of being three years old and sitting at the dinner table while her mother and father screamed at each other. She tried to stop them but couldn't. She remembered leaving, unnoticed, and going to her room alone.

While singing together during a therapy session several weeks later (again vocally improvising without words), another memory surfaced. Once again it was the 'loud, high pitched sounds' that triggered her memory and the accompanying feelings. The image she saw was her mother holding a knife while standing over her. She had talked about this experience before but felt 'numb' while describing it. This time, however, Liz was able to feel some of the terror that she was not strong enough to manage as a child.

I also felt the terror and my eyes filled with tears. Some of my feeling was countertransferential. I could identify with her feelings because of events that took place in my own childhood. Some of my tears were empathy for a helpless, terrified child. Mary Priestley (1994) referred to this kind of empathic countertransference as 'e-countertransference', a state in which the therapist resonates with the client's feelings.

Liz was able to cry and feel some compassion for herself as a young child trapped in a terrifying situation. She said: 'Seeing you cry is helpful –

it's like reality testing…yes, this really did happen and yes, it was *very* upsetting.'

Liz avoided singing in her upper register in subsequent therapy sessions. Then, several months later, she arrived looking flustered and said that she was feeling anxious and out of control. She talked about school and a professor of hers who was intrusive and critical. As Liz talked, she became aware of feeling anger toward her teacher: 'Something in her tone of voice sets me off…she sounds sweet but there's something underneath… I feel like she's invading my space, controlling.'

I suggested that she play her feelings. She agreed and chose the drum. She asked me to play the piano. I played C7 to G7 (without the third). Her drumming was strong and steady. After several minutes she began singing ('ah' and 'ee') and I joined and supported her by singing in unison, harmonizing and, at times, mirroring her phrases.

Her singing grew louder as she moved upward in her register. We were soon singing the 'loud, high pitched sounds'. I wondered about the connection between her professor and her mother. I am always on the lookout for connections between the past and the present, for re-enactments and projections. Liz's description of the teacher and the tone of her voice made me think of the way Liz described her mother. I also wondered if her voice would 'crack' again. I felt a shiver run through my body as the sound became piercing and then slowly decreased in volume and intensity.

When we discussed the music, I asked Liz if her teacher reminded her of her mother. She said yes, she had that thought while singing. She never knew when her mother would change from 'nice' to 'violent'. Her teacher was somewhat moody and sometimes had a sharp, critical edge in her voice (like a knife, I thought). I commented on Liz's ability to hold the high notes and to go up and down her register without breaking. This seemed significant to me on several levels. Liz said that at one point in the music she decided to become her mother to overcome the fear of her mother's loud, high pitched voice: 'It felt sort of like desensitization… I've been building up my strength – vocally and psychologically – to take on this sound.'

We discussed the fact that this 'sound' was both literal and symbolic. It represented aspects of the negative mother archetype and her own personal mother when she was abusive and full of rage. It seemed that in order to heal the split (break) in her voice, Liz had to confront her fear of her mother. To accomplish this, Liz needed to acknowledge and express her anger. Her anger gave her access to her power and enabled her to disidentify with the frightened child aspect of herself ('the victim'). Liz had always been afraid of her anger – that it would emerge as rage, overwhelming and out of control. Drumming in previous sessions had been a safe way for Liz to begin to express anger in a creative, contained form. Her drumming in this session supplied additional grounding for her vocalizations.

In the following months Liz continued to work on identifying and expressing feelings and needs musically and verbally. As her confidence in her ability to express herself in a related way grew stronger, Liz was successfully able to confront her teacher and her boyfriend when she felt unheard or intruded upon. She began to realize that she could have feelings and express them without becoming her mother and 'going crazy'. Liz was in the process of depotentiating the negative mother complex (or negative introject) and claiming her own voice.

After one therapy session, during which Liz had sung in her upper register for a significantly long time, she said: 'Screaming to me was always taboo because of the amount my mother screamed, and singing so loud on those high tones feels like screaming in a way…but the fact that I can sing in the high part again – that's amazing to me. It means this is a part of me that I can have control over and it doesn't mean that I'm going to lose control if I use that part of my voice.'

The metaphor here is striking in its clarity. In accepting her 'high pitched voice' I think Liz was becoming more accepting of her intense feelings – her anger, her terror, her grief. In the beginning stage of therapy Liz didn't want those sounds. In her words, 'I didn't want that part of myself…as soon as I got to that place my throat would just shut off. I would stop the sound.' Within a Jungian framework, this aspect of Liz's voice represents the 'shadow' archetype (the unwanted, repressed parts of the personality). It is in the shadow, however, that the person finds what is most essential to her next stage of development (Jung 1968).

When Liz spoke of being able to move back and forth between the highs and lows of her vocal range, it seemed symbolic of her increased ability to modulate her affect states. Instead of 'all or nothing', Liz now had access to a wider range of feelings with increased flexibility of self-expression.

CHAPTER 10

Vocal Holding Techniques

'Vocal holding techniques' is the name ascribed to a method of vocal impro-visation I have been developing and refining since 1994 (Austin 1996, 1998, 1999a, 1999b, 2001). During the writing of this book, I discovered ways in which I had expanded and amplified these techniques. I also became more aware of their effectiveness as an intervention with a variety of clients and for a variety of symptoms and psychological issues. I was surprised by how frequently I used them as interventions. I often improvised with clients using these techniques. Numerous examples can be found throughout this book whenever I refer to vocally improvising with or without words over two chords.

Vocal holding techniques involve the intentional use of two chords in combination with the therapist's voice in order to create a consistent and stable musical environment that facilitates improvised singing within the client–therapist relationship. This method provides a reliable, safe structure for the client who is afraid or unused to improvising. In Sandy's words, 'As a classically trained singer it used to be hard for me to improvise and to not care about what came out or how it sounded when it came out.'

Vocal holding techniques also support a connection to self and other and can be used to promote a therapeutic regression in which unconscious feelings, sensations, memories and associations can be accessed, processed and integrated. As Joseph said:

> At first it was not easy to sing in therapy. Although I loved music, I feared my voice and the tunes that might emerge. I was afraid it would make me too vulnerable and unprotected. I was afraid of being crushed. But I sang, and

the little child that emerged was not crushed. He was held by the piano chords and your voice and the safety of the room. The child felt free.

These unconscious experiences are directly related to parts of the self that have been split off and suspended in time due to traumatic occurrences. When contacted and communicated with, these younger parts can be reunited with the ego and the vital energy they contain can be made available to the present day personality. Developmental arrests can be repaired and a more complete sense of self can be attained.

Unlike jazz or other forms of clinical improvisation where shifts in harmonic centres are to be expected, this improvisational structure is usually limited to two chords in order to establish a predictable, secure musical and psychological container that will enable clients to relinquish some of the mind's control, sink down into their bodies and allow their spontaneous selves to emerge. The simplicity of the music and the hypnotic repetition of the two chords, combined with the rocking rhythmic motion and the singing of single syllables (sounds, not words, initially) can produce a trance-like altered state and easy access to the world of the unconscious. The steady, consistent harmonic underpinning, the rhythmic grounding and the therapist's singing encourage and support the client's vocalization. Within this strong yet flexible musical container the client can explore new ways of being, experience the freedom of play and creative self-expression and allow feelings and images to emerge (Austin 1996, 1998, 1999b). The client's voice, feelings, and emerging aspects of the self are all held within this musical matrix.

This method is especially useful in working through developmental injuries and arrests due to traumatic ruptures in the mother–child relationship or empathic failures at crucial developmental junctures (Austin 2001). After vocal holding, Ann said she felt accepted. 'I didn't have to do anything amazing, sing louder or better… I was enough!' This was very therapeutic for Ann who grew up with critical, perfectionistic parents who expected so much from her. This perfectionism often prevented her from enjoying her own music.

Interpretation and illumination of psychic conflict is of minimal value in working with adults traumatized as children, until the link between self and other is rebuilt and the client's capacity for relationship is restored (Hegeman 1995; Herman 1992). Cindy felt she couldn't hide in the simplicity of the music:

> I felt you really saw me. I was shy at first but then it felt so reassuring. I wasn't alone and you felt safe... I could hear and feel you singing – you were really there with me and for me, just for me.

Improvised singing seems ideally suited for this reparative work. Babies begin to vocalize at around five weeks of age and the attachment between the infant and its caretaker develops slowly over the baby's first year of life through physical closeness and an ongoing dialogue of cooing, babbling, gazing and smiling. The gaze between mother and infant contributes to the vocal rapport between the two (Bowlby 1969; Winnicott 1971). Vocal inter-action between mother and child fulfils a basic need for both in that it nurtures connection and affects the child's development (Newham 1998). Tomatis (1991) has even suggested that the mother's voice is just as important to the child as the mother's milk in providing adequate relational bonding. The importance of the voice and vocal holding in building and repairing the connection between self and other has significant implications when working in depth with clients suffering from the consequences of pre-verbal wounds to the self. In Marie's words, 'I felt safe, connected to you physically and musically, and when I looked into your eyes it was almost like you were feeding me. I could imagine soup, hot soup.'

Winnicott describes the optimal situation between mother and baby. The baby looks at the mother and sees him- or herself. What the mother looks like is related to what she sees in the baby's face. But the situation is not always optimal. Some babies look at their mother and the mother reflects her own mood or the rigidity of her defences. Then the babies do not see them-selves. Then, 'their own creative capacity begins to atrophy, and in some way or other they look around for other ways of getting something of themselves back from the environment' (1971, p.112). Babies may feel reflected through other senses than sight (sound, for example) but when the mother is in need of reflection herself, probably because her childhood needs for mirroring were not met, then the babies get accustomed to seeing the mother's face instead of their own.

> The mother's face is not then a mirror. So perception takes the place of apperception, perception takes the place of that which might have been the beginning of a significant exchange with the world, a two-way process in which self enrichment alternates with the discovery of meaning in the world of seen things. (1971, p.113)

Vocal holding techniques are not meant to be a prescription or recipe and are not necessarily used in the order that follows. For the sake of clarity, I will describe the process as it appears to complement the developmental stages. As with any therapeutic intervention, however, the client's history, diagnosis, transference reactions and unique personality and needs should determine the approach taken to accomplish therapeutic goals. For example, when improvising, Ann initially felt more comfortable using words and may have experienced vocal sounds as more regressive and associated with loss of control. Marie felt more comfortable in the open realm of non-verbal singing in our earlier sessions perhaps because she had difficulty finding words to express herself and because she often regressed to a pre-verbal place. At other times, she seemed to need more structure so pre-composed songs were more effective.

In the initial vocal holding phase the client and I sing in *unison*. Singing together on the same notes can promote the emergence of a symbiosis-like transference and countertransference. This is important for clients who never had a satisfactory experience of merging with an emotionally present, attuned mother. Through a replication of early mother–child relatedness, these clients can eventually internalize a stable sense of self and then gradually renegotiate the stages of separation and individuation. Sometimes sounds and phrases emerge that are reminiscent of the babbling sounds of a three- to six-month-old (Gardner 1994).

In our initial vocal holding experiences, Marie preferred singing in unison with me. When I moved to another note to harmonize with her, she followed me. Over time, she allowed me to leave her note and sing in harmony with her and gradually she began to explore more of her vocal range and create more expressive melodies. The second stage, *harmonizing*, creates the opportunity for the client to experience a sense of being separate yet in relationship. Marie's music mirrored her psychological growth. As her early needs for containment and safety were met and she felt truly seen and heard by me, her sense of self grew stronger. She gradually began the process of separation and individuation.

Marie and I sang together at the piano. She picked out chords to improvise over – A minor 7 to G major 7. We sang on 'ah' in unison and in harmony. Her melodies now had more variety than in the past. I also noticed that her voice had become more resonant and less breathy. Her voice sounded stronger and I thought about the way it mirrored her psychological growth. Marie had grown stronger as well. She seemed more solid and three-dimensional to me. I felt some sadness in the music. I had a sense that her inner child was around. At times she sang up a minor third and a minor sixth. I mirrored her melodies. They had a yearning quality to them. When we stopped singing we sat quietly for a while. Then she said, 'That was very powerful... I had a deeper awareness of something, it's hard to find words, to pin down because it comes through the feelings but the image is the most important thing. I saw my child. She feels left and I suddenly felt sad for her, for leaving my own child, for leaving the dark place, the floaty place... I think she feels sad because I don't need to go there anymore. I don't want to...' Marie began crying. 'I feel some loss, some relief, so many things – after so long finally there's this change – that place, the quality of being there was so beautiful.' I asked her what she replaced the dark floaty place with. Marie said, 'I guess the real world, being able to find it with real people, being here and finding it here with real people.'

Singing in unison can be very soothing and useful when clients need comforting or closure at the end of an emotional session. It is also a way to encourage clients to improvise. They may feel safer because they are not alone or exposed and they can draw on the therapist's voice for support.

Today while singing with Ann, I was enjoying the unison singing – it felt so right – the way our voices fit and soared together but I was aware of this and moved to harmony at one point quite consciously for fear that it might be *my* need for unison... Afterwards she said the unison was the most powerful part of the singing for her. 'I felt so much support, so much freer to sing and take chances.'

Mirroring occurs when a client sings her own melodic line and I respond by repeating the client's melody back to her. I often used mirroring with Cindy to support her in finding, strengthening and staying grounded in her authentic voice (for example, when she felt frightened to confront her uncle). Mirroring also helped her to hear and accept new parts of her personality, like the happy child, when they emerged. This musical reflection provides encouragement and validation.

Grounding, when I sing the tone or root of the chords, often provided a base for Cindy's vocalizations later in the process. She would improvise freely and return to 'home base' whenever she wanted to check in. One client referred to the grounding tones as 'touch tones'. This musical intervention is reminiscent of a typical pattern of interaction between the child and the maternal figure that occurs when the child begins to move away from the mother to explore the environment. In the ideal situation, the mother stays in contact with the child and supports and encourages her increased efforts to individuate; otherwise the stages of separation–individuation become associated with object loss. Cindy expressed it this way:

> It felt like time and space were being stretched and opened. I could take as long as I wanted to get out what I wanted to get out and go as far out as I needed to but if I wanted to return I could…the music never left.

Vocal holding techniques are introduced into the music psychotherapy session in various ways. With clients who are especially anxious about improvising but want to try, I might explain this method in detail. Usually, however, I give a minimal description or simply ask: 'Would you like to try singing about this (person, situation, feeling, etc.)?' I then ask clients if they want two or more chords. They sometimes choose the exact chords or give a general description ('something minor'), but if they have little or no knowledge of chord structure or need help finding the sound they want, I might play examples of different chord combinations (major, minor, suspended, etc.) and ask for their preference. Occasionally, clients will describe a mood or feeling they would like to evoke and together we search for and find the fitting chords (Austin 1999a). The clients may also suggest a rhythm and a piano setting (I use a Clavinova that has various settings such as organ, strings, etc.). Giving choices and working collaboratively empowers clients and helps to create a safe therapeutic environment.

We begin by breathing together. As previously described, deep breathing is critical in focusing, relaxing and grounding clients in their bodies. Breathing together begins the process of vocal attunement that continues as the therapist attempts to match the client's vocal quality, dynamics, tempo and phrasing. Being present to clients as an empathically attuned companion may also involve matching their physical movements (for example, rocking together) and making eye contact. Eye contact can reinforce the intimacy engendered by singing together but may be too intense an experience for some clients and even distracting for others.

Many clients benefit from vocal holding techniques, sometimes for different reasons. The following categories describe the kind of clients with whom this intervention is most effective:

1. Clients who want to vocally improvise but have little or no experience: The predictable repetitive chord structure frees these clients from over thinking and worrying about scales that fit with

the more complicated and rapidly shifting harmonies of jazz and other forms of vocal improvisation.

2. Clients who are very skilled improvisers but are disconnected from their emotions: These clients can hide in their technique and take cover in complicated rhythms, melodies and harmonies, thus remaining in their heads and avoiding feelings.

3. Clients who have difficulty being playful: The two chords and the therapist's voice and presence create a safe, musical playground where they can let go, surrender to the music and allow their spontaneous selves to emerge. They can experience the pure sensation of singing and the pleasure of making all kinds of sounds, something they were often not allowed to do as children because of direct or indirect messages to be quiet, good or to suppress their feelings. The musical environment and the therapist's encouragement can ameliorate the internalized judgement of being childlike, silly and emotionally expressive.

4. Clients who have early attachment or bonding issues and need to experience a direct involvement on a sensory and feeling level with a positive (mother) therapist: This technique facilitates a therapeutic regression and creates a space for a reparative experience to occur.

5. Clients who experience the repetition of the two chords in combination with the rocking rhythmic motion and the singing of single syllables as a stimulus for the spontaneous flow of imagery that uncovers unconscious contents: These clients respond to vocal holding techniques much like they respond to the 'Bonny method of Guided Imagery and Music (GIM)' (1986), a receptive form of music psychotherapy in which clients listen to taped classical music carefully selected by the therapist, to evoke emotions and symbolic images related to the client's therapeutic issues. In both vocal holding and GIM, clients are able to relax the body and mind and allow feelings and images to unfold at their own pace in a stream of consciousness reminiscent of a waking dream.

6. Clients who experience dissociation: These clients are often able to 'return to their bodies' through the combination of deep breathing

that is necessary to sustain tones and the vibrations that resonate deep inside and increase body awareness.

Following are some of my reasons for using vocal holding techniques as interventions in the clinical process:

1. to build trust and create a positive mother transference

2. to soothe and comfort clients

3. to offer an experience of being seen and deeply listened to

4. to encourage vocal play and spontaneity

5. to work through resistance to feelings

6. to create an opportunity for the client to undergo a therapeutic regression in order to re-experience and repair early developmental injuries

7. to access unconscious feelings, images and associations

8. to release feelings

9. to lead into and out of free associative singing (vocal holding with words).

Case example: Vicky

Vicky, a 28-year-old professional cellist, sought out music psychotherapy for what she believed was a psychosomatic illness. Approximately two years ago, after a successful performance, she awoke to find she could not move her right hand. Since that episode, she had been suffering from periodic pain in both her right hand and arm that was seriously affecting her ability to practise and perform. Vicky had been to the best doctors and physical therapists, who found nothing wrong with her. She felt she was losing her 'musical self' and she was now convinced the problem was not in her body but in her mind. She was very ashamed of acknowledging this.

Vicky described her family as 'normal'. Her mother worked full time as a high school principal and her father had his own medical practice. She had a brother three years younger who still lived at home. Initially, Vicky was reluctant to discuss her family and only wanted to talk about her music and her physical ailment. She appeared to be very bright, serious and responsible, a person driven to constantly achieve, and pursued by a harsh perfectionistic inner critic. She seemed to live in her head and spoke very quickly in a high pitched, monotone voice seldom taking a deep breath or leaving any space for feelings to emerge. I sensed a great deal of anxiety and fragility underneath her confident manner.

Vicky was interested in her dreams and usually brought at least one to each session. The majority of these were archetypal 'trauma dreams' (Kalsched 1996) with images of car crashes, wounded animals and dismembered bodies. I felt the dreams were providing us with a picture of what was happening to Vicky intrapsychically, of the severe split between her mind and her instinctual self.

As the therapy progressed, Vicky came more into focus as a 'parentified child' (Miller 1981) who took care of her emotionally immature and unavailable parents by 'holding herself together' and relinquishing her needs and her young, feeling self in the process.

Her music was the one area of her life in which she felt free to express her feelings. Listening to Vicky describe her situation and hearing the desperation in her voice, I was reminded of my senior year of high school when I developed vocal nodes. I remembered how devastated I felt. Like Vicky, I depended on my music (singing in my case) to provide an outlet for feelings that were otherwise too difficult and frightening to express.

I had the sense that Vicky's psychosomatic symptoms were related to the shame and guilt she felt acknowledging her feelings and the problems within her family; that it was all right to complain about physical problems but not emotional ones. Intuitively, I felt that her hand was carrying all her unresolved grief and rage. Vicky's dreams provided information about her unconscious processes but her associations to the material remained on an intellectual level. I felt we needed to access the feelings connected to the dream images. I often use music to work with dreams. Since music and dreams speak a similar language (symbolic), and both directly access the unconscious, it is as if no translation is necessary for the music to resonate in the heart of the dream image and release its affective component.

I thought singing would be an effective way of working with Vicky because she was not identified with her voice, there was no performance pressure associated with singing and her hands would not be involved. It was a conflict free area. Vicky had enjoyed singing in choirs during her school years but had never improvised using her voice before. During one session I introduced her to vocal holding techniques and when we stopped singing she said, 'I felt a chill, like a ghost came into me... I've always been two people, one is independent and rational, the other is all energy and emotion…it's like they came together for a minute.' Vocal holding techniques are especially useful when working with dissociative defences and the kind of mind–body splits so prevalent in traumatized clients (Austin 1998, 1999b). The two parts that Vicky experienced coming together during the singing symbolized a moment of integration that would have to be repeated over and over again to be resolved.

The session that follows took place during our third month of working together. Vicky had just returned from a weekend with her parents. When I asked her how things went she said: 'Fine, but my hand started hurting again when I was practising Sunday.' When I inquired further about her interactions with her family and any feelings she had experienced during the weekend, she was vague and changed the subject. She was speaking very fast and in an excited manner but with little real affect. She kept changing topics. I had the thought 'a moving target is hard to hit'; that she was defending against delving too deeply into any subject. At one point she mentioned a past dream she'd had and I asked her if she'd had any dreams this weekend. She reported the following:

> I am at the airport and I'm all excited watching the planes taking off. A plane takes off right in front of me but then turns to the right suddenly and crashes into a building. The plane goes up in flames and I start yelling for help. Men come out of the airport with stretchers and I go with them. There are people badly burned lying on the ground. Then I see a baby. I'm not sure if it's alive or dead. It's all shrivelled up.

Instead of asking Vicky for her associations to the dream or offering any interpretations, I asked if she would like to try exploring the dream in the music, using two chords and singing. She agreed and came to the piano to sit beside me. I suggested either singing the overall feeling of the dream or an image that felt particularly meaningful to her. She wanted to focus on the image of the baby. I asked her what chords she would like and she said she wasn't sure. I played different combinations for her and she settled on A minor 9 to F major 9. We began by breathing together several times. Breathing helps the client (and the therapist) release excess anxiety, get grounded in his or her body and begins the process of vocal attunement. It also serves as a transition state between speaking and singing.

I played slowly and softly in the middle register of the piano. The tempo, dynamics, repetitious rocking rhythm, chord voicings (suspended ninths that resolved) and occasional arpeggios seemed to support her voice and create a feeling state that complemented the dream. I liked this music. It felt soothing to me yet conveyed a particular kind of sadness mixed with longing.

She began singing 'ah-h-h', holding the tone – stretching it out. The tone she chose and the open sound suggested a willingness to explore her feelings. I joined her immediately and we started singing in unison. She seemed comfortable with the unison, as if taking in my support and gathering strength by merging or joining with me before beginning to move on her own. She slowly began a descending melodic line, which I mirrored and then harmonized with and then we returned to unison. Her singing voice was softer, breathier and had a more feeling, receptive quality than the music of her speaking voice, which was usually monotone, fast and staccato. At moments, her singing sounded frail and vulnerable to me and seemed to give voice to her young, wounded feminine self. At one point she began an ascending melodic line and I remember thinking she needed a firm grounding base to support this upward movement. I held a low tone while she ascended. I had an image of a little bird whose spirit had been broken but who kept trying to get off the ground. I believed the baby in the dream was her young, feeling self that was suspended somewhere between life and death.

This belief was grounded in experience both professional and personal. I had spent many years in psychotherapy working to reclaim and integrate the young dissociated feeling parts of myself. The image of the shrivelled up baby filled me with sadness and compassion.

Vicky's singing became dissonant at one point alternating between the flat five and the fifth of A minor 9, and then alternating between the dominant seventh and the seventh of F major. She may have been influenced by my use of suspended ninths to create tension and resolution. I was playing whole steps to produce this effect, whereas she was singing half steps and creating even more tension by alternately singing tri-tones. I think the music was reflecting her pain and perhaps her ambivalence about living. The music built and then diminished in volume and intensity as she sang descending and ascending melodic lines. I alternated between unison and harmony, sometimes mirroring and overlapping into unison and harmony again. The music felt sad to me and filled with yearning. We 'pulsed' together in unison and harmony. The volume and intensity increased as we ascended up the scale. I felt connected to her. I noticed that when singing she utilized a vocal range of over an octave – a contrast with the fairly monotone range she spoke in. We descended again and her voice grew soft. I began playing in the high register of the piano and arpeggiating the notes in what felt like a sort of music box sound. She changed from 'ah-h' to 'hm-m-m'; a more closed sound which seemed more regressive and perhaps protective. I joined her singing. I saw that she was rocking back and forth and I matched her movement. The singing grew softer and we breathed together and came to a close. We sat in silence for a few moments when the music ended.

I then asked her what she was experiencing. She said, 'It's like we were waking up that dead baby.' She began crying and continued, 'Everyone thinks I'm the happy one and my life should be so good… I feel sad for my brother and my mother, I worry about her.' Vicky began to talk more openly about her family and how they affected her. Her father emerged as a self-centred person with severe mood swings who could be verbally abusive at times and more loving at other times. Over the weekend he was extremely critical of her playing and told her she should give up the cello and pursue another career. At the end of the session, I reflected how unsafe she must have felt growing up with such an unpredictable parent and how difficult it has to be to express herself in such a critical atmosphere. I believe the vocal holding created a nurturing safe environment that enabled Vicky to dialogue with her unconscious so that she could retrieve a piece of what had been lost to her: an image from the depths and the feelings connecting her to the part of herself contained within the image.

This session was at times difficult for me. I could easily empathize with aspects of Vicky: the perfectionism and the accompanying performance anxiety, the successful persona and the fragile child underneath. I attempted to use my countertransferential feelings to understand and connect with her. I was also aware of the dangers of overidentifying with Vicky and losing my therapeutic stance and with it the ability to be fully present to Vicky and her experience. I reminded myself that although we had some similar wounds we were different people at different stages in the healing process. Deep breathing also helped me to tune in to my own feelings and physical sensations, stay grounded in my body and maintain my boundaries.

Hear audio example at www.dianeaustin.com.

CHAPTER 11

Free Associative Singing

'Free associative singing' is the term I use to describe a technique that can be implemented when words enter the vocal holding process. It is similar to Freud's (1938) technique of free association in that clients are encouraged to verbalize whatever comes into their head with the expectation that, by doing so, they will come into contact with unconscious images, memories and associated feelings. It differs from Freud's technique in that the client is singing instead of speaking, but more significantly, the therapist is also singing and contributing to the musical stream of consciousness by making active *verbal* and musical interventions. The accompaniment (two-chord holding pattern or repetitive riff) and my singing continue to contain the client's process, but the emphasis now is not only on 'holding' the client's emerging self and psychic contents but on creating momentum through the music and the lyrics that will propel the improvisation and the therapeutic process forward.

The progression to words and the more active role I take on generally promote a greater differentiation between the client and myself. When I begin questioning, reframing and adding my own words to the improvisational dyad, the transference and countertransference can become much more complex. The client may experience me not only as the 'good-enough' mother, but in other roles as well (figures from the client's interpersonal and intrapsychic world).

In its simplest form, free associative singing involves clients singing a word or phrase and my mirroring or repeating the words and melody back to them. We always start with deep breathing and sometimes ease into this new stage by first singing without words. The vocal holding techniques of singing in unison, harmonizing and grounding add additional and various kinds of support and containment. There are many examples of free associative singing throughout the book. Since its inception, however, this technique has evolved along with the ways it can be varied to suit the individual needs of each client.

I begin the process of vocal attunement by breathing in unison with the client:

> Ann and I begin by taking a deep breath in and exhaling while allowing sounds to emerge. We continue this for several minutes. Sounding helps Ann to relax and release some of her inhibitions related to singing.

> I ask Cindy to breathe in deeply as if sipping through a straw and exhale on an f-f-f-f sound to slow down her inhalations and exhalations. I join her.

> Marie and I breathe together before singing. I notice how shallow her breathing is. I help her by asking her to sit up straight, relax her shoulders, and sing from her lower abdomen. I demonstrate for her and then we continue to breathe together.

As we sing together I attempt to match the client's vocal quality, timbre, dynamics, tempo and phrasing:

> It is often hard to distinguish my voice from Cindy's. Our voices blend so well together.

> Marie's voice is so soft. I feel like I'm almost whispering when we sing together.

> Ann said, 'I felt like our voices were weaving and melding together. When we sang loudly I felt an intense vibrational sound connection with you.'

With the movement to words there is often a need for more variations in the music. The two chords remain the basis for the musical improvisation but changes in the client's feeling states and emotional intensity often require a broader musical palette. Variations in dynamics, tempo, voicings, arpeggiation, rhythm, accents, rests, alternate chord substitutions and chord extensions (adding 7ths, 9ths, 11ths, 13ths) enable me to reflect and support the client's experience. In this way, I use not only my voice and the lyrics but also the music to deepen the vocal improvisation and the therapeutic process.

Throughout the improvisation I am making critical decisions about when, how and what to sing with the client. This is especially true when I move beyond simply mirroring the client's lyrics and music and begin to vocally provide empathic reflection, make gentle interpretations by singing thoughts and feelings clients may be having but are not yet voicing, and use repetition to emphasize important words and help the clients digest the meaning in the words.

Essential to the effectiveness of this method is the use of the 'double' (Moreno 1994). The 'double' is the inner voice of the client. The therapist sings as the double in the first person using 'I'. Drawing on induced countertransference, empathy and intuition as well as knowledge of the client's history, I give voice to feelings and thoughts the client may be experiencing but is not yet singing, perhaps because the feelings and thoughts are uncomfortable, unconscious, or the client has no words for them, or no ability to conceptualize the experience. When the doubling is not accurate it still moves the process along as clients can change the words to fit their truth. When it is accurate, it provides clients with an experience of being truly seen and understood. It also encourages a bond between client and therapist and over time strengthens the client's sense of self.

This intervention is especially useful for clients working to integrate thinking and feeling or a mind–body split. Doubling offers an effective way to breathe feelings into words and supply words for feelings. In addition, the naming or labelling of unprocessed trauma material can aid in preventing uncontrolled regression and re-traumatization (Hudgins and Kiesler 1987).

'Essence statements' – statements that begin with 'I feel', 'I need', 'I want' – are effective in deepening the therapeutic process because they are fundamental expressions of self-awareness and building blocks to identity. Therapists can sing the complete phrase, such as 'I feel sad', if they believe this is an accurate observation of the client. If this is true, the client will repeat and/or add to the statement; if not the client will change the word usually to the way he or she is feeling. Or the therapist can simply sing 'I feel…' leaving space for the client to supply the missing word.

Repetition also plays a significant role in free associative singing. What would sound ridiculous in verbal psychotherapy – the client and therapist repeating the same word or sentence over and over again – is filled with meaning in vocal psychotherapy. Each time the word or phrase is repeated by the client and echoed by the therapist, the affect contained in the word is intensified. It is as if the word and the meaning attributed to it has time to sink deeper down into the body-self where it can be fully experienced. The therapist's echoing reinforces the validity of what the client is singing and supports the integration of mind and body.

Working with many clients from other countries, whether using free associative singing or singing songs, I became aware of the importance for clients to sing in their 'mother tongue' at some point in the therapy. I realized that singing in English was safer for them because it created distance. After all, most of the experiences we sang about occurred in their native culture and most of the emotional and psychological language they learned was in English. When I asked them to sing in their own language they often could not find an equivalent translation and doing so required thinking which could distance them from or dilute the emotional experience. In the beginning of therapy, this distance was often helpful because it helped them overcome their fears of direct feeling. However, at a certain point in the therapy it often became important for them to sing about their feelings, for example 'I never really felt seen by you' to their mother (or some other significant person), in their own language in order to take the process deeper. When Akiko sang in Japanese she cried for the first time. 'It makes it feel closer, more raw,' she said. 'In English it's not so primal.'

Of course it would have been easier for her to sing a song from her childhood in Japanese and I often encourage clients from other countries to sing significant songs in their own language. In free associative singing this is obviously much harder. When using free associative singing with Akiko, I sang with her less frequently and when I did I tried as best I could to imitate the sounds she made. If I couldn't imitate the sounds of the language, I would just sing the melody. Akiko told me that she felt very supported by this and was touched by my effort to sing in her mother tongue.

By taking a more active role in musically facilitating the therapeutic process and with the singing of words, I can help the client understand and make meaning out of what he or she is experiencing in the present and what he or she experienced in the past and how these events affected his or her sense of self. Old, negative self-concepts can be replaced by new, realistic ones resulting in self-acceptance and increased self-esteem.

Vocal holding is often an effective way to lead into free associative singing and similarly to provide closure at the conclusion. When clients have experienced an intensely emotional session, non-verbal vocalizations can provide them with lullaby-like comfort and time to digest and begin to integrate what has occurred. Therapist and client can sing together or the client may prefer to be sung to.

Case example: Michelle

The first thing I noticed about Michelle was her voice. It was very soft and airy and seemed to be coming from far away. Like her voice, Michelle seemed more spirit than flesh. She appeared to be disembodied, had low energy, and looked younger than her age. Although she said she had 'a happy childhood', over time I learned that she was extremely neglected as a child and spent a lot of time alone in her own world dissociated from her feelings. She could not remember many concrete details of her early life except that the family moved frequently. One move from her grandparents' home in Italy back to Canada was very traumatic for her. She remembered being happy in Italy but returning to Canada after a year and continuing her isolated existence. 'I had a glimpse of life, then lost it again.'

As our work progressed, Michelle began to connect with dissociated aspects of herself, primarily through songs and free associative singing. During the following session she was able to contact an isolated young part of herself, begin to accept the truth about her childhood, and feel compassion for the sad and lonely girl she was.

We begin with vocal holding. Michelle prefers minor chords. Today she chooses B minor to E minor. We sing in unison on 'ah' for several moments and then move in and out of harmonizing. She closes her eyes and seems to enter an altered trance-like state. She begins singing words, and I begin echoing her words and melody.

Michelle:	I see the trees
Diane:	I see the trees
Michelle:	and the river
Diane:	and the river
Michelle:	and I'm looking
Diane:	and I'm looking
Michelle:	in the woods
Diane:	in the woods
Michelle:	alone
Diane:	alone
Michelle:	but there never seems to be anything to do
Diane:	anything to do
Together:	anything to do

I notice that her vocal range is limited and that her melodies contain a lot of descending thirds and fourths and have a childlike quality to them. After several minutes I begin introducing other words and phrases that might be true for her instead of simply mirroring back (repeating) her lyrics.

Michelle:	I'm wandering
Diane:	all alone
Michelle:	just the trees and the water
Diane:	I'm alone
Michelle:	I'm alone
Diane:	it is peaceful
Michelle:	all alone
Diane:	and I'm sad
Michelle:	and I'm sad

I use my induced countertransference to make the musical intervention 'and I'm sad'. I feel sadness pass through me before singing these words. When Michelle repeats them, I feel she is acknowledging the sadness as her own. She now has words and validation for this feeling. I continue to make more active interventions lyrically and musically to move the process forward. I pick up the tempo slightly and sing a little louder.

Diane:	Where is everybody?
Michelle:	Where is everybody?
Michelle:	I know they're not there
Diane:	all alone – where is everybody?
Michelle:	I am here but alone and I know they won't come here
Diane:	and I know they can't see me
Michelle:	they can't see me
Diane:	they can't see me
Together:	they can't see me!
Together:	they can't see me!

I think this last phrase is connected to Michelle's early childhood experi-ence of feeling invisible. I doubt she ever felt really seen, heard, or under-stood as a child, so now she struggles with identity issues and an inability to know and act from her authentic feelings and needs. We continue to sing. We sing about whether she is ready to leave or not and that she does not have to hide any more. She has a choice.

Michelle:	I wish I could go back, back to school
Diane:	back to school
Michelle:	and learn again, how not to be alone
Diane:	I wish my mother had taught me
Michelle:	had been there
Diane:	to help me
Michelle:	to give me what I needed to grow
Diane:	no one really was there
Michelle:	no one really was there
Diane:	to understand what I felt
Michelle:	that's the truth
Together:	that's the truth
Michelle:	no one helped me
Diane:	no one helped me
Michelle:	no one listened
Diane:	no one knew
Michelle:	how sad and lonely I was
Diane:	no one helped me
Michelle:	to feel
Diane:	to feel
Michelle:	that's the truth!
Diane:	that's the truth!
Together:	that's the truth!
Together:	that's the truth!

Adaptations of free associative singing

As previously mentioned, free associative singing can be very effective in eliciting a therapeutic regression and connecting with repressed or dissociated feelings.

For that reason it is a powerful technique that requires advanced training. For the beginning vocal psychotherapist, there are simpler adaptations that can be used. For instance, the subject being sung about can be limited to categories that offer more structure such as: I need…, I wish… or I can. The therapist joins in the singing and repeats the lyrics back to the clients using the vocal holding techniques of singing in unison, harmonizing and grounding to add additional and various kinds of support and containment.

Free associative singing can also be the container for affirmations that allow clients to connect with their positive attributes. For instance, Sarah sang lyrics like, 'I am smart, I am helpful, I can cook.' Some clients need more supportive affirmations like, 'I am good enough, I can do this, I can ask for help.' These sung affirmations are valuable for clients who suffer from low self-esteem or fragile self-images. They can be recorded and used by clients in between sessions when their egos need bolstering or when they feel attacked by persecutory thoughts.

The gratitude list, a technique borrowed from twelve-step programmes such as Alcoholics Anonymous, can also be sung. Clients are asked to think about things in their lives they are grateful for and sing them over two or three chords. Sometimes these things may seem small at first and clients might need the therapist's support in validating them or even coming up with ideas. An example comes from Peter who always complained about his life and his bad luck. For Peter the glass was always half empty. When asked to sing about things he was grateful for, he had difficulty thinking of anything. I reminded him that he had a date next week. After that, he got the idea and began to sing about his good health, the fact that he could pay his rent and other positive things in his life he took for granted.

Resourcing

Resourcing is a term used in trauma work (Hudgins and Kiesler 1987; Levine 1997) and refers to the process of helping clients connect to inner and outer sources of support and strength. Clients may need resourcing at the beginning of the session in order to be more present in their bodies before talking, playing or singing. Sitting quietly and breathing together can help clients feel less anxious and more grounded. This is a simple technique that clients can use on their own when they feel panicky or frightened. The resource is within them and realizing that they have the ability to calm and nurture themselves is empowering. Some clients find deep breathing is even more effective when they exhale a sound. The exhalation may also be prolonged through the use of sighing, moaning or allowing whatever needs to be released to come out.

Many clients have inner resources they are unaware of and need help identifying. I will sometimes ask, 'What helped you survive your childhood?' or 'What inner qualities or strengths do you possess that helped you get where you are today?' These questions provoke introspection and self-examination.

When clients answer 'my sense of humour', 'my anger', 'my courage', etc., I then ask if they can put that quality into a sound and movement. If they can, I mirror them and we repeat this several times. Sometimes it is easier or preferable for them to think of a song that conveys this quality and then they, or we, will sing it. Sometimes, I will invite them to vocally improvise over two or three chords, about the quality, to the quality or as the quality. For example, Josh sang as his 'determination'. Some of his lyrics were 'I won't let him stop me from growing… I don't have to be a fuck-up like you.' The embodiment of the quality and hearing the words out loud help clients to become more aware of strengths they possess and aid in the integration of these resources.

The therapist carries the client's history and usually has knowledge of the client's assets that can prove valuable in moving a client from a weakened state to a more empowered one. An example of this is when Yuriko was preparing for a conference presentation and felt overwhelmed with anxiety. We used free associative singing to uncover the source of her fears. What emerged in the singing was a chorus of critical voices telling her: 'You can't do this… You don't know enough… You have nothing to offer.' Afterwards we discussed the genesis of these criticisms and judgements. We both knew the source but she needed resourcing now. I asked her to close her eyes, take a deep breath and see if there was anything she had done recently that she felt good about. After a few moments a big smile spread across her face. 'My workshop I did in Canada,' she said. I asked her to tell me more. 'The audience was terrific. They asked great questions… I felt like I really gave them something.'

I asked her how her body felt now. 'Calm,' she said. 'Happy…it was so much fun and I did a really good job!' I asked her to stay with those thoughts and feelings and put them into a sound and movement. She stood up, opened her arms wide and hugged herself. Her sound was strong and expansive. 'AHHHH.' I imitated her and we did this together several times. I then asked her if she could talk back to those voices now. 'I did well,' she said. 'I know things… I can do this!' 'Remember this moment,' I said. 'Put it in your heart and keep it there.'

Clients also have outer resources they may or may not be aware of that fall into three categories: places, people (or animals, objects) and spiritual support. I will, for example, ask clients if there is a place where they felt safe as a child or a place where they feel safe now. I will ask them to describe it in detail and imagine that they are there. Again, I might suggest they express this safe place in a sound and movement, a song, or an improvisation. Other options are to write a song together or to hold this place somewhere in the body and find a tone that resonates with that area. I will then support them by joining in the toning.

I work similarly with the other two categories: 'Was there a person you could go to when you needed help or felt unsafe? Is there someone now?' If the answer is 'no', which is not uncommon with traumatized clients, I ask if there was (is) an animal (a pet) or a special toy. One client I work with, Sara, has a doll she received from her grandmother when she was two years old. She is now 35 and still finds comfort in talking to this special doll when she is deeply depressed or anxious. She sometimes brings the doll to therapy sessions when she is feeling regressed. When Sara is confused or unsure about what she feels or thinks I will sometimes ask her doll for help. The doll clearly represents a dissociated aspect of Sara, a part that is strong and wise. Sarah often sings about the doll, to the doll or as the doll. The singing helps her connect with this split-off part of herself, relate to it and work towards integrating it.

When exploring the third category, I usually ask clients if they have some kind of a higher power – a term used in Alcoholics Anonymous and other twelve-step groups to describe 'God' or a belief in something transcendent, religious or spiritual. Again, we then take this source of support into the music. We tone, sing songs, improvise music, or listen to music that evokes the spiritual dimension of the client's life. All of these outer resources are potential inner resources that with time clients can access in difficult moments and draw strength from.

CINDY

Cindy is a professional singer. She has fears of success tied up with separation anxiety and abandonment issues that hold her back and keep her from becoming more visible in her field. Like many people with this issue, she equates success with being alone; leaving behind her emotionally disturbed mother and her rejecting father and being on her own without support.

Cindy was sexually abused by her uncle between the ages of five and eight. Even though she knows rationally that her parents never protected her from the sexual abuse or supported her growth, the child in her still feels dependent on them and fears losing them. Cindy believes her abandonment feelings are exacerbated by the abuse and the fact that it was never talked about.

Cindy tells me she feels ready to work on her feelings about the abuse. I suggest we do some resourcing first. Since we are returning to her past, my questions are related to her childhood. I begin by asking her if there was a safe place she could go to when she was a child. She says, 'No. My uncle lived down the street and was always hanging out at our house.' I ask her if she was religious or had some notion of a higher power. She says her parents went to church occasionally but that she felt no desire to go with them, that they didn't seem to get anything from going.

Then I ask Cindy, 'Was there anyone you could talk to that you felt safe with?' She shakes her head and says 'no'. 'Did you have a pet or a favourite stuffed animal?' Again she says, 'no'. I am feeling sad for her and trying to think of what might have helped her to survive when she says, 'There was a tree'. I ask her to tell me more about it, and she says, 'It was huge and beautiful and right outside my bedroom window… I guess the tree was my friend growing up.'

I ask Cindy if she would like to sing as the tree, to the tree, or about the tree. My intention is to put her in touch with a resource she has – an image she can return to when she feels unsafe. I also want to give her choices. Giving choices is empowering and is especially important when working with traumatized clients. She wants to sing as the tree and asks me to play something 'soft and warm'. I try a few chords and she chooses C, F/C, G/C. She likes the pedal tone sustaining throughout. I suggest we begin by breathing together several times. My intention is to help her relax and ground her in her body. She starts by singing 'ah-h-h'. I join her briefly in unison and then in harmony. She begins to cry softly and sings:

Cindy: Sweet little girl I hear your tears

Diane: I hear your tears

Cindy: I see you crying

Diane: I see you crying

Cindy: and I wish my arms could hold you – reach around and hold you close to me

Diane:	and hold you close to me – reach around and hold you close
Cindy:	but my arms can't move that way and my arms can't give you that touch
Diane:	but I'd like them to – reach around, reach around, reach around to you
Cindy:	maybe you can look at me and see you're not alone
Diane:	maybe you can look at me and see you're not alone

I repeat her words and melodies – echoing them back to her, but when I sing, 'I'd like them to', I am offering a reparative experience as a mother-tree. At the end of 'you're not alone' my melody resolves the phrase and feels comforting to me, and I hope to her.

Cindy:	Maybe you can see my arms reaching up, reaching out, maybe you can see my strength, maybe you can see me connecting to the earth. (Her singing becomes stronger, her melody soars up, building and she sustains the last note for two measures)
Diane:	the earth. (I join her in unison)
Cindy:	can you see me?
Diane:	can you see me? See my arms?
Cindy:	I'm just staring at the bedspread. (She's now singing as her little girl)
Diane:	staring at the bedspread.
Cindy:	the spread turns into different patterns, what a bore, what a bore staring at my bedspread.
Diane:	wouldn't you like to play says the tree, wouldn't you like to play with me, climb up in my branches, put your arms around me?

I decide to continue to sing as the tree – the nurturing, positive mother figure that offers her support. I also sing an entirely different melody. Her melody consists of three repeated notes, the sound of boredom. I sing of play and my melody reflects that by jumping up to a fourth, then to a sixth and creating a singsong effect.

Cindy:	I'm afraid. (She cries)
Diane:	we could just sit then, it's okay to be afraid, it's okay, it's okay, it's okay. (Cindy cries and blows her nose)

Diane: I will stay here outside your window and you can cry if that's what you need to do. (My singing has a lullaby quality to it, both my voice and the melody; again, I am offering a reparative experience – an empathic mother-tree who is accepting and understanding)

Cindy: But what if lightning strikes you down?

Diane: (I pause here – stuck for a moment, how do I answer that? I wasn't expecting it but she needs to know I won't be destroyed by the lightning or the intensity of her needs)

Diane: My spirit will always be here with you.

Cindy: you'll be here with me?

Diane: I'll be here with you. (I feel relieved that I came up with an acceptable answer; I feel very close to her – very moved by her)

Free associative singing in supervision

I have been supervising professional music therapists for the past ten years. Not all of them are in private practice so the issues they are dealing with are diverse. However, there are times when every therapist has similar needs. For instance, the need for practical problem solving: 'How do I get kids to come to my groups?' 'What are some interventions for anger management with adolescents?' 'How do I make my schedule work so that I have time to take notes?'

Education is also a part of supervision even for music therapists who are professionals, for we all need to continue to learn in order to grow as clinicians. This is especially true when working with a new population. So I sometimes educate the therapists I work with about diagnoses, symptoms, interventions for specific personality disorders, working through different stages of therapy and the like. I also recommend books and articles that will enhance their knowledge.

Another need shared by therapists in supervision is the need for validation, support and empathy. Having someone who understands and has 'been there' is important to combat feelings of isolation; feelings that are not unusual in private practice but are also experienced by many therapists who work in schools and institutions. Feeling understood and appreciated and having a safe place to talk or sing and play about uncomfortable feelings toward patients or staff can also help prevent burnout.

I have found free associative singing to be extremely effective when working with more in-depth issues like resistance, transference and countertransference. Supervision, in this case, is similar to vocal psychotherapy. The spontaneous singing of lyrics and melody can cut through to the essence of a feeling, thought or action.

Case example: Brenda

Brenda was working with a new client, Courtney, a 16-year-old adolescent who evoked strong emotional reactions in Brenda. In the beginning of treatment, Brenda felt annoyed by Courtney's 'victim' persona and even wondered if she could work with her. Through free associative singing with me, Brenda realized that she was projecting feelings about her mother, who played a martyred victim in need of rescue, onto Courtney. Brenda always resented feeling she had to rescue her mother so these feelings of having to rescue Courtney were especially irritating and inhibited Brenda from working effectively. Once Brenda realized and worked through her countertransference the therapy progressed.

Several months later, Brenda said she needed to discuss Courtney again. This time, Brenda was concerned about her strong protective urges toward Courtney. Brenda suspected that she was overly invested in this case and that her maternal attitude was affecting her ability to assume a more neutral stance and might be getting in the way of seeing Courtney clearly. We decided to explore her feelings through free associative singing. I am only including a brief exchange from this session. An audio example can be heard at www.dianeaustin.com.

Brenda:	Courtney, you touch my heart
Diane and Brenda:	(in unison) Courtney, you touch my heart
Brenda:	And I want to teach you, help you, guide you, show you the world.
Diane:	Teach you, help you, be with you, it's been so rough for you.
Brenda:	It still is.
Brenda:	You're just starting your life.
Diane:	(harmony) Your life

Brenda:	Courtney, you could do so much if you had someone to guide you. Someone who cared. Someone. Someone. Someone.
Diane:	You don't have anyone.
Brenda and Diane:	(harmony) Courtney, you touch my heart
	You touch my heart
	You touch my heart
	You touch my heart
Brenda:	I see your pain.
Diane:	And I understand it.
Brenda:	And I get it. I think I get it.
Diane:	I can relate.
Brenda and Diane:	(harmony) I can relate. I can relate. I can relate.
Brenda and Diane:	(unison) I understand
Diane:	I have a heart like you.
Brenda:	I have a part like you.
Diane:	Who's scared
Brenda:	Who's scared
Diane:	And sad
Brenda:	And sad. (cries) A kid like you, who lives deep inside of me, who's sad and mad and hurt.
Diane:	So hurt.
Brenda and Diane:	(harmony) So hurt.
Brenda and Diane:	(unison) Courtney, you don't know how much you touch my heart
Diane:	You touch my heart
Brenda:	Because you're me.

When we finished singing, Brenda continued to cry. We sat in silence for a while. Brenda said, 'It's funny, first she reminded me of my mother, now she reminds me of me! But she is neither of us. She is Courtney.'

Psychodramatic singing

Psychodrama has interested me for years. I have a background in theatre that led me to take courses in drama therapy and psychodrama during my graduate studies at New York University. I returned to it six years ago after attending a workshop and learning that many psychodrama therapists are working effectively with trauma survivors (Bannister 2000; Dayton 1994, 1997; Hudgins and Kiesler 1987; Kellerman 2000).

There is a relationship between free associative singing and psychodrama. I realized during my psychodrama training that a technique I use frequently and find invaluable, that I had referred to as an 'alter-ego' (Austin 1998, 1999b), was actually a musical version of the psychodramatic 'double' (Moreno 1994). In psychodramatic singing, besides singing as a double I also take on (sing) roles from the client's story as it unfolds in the improvisation. The client may also switch or take on different roles as illustrated in the case example on pp.169–170.

Following is part of an excerpt taken from Cindy's next vocal psychotherapy session. It illustrates psychodramatic singing.

CINDY

Cindy feels ready to confront her perpetrator, her uncle. We spend extra time breathing together until she feels grounded in her body. I ask her what chords she would like and she replies, 'Something in A minor, maybe something modal'. I begin playing A minor to D minor, medium tempo and dynamics. Cindy begins singing.

Cindy:	Okay, I'm ready. He is sitting on the bed looking out the window. He knows, he knows why we're coming. He's very sad.
Diane:	He's very sad.
Cindy:	He's very ashamed.
Diane:	He's very ashamed.
Cindy:	We walk in – Mummy takes my hand. (I realize that she is singing as her little girl accompanied by her adult self-mummy, and me)
Cindy:	And they're both crying.

Diane: They're both crying, they're both crying, Mummy takes my
hand, they're both crying – he knows what he's done – he
feels so ashamed.

Cindy: I know you're very sad – I know that you were hurt, but you
can't do this any more – not to my little girl, not to my little
girl. (Cindy is now singing as her adult self mothering her
younger self)

                (I change my piano accompaniment. It is very rhythmic with a
strong moving bass line. I am playing parallel 5ths so there is
lots of dissonance. The chords are modal 7ths, 9ths, 11ths and
13ths.)

Cindy/
Diane: (I join her as her adult self) not to my little girl – NO NO NO!

Diane: NO!

Cindy: Keep your hands off of her!

Diane: Keep your hands off of her!

                (The music supports the intensity of our singing)

Cindy: You will have to answer to me – I'm taking care of her now!
You keep your hands off, I'm warning you – I'll make your life
miserable. I'm not kidding.

Diane: (I am now singing as myself, supporting her adult self) He can
see your power. He knows you're not kidding. He can see it in
your eyes.

                (I am playing loudly to match her singing. The polyrhythms
and syncopation support and encourage the expression of her
anger.)

Cindy: He can see my power.

Diane: He can see your power.

Cindy: He knows he's gotta feel – this pain and sadness for a long
time, he's gotta feel – remember what he did to me – he's gotta
feel the pain – He's gotta feel what he did to us, so he's feeling
it and he's hurting, hurting, hurting, hurting, hurting, hurting
inside – and that's the only way he's gonna face himself. He's
gotta face what he did, he's gotta make retribution on his soul
– and that's all right with me because I carry all my burdens by

myself – I don't ask anybody to let me off the hook – so you go ahead and feel it, you go ahead and feel it, you go ahead and feel what it felt like to have my uncle treat me like I was his lover – I'm not carrying it for you – It's yours.

Diane: It's yours, it's yours, I'm gonna give it back to you. It's not my burden.

Cindy: It's not my burden.

Cindy/
Diane: not, not, not, not, not, not – I wanna go on and be a woman.

            (We are singing in unison and harmony)

Diane: On and be a woman, I wanna go on.

Cindy: I wanna grow stronger.

Diane: Stronger… Stronger… This guilt is yours.

Cindy: It's yours and I won't carry it any more. I'm putting it down now.

Cindy begins to cry softly and rock back and forth. I sing 'hmmmm' and return to A minor 7 and D minor 7 chords. I am playing slower and softer now. I sing in a lullaby-like fashion. I am also taking deep breaths to resource myself, as this was a very emotional process for me as well. Then we both continue singing on 'm-m-m' for several more minutes. This is an important time, a time for Cindy to take in what just occurred and to come to closure with it, at least for this session.

The empty chair

The 'empty chair' is a psychodramatic technique that originated with Moreno (1994) and was later adopted by gestalt therapists (Blatner 1988). The chair is placed in front of clients and used to symbolize another person, part of the self or a meaningful object. This technique is deceptively simple but very effective at revealing the projections of clients, helping them clarify and express feelings and providing an opportunity for catharsis.

The empty chair can also provide clients with a chance to work through unfinished business, for example, saying goodbye to a deceased parent. Anyone can be placed in the chair and spoken to: a fictional character, a future husband, someone from your past, God. The enactment is more complete, and more can be learned about projections we place on others, when clients reverse roles. Speaking from the point of view of the other enables clients to gain a different perspective on the relationship through insights into the other person's feelings and thoughts (Blatner 1988).

I have adapted the empty chair technique and use it in psychodramatic singing. When clients are discussing someone they have unfinished business with, or a person or part of themselves they need to talk to, I ask them to look around the office and pick something to represent that person or aspect of themselves. There are many 'actors' in my office: stuffed animals, dolls, hand puppets, musical instruments, tin soldiers, little statues of Gods and Goddesses from various cultures and a small collection of minerals, seashells and *objets d'art*. Some clients might also want to pick an ally – someone or something to support them that they can place nearby or hold on to while they sing. I also have a huge bowl of brightly coloured scarves and occasionally clients will pick a scarf that they can drape around themselves, in a colour that reminds them of an inner resource they possess.

I then invite them to the piano and ask them to sit down next to me. The top of the piano becomes the empty chair where they place the object. I often learn a lot from seeing the object they pick. Phyllis described her father as a stern patriarch but she picked the glass dog to represent him. Sometimes we discuss their choice before we start, sometimes later or not at all.

I offer the clients choices. They can sing about the person, as the person or to the person. When they pick 'to the person' I tell them the rules. Phyllis decided to sing to her father. I tell 'him' he has to stay and he cannot speak or interrupt in any way. He must listen to her. Even though this encounter is happening in a transitional play space, these rules are important for safety. As mentioned earlier, when using free associative singing, it is easy to enter a trance-like altered state where what is occurring feels quite real.

Clients often choose to sing to parts of themselves, like 'the little girl', 'the witch', 'the wounded artist', and picking objects to represent them can make the experience more compelling.

MARIE

Marie wanted to sing to her very young part in this session. It is the part she sometimes describes as her 'small voice'.

Marie looks over at the shelf where I keep stuffed animals, dolls and other objects and asks me if my stuffed animals have names. I tell her they don't and ask if she would like to look at them up close. She says 'yes!', gets up from the bench and goes over to the shelf. She picks up and examines the different stuffed animals and puppets. She says she likes the moose. She likes the colour and size of his horns. I tell her she can bring him over if she wants to. Marie brings the moose to the piano and sits him on top of the keyboard.

She wants to sing as the moose and picks minor chords. She sings about how the moose feels invisible and ignored. Marie doesn't understand how this could be when 'my horns are so big, how could they not be seen?' I double her and repeat her lyrics. I sing about how sad it is when you aren't seen or heard. She repeats my lyrics. She sings about not knowing if she is bad. Maybe that's why they ignore her.

I switch roles and sing as adult Marie and comfort the moose. I tell her she is not bad. They are all so self-absorbed in their own problems they just don't notice her. It's not her fault. I ask what would help her (the moose) feel better. She sings, 'To feel welcome.' I sing, 'Welcome moose, I am so happy to see you.' I repeat this several times. Marie's eyes fill up with tears as she looks into my eyes for the first time.

CHAPTER 12

Songs

What's the first song you remember? Perhaps it's a song your mother or father sang to you, maybe a lullaby. Do you remember your first favourite song? Where you were when you heard it? What you were doing? Who you were with? What about the songs that remind you of your first romance, your first breakup, songs you listened to in high school, in college, at a loved one's death? Is there a song that comes to mind when you think about major events in your life, like leaving home, falling in love, getting married or when you remember people who were or still are important to you? There are songs that are significant because we played and often sang them over and over again when we were happy or sad or because they reflected what we were feeling at different points in our lives.

As I write this I'm reminded of the first song I loved, 'Where Is Your Heart?'

It was the first song I ever sang on stage. I was about nine years old at the time but I can still remember the room and the way I felt. I also remember the lyrics to a song I played for weeks on end when I broke up with my first boyfriend. I would put on the recording and cry. I was about 14 at the time and deep into the angst of adolescence. I can remember laying on my porch and crying as I sang about my loneliness. All through my life there has been a song or songs that reflect where I am in my individuation process. When I was a professional singer 'My Funny Valentine' was my signature song. Whenever I sang it, it brought tears to my eyes. I knew this song contained some special meaning for me but I wasn't sure what that was. Then one day in therapy while talking about my father, it occurred to me that 'My Funny

Valentine' had to do with my need/fear of emotionally separating from him and pursuing a career that was different from his. This is an example of the symbolic value of songs and one of the ways they can illuminate issues in vocal psychotherapy.

Songs also elicit projections and transference reactions from both client and therapist and can easily promote an exchange of unconscious contents between both parties (Nolan 1998). The intermingling of unconscious feelings and associations is deepened in the intimate environment created when client and therapist sing together.

The reasons singing is such a powerful intervention are discussed in Chapter 1 as well as the chapters on vocal holding techniques and free associative singing. Singing pre-composed songs, however, is a safer intervention than improvising music and lyrics. The song is known to the client and therefore predictable, so there is a greater sense of control and less a feeling of risk taking. The sense of exposing oneself in the more precarious world of vocal improvisation is greatly reduced. The structure inherent in a song offers more containment than spontaneous singing especially when improvised lyrics are part of the process. There is less anxiety about revealing something prematurely or being overtaken by emotions because the music and the lyrics are familiar as are some thoughts and feelings about them.

The repeated singing of a song can help clients work through the feelings or issues the song evokes or 'increase clients' tolerance for the words, ideas or feelings' the song gives voice to (Dvorkin 1991, p.258). Sometimes clients repeatedly sing songs that have qualities or ideals they want to introject. These kinds of songs can be inspiring and provide a resource (an inner or outer source of support and strength) for those who need it but can be especially beneficial for the traumatized client.

Dvorkin (1991) discusses the use of songs as transitional objects (Winnicott 1971) – objects the child uses in the course of emotional separation from the mother (or primary caretaker) that substitute for her and relieve stress especially at bedtime. These special objects can counteract feelings of loss and abandonment and 'preserve the illusion of a loving, comforting and soothing mother' (Moore and Fine 1990, p.207).

I have often made recordings for clients of us singing one of their favourite songs; sometimes they ask me to sing alone. Some clients listen to their recordings to help manage their anxiety when I am away or on vacation. One client found it helpful to listen to the recording in between sessions, when we had just begun working together. Hearing my voice every night helped her build a sense of object constancy. Another client who often suffered from agoraphobia and separation anxiety played our song on her iPod while travelling on the subway or long distances. She said, 'Hearing your voice singing that soothing music helps me...it's relaxing and I don't feel so alone. It's almost like you're here with me.'

Songs have the capacity to tell our histories. They can transport us back in time, remind us of the people, places and events that helped to shape our lives and reconnect us to feelings we may have lost touch with. Many music therapists, including me, have given their students or clients the assignment to tell their life stories through songs. This assignment had a powerful effect on the students and many were surprised by the intensity of the feelings and memories that emerged through the music as well as the insights into their lives that the songs gave voice to.

> Songs are ways that human beings explore emotions. They express who we are and how we feel, they bring us closer to others, they keep us company when we are alone. They articulate our beliefs and values. As the years pass, songs bear witness to our lives. They allow us to relive the past, to examine the present, and to voice our dreams for the future. Songs weave tales of our joys and sorrows, they reveal our innermost secrets, and they express our hopes and disappointments, our fears and triumphs. They are our musical diaries, our life stories. They are the sounds of our personal development. (Bruscia 1998, p.9)

Sometimes I suggest that clients bring in a significant song; a song that is important to them or that relates to an issue we are working on. They bring in CDs or songs on their iPods that we listen to and often sing along with. These songs are usually revealing and can open doors to new information or take us deeper into difficult subjects and feelings. The clients may or may not realize the symbolic meaning of the song or why it is important to them until we listen to it together or sing it. An example of this is when Julie brought in the sheet music to 'I Can't Make You Love Me'. She said it was about her last boyfriend who broke up with her unexpectedly. She was still trying to accept that it was over.

When we sang the song together it was a very emotional experience for her. Afterwards we talked about the lyrics and I asked her for associations. She said she felt abandoned by him. I asked if she had ever felt this way before (a classic question). She replied, 'I don't know...I guess I felt this same kind of loss with another guy I really liked but it didn't work out either.' We talked some more and I questioned her about other feelings of loss she had experienced. Then I suggested we sing the song again and see if any other images or feelings emerged. By the end of the session Julie made a connection to how she felt when her parents divorced. She was only nine years old at the time and was very close to her father. He remarried shortly afterwards, started another family and moved to another state when she was 13. She saw him infrequently after he moved. It was a huge loss for her. She had told me the details of the divorce before but in a matter of fact way. This time she was crying and connected to the effect this experience had on her life.

Sometimes clients bring in songs in which the meaning is self-evident. They bring them in because they want to tell me something the song conveys. They bring them in because they want me to witness the feelings the song evokes in them. They bring them in so that we can sing together and they can enlist my support and encouragement. This was the case with Nan when she was tired of being a good girl and was finally getting in touch with her anger. We had a great time singing 'I'm Not Ready to Make Nice', her favourite empowerment song.

Listening to songs

When I began my private practice in music psychotherapy, it was improvisationally based. Clients would discuss an issue and we would sing and play in order to elicit feelings, insights and associations to the subject matter. Improvising is a form of free association and a road to the unconscious. I never know where the music will take us. Sometimes it deepens the topic under discussion and sometimes it leads us around a corner and into an unfamiliar place.

My approach initially stemmed from my training at New York University and their emphasis on music psychotherapy and improvisation. The theorists I resonated the most with were Florence Tyson (1981) and Mary Priestley (1975). They both utilized music and verbal processing to enable the client to gain insight into unconscious material. I was excited by Tyson's application of psychodynamic principles (Balint's theories in particular) to music therapy practice with regressed borderline and schizophrenic patients. I related to Priestley's use of improvised music to access unconscious feelings and associations as well as her emphasis on the use of countertransference in music therapy.

In 1992, I began a music therapy programme for adolescents in foster care. The programme took place at Turtle Bay Music School in New York City every Friday night. I had never worked with adolescents before and thought it would be a nice balance to the in-depth work I was doing in private practice. I had no idea how difficult it would be to work with this population and the amount of resistance I would encounter.

Before I began working at Turtle Bay one of my fantasies had been that we would create songs and poems about the lives of these adolescent girls that would culminate in a musical drama. Throughout the year, however, I often found myself sitting on the floor and listening to CDs with my groups and my individual clients. During those moments I remember questioning if what I was doing was even music therapy. This wasn't what I learned in school and wasn't the kind of in-depth vocal psychotherapy I conduct in private practice with adults. I didn't see the therapeutic value of sitting and listening to songs, many of which I could not even understand. Some of the lyrics used slang I was unfamiliar with and some of the songs were about sex and violence and the lyrics were garbled. Adding to my frustration, the girls would not talk about the songs, why they liked them or what lyrics related to their own lives and experiences.

Around this same time, in what could be called a parallel process, I brought a song with me to therapy. It was a tape and I even brought a tape recorder since I knew there wasn't one in my therapist's office. I felt it was an important song because I had been playing it for weeks and, every time I played it, it evoked strong feelings in me.

I told my therapist I wanted to play it for him and why. He looked stymied. He said something like, 'What do you want me to do?' I looked at him in disbelief. 'Listen to it with me!' He sat quietly for a few moments. He seemed uncomfortable. Maybe because this was my area (music therapy), maybe because he had never been asked to do this before, or maybe he felt confused because I didn't necessarily ask him to analyse it or *do* something with it. He then said he was concerned about the sound leaking into the office next door. Not ready to give up, I said I would play it softly and he acquiesced.

This experience was pivotal in terms of my remembering why it was so important to listen to songs with clients (I used to do this when I gave therapeutic voice lessons). It also made me appreciate the value of listening to songs as an intervention in vocal psychotherapy. As music therapists we have the ability not just to hear but to listen, listen to something that someone else feels is important. Maybe because music is our medium, our clients trust that we will understand why their songs are so significant to them.

I realized my countertransference to the girls and the music was blocking the therapeutic process. I stopped judging myself and the adolescents I worked with. I listened with them and to them. I asked them to explain the lyrics I didn't understand. They enjoyed teaching me words from their world. Something positive was happening. The girls were opening up to me and to each other. The songs were a catalyst for feelings, thoughts and sensations and a safe way for these girls to begin to put words to their experiences. They slowly began talking about difficult issues, such as what it was like being in foster care.

Sometimes they brought in violent songs. Since they were listening to them anyway, I believed it was better if they listened to them with me so that we could talk about the feelings and issues that the songs evoked. When we discussed the songs, some important information emerged. I learned that Karaar's father was in jail for killing her brother, that Tania and her sisters had been brutally beaten by their mother and that all of these girls had a legacy of pain and anger that made life incredibly difficult for them.

Songs play a central role in the lives of nearly all adolescents. Songs can provide them with a form of object constancy (Hartmann 1952) in that their music and favourite singers are always available to them in ways that their parents and foster parents are not. With the flip of a switch they can be enveloped in sounds that are familiar and reliable, sounds that can energize and comfort, and rhythms, melodies, harmonies and lyrics that can create a cocoon of safety which allows them to block out the harsh realities of their lives.

Adolescents identify strongly with their musical choices and their favourite singers often become role models. These identifications can bolster a compromised sense of self and play a part in building peer relationships (Frisch 1990). The songs they gravitate towards are most revealing in the ways in which they mirror, reflect and validate the inner and outer worlds of the adolescents.

Of course, some of these observations about listening to songs hold true for other clients as well. When clients choose a song to listen to in your presence, they are often telling you something about their emotional, psychological or spiritual state. They could also be revealing something about the transference. They are revealing something they cannot say because either they aren't consciously aware of it, or they don't have the words to say it, or they do not feel safe enough to talk about it. But they are disclosing thoughts and feelings, nonetheless. Thoughts and feelings they want you to listen to and probably empathize with. The first song they bring in, the presenting song, can be like a presenting dream in analysis in that it can foreshadow the main issues that will emerge in the therapy (Austin in Rolla 1993). Thus, songs can also be useful in assessment.

Case example: Leslie

Leslie, a 32-year-old investment banker, began vocal psychotherapy by bringing in CDs every week for us to listen to. She was painfully shy and self-conscious and had a hard time talking about her history; in fact, it was difficult for her to talk about anything that might elicit feelings. That was why she wanted to try vocal psychotherapy even though she said, 'I'm not talented at music… I just like to listen to it and sometimes sing along.'

By the third session I noticed that she brought in fast, upbeat songs every week but the theme of the lyrics was incongruent. The songs were all about being alone, being rejected, wanting someone to take her home and stay with her. When I questioned her about the lyrics she said, 'I just like the music, it's fun to dance to.' Several weeks later when she seemed more comfortable with me, I talked about my transference to the music, that the songs gave me the impression of someone who was sad but trying to act happy. She sat in silence for several minutes and then said, 'The happy music helps me tolerate the sad lyrics…no one wants to be around someone who is sad all the time.' This discussion opened up a channel for her to begin to talk about the root of her sadness.

Your inner soundtrack

Do you ever find yourself humming or singing a song and then realizing it is relevant to how you are feeling or what is occurring in your life at the moment? If you do, you are not alone. According to Rolla (1993), 'Everyone experiences the inner music phenomenon, not because of inherent musical values or talent, but as a result of the function of memory and its significance to individuation' (p.12). Many of us don't pay attention to these subtle messages from the unconscious as we rush from one task to another in our busy lives but Rolla (1993) speculates that 'The unconscious may possess the ability to reveal its contents through the music memory patterns which emerge from it at random' (p.11).

My husband has an uncanny ability to communicate what's on his mind or how he's feeling through the unconscious selection of a song. Sometimes I hear him singing around the house and I am astounded by the amount of information he must be processing. I often ask him if he is aware of what he's singing and he catches himself and laughs because of the relevance of what he's singing to what is happening or what he is feeling at that moment. I have a student who is similarly attuned to the songs that bubble up from her unconscious and the self-knowledge they give her. She calls this phenomenon her 'inner DJ' and says it is incredibly accurate. She does have the advantage, however, of possessing an enormous inner jukebox.

Theodore Reik (1953) observed that 'in this inward singing, the voice of an unknown self conveys not only passing moods and impulses, but sometimes a disavowed or denied wish, a longing and a drive we do not like to admit to ourselves' (p.10).

Diaz de Chumaceiro (1992, 1998) has written extensively on what she calls 'induced song recall'. She studied songs that spontaneously arise in the client's mind during sessions and found they are valuable clues to unconscious issues and dynamics such as transference reactions. The results of two research studies in Latin America supported her own conclusions that a relationship also existed between transferential and countertransferential song evocations in terms of feeling states, unconscious conflicts, and transference reactions.

Reik (1953) was the first psychoanalyst to point out and describe the importance of therapists' affective responses to patients revealed in music evocations. He analysed songs that arose in his mind when he practised psychoanalysis in order to discern countertransference reactions to his patients.

> They not only convey contents unknown to the analyst's conscious thinking but also communicate to him something of the hidden emotions that he has not yet been able to catch while he listens to his patient. The tunes stand in the service of the agents responsible for the communications between the unconscious of two persons. These melodies present themselves clearly or dimly to the mind, but what they have to convey becomes comprehensible only when the analyst listens with the 'third ear'. (Reik in Nolan 1998, p.392)

The following case illustrates the combination of vocal holding, free associative singing and unconscious song recall.

Case example: Liz

Liz is a 28-year-old pianist who, at the time of treatment, was completing her Master's degree in Music Therapy. She entered therapy because of 'intimacy issues' with her boyfriend. She felt stifled in the relationship, yet the thought of leaving him triggered anxiety and feelings of abandonment.

Liz had grown up in an alcoholic family where she never felt safe. 'The constant chaos and confusion…everyone screaming all the time… I couldn't wait to get away.' Her mother's emotional intensity frightened her and she was afraid she might be the same way if she expressed her feelings. This was an issue we had been working on.

The session I will now describe took place during the tenth month of Liz's therapy. Liz arrived late for her appointment and seemed distant. She said: 'Things aren't working out with Peter… I think I want to break up with him.' She had a blank look on her face and spoke with little affect. We talked about how Peter sometimes said or did things that reminded her of her mother. I felt that we were not getting to the feeling content in her words so I suggested music. Liz said that she wanted to sing and wanted me to play the piano and sing with her. She requested a 'light pop' sound and together we came up with a vamp on C major, D minor and E minor. Liz began to sing without words, using 'ah's, and I supported her using unison, harmony and mirroring.

I was struck by her choice of rhythm and harmony. The music did not match what I imagined her inner state might be. The upbeat music combined with Liz's lateness made me wonder if she was resisting her feelings about the conflict and potential loss of her relationship with Peter. In a trauma model, however, what looked like resistance could actually be resourcing (Herman 1992; Levine 1997). In other words, Liz often defended against painful and difficult feelings by dissociating. The deep breathing required for singing was very useful in helping Liz calm her anxiety and gradually enter her body and ground herself. Experiencing her own body producing strong, full sounds was empowering for Liz and put her in touch with her inner resources.

After several minutes of singing on 'ah' and 'oo', Liz sang the word 'somewhere' and then 'somewhere, where?' She stopped singing and said: 'Something in the music reminds me of that song, Somewhere Out There.'

I knew about the significance of songs that spontaneously come to mind. These songs contain messages from the unconscious. I stopped playing and worked out the chords to the song and then Liz and I began to sing 'Somewhere Out There'. Halfway through the song, Liz stopped and said: 'I'm blocking out the words… I can't remember them all.' One could look at this as another layer of resistance *to* the music while simultaneously working through resistance *in* the music (Austin and Dvorkin 1993).

I suggested that Liz make up her own words to the song. We had done this with various songs in the past and Liz never found it difficult. Today, however, she felt reluctant to do this, so I asked: 'What is the most meaningful lyric in the song?' She replied: 'We'll find one another.' At this point, my therapeutic intervention was to use the two-chord holding technique. I used the opening chords to 'Somewhere Out There': B flat major 7 to C minor 7/B flat. Liz began singing 'We'll find one another' and then began to vocally free associate. I mirrored her melodies exactly at some points and sang variations of her melodies at other points. At moments, we came together with unison and harmony. I also matched and attuned my voice to hers in terms of breathing, vocal placement, quality, dynamics and emotional affect.

Initially, I repeated her lyrics exactly: 'I want to find you… where are you?' Repetition is used differently in vocal psychotherapy from in verbal psychotherapy. I use repetition in vocal improvisation to deepen affect. It is as if each time the word is sung, it works its way from the head or throat down deeper into the body and the feeling realm.

As I continued to sing with Liz, I noticed that I began to feel sad. I decided to use what I felt was induced countertransference. I sang an essence statement involving feeling: 'I feel sad.' Liz's voice took on more feeling. She sang 'Where are you?' several times. I then sang: 'Will I ever find you. I need…' (another essence statement). She picked up 'I need' and started crying. Liz's crying intensified as she sang: 'Sometimes I feel like I can't even find myself for looking… I get so lost in looking… I get so lost in the feeling of sadness.'

Then she returned spontaneously to a non-verbal holding state. We sang 'ah's in unison for several minutes before adding an occasional harmony. I attuned my breathing to hers. I felt emotionally and musically available and responsive to her. At one point, we were rocking back and forth in synchrony. Liz continued to cry but kept singing. I felt that she was regressing to a younger, pre-verbal stage. The singing seemed to calm and soothe her. I was being the good-enough mother-therapist, holding her vocally and helping her to contain and metabolize the grief she was experiencing. I was companioning her and accepting her feelings in a way her mother had not been able to. Once again, Liz had a therapeutic experience in which she could have feelings without being engulfed by them. She could cry without drowning in tears, in the same way that she could feel angry without becoming abusive.

During our processing of the music, I said, 'I think that the title of our improvisation could be somewhere *in* there.' Liz agreed: 'Yes, it's not somewhere *out* there, it's somewhere *in* there. I've always looked for someone or something outside of myself to make me whole, and really it's inside of me… I've been afraid to go too far inside myself, afraid of the hurt part, that the hurt part would take over and that's all I'd be…but maybe I don't have to be so afraid.'

We can look at the emotional content in Liz's singing on several levels. On a conscious level, her feelings are related to loss and abandonment brought up by the pending separation from her boyfriend. On a deeper, more unconscious level, her feelings of grief are related to the initial abandonment by her mother. On an intrapsychic level, we can look at this session as another step in Liz's journey to integrate the dissociated parts of herself into a more cohesive, authentic self.

> Big eyes looked into mine
> And a small voice came out to meet me
> 'It's safe here,' I sang
> The notes made a nest
> That cradled her and kept her warm
> I fed her with sound and simple melodies
> And her small voice grew stronger each day
> 'I'm ready to try my wings,' she sang
> And in a flurry of song she flew away.

Songs from the therapist

Sometimes to soothe clients who are crying or who seem especially vulnerable near the end of a session, I might offer to sing them a song. If this idea appeals to them, I will usually invite them to the piano so that we are in closer contact. I have several songs I have found to be effective over the years in comforting clients and helping them feel held, contained and ready to go back out into the world. One has a simple melody and repetitive rhythm similar to a lullaby. They all have lyrics that relate to being mothered, protected or companioned through some difficult journey (one example is 'Not While I'm Around' by Stephen Sondheim). During particularly challenging times and transitions, clients might ask me to sing one of these songs again or a favourite song they have brought in and taught me. Sometimes we record the song and it becomes a transitional object, available to them when they are feeling stressed or anxious.

I have had clients ask me to pick a song for us to sing that relates to what they are experiencing and I have occasionally offered them a song spontaneously that I thought they would like. This is, as you might imagine, a risky intervention. They could be testing me to see if I am accurately perceiving them and even if that is not the case, I might not know or be familiar enough with the kind of songs they prefer. I might choose appropriate lyrics but the music may not be to their liking. Then there is always the possibility of my countertransference to the song. My positive or negative feelings and associations might prevent me from making a more informed choice.

I have often had good luck when a song comes spontaneously to mind when I'm sitting with a client. This happened with Meg. She spent most of the session talking about being 'fed up with being so compliant all the time'. I asked her if she had ever heard 'Sing' (my sister's sing) by Annie Lennox. She said no but it sounded interesting. I sang it for her and she immediately wanted to see the video. We found it on 'Youtube' and we sang along with the video until the session ended.

This wasn't the case with Cindy but our relationship grew stronger through our discussion of an inappropriate song choice I made.

CINDY

Cindy said she felt happy to see me. 'My little girl has been jumping up and down at the thought of coming today…it's my birthday!' I asked her what she would like to do to celebrate. She said she had been singing 'Happy Birthday' to herself all morning. I asked if she'd like to sing it. 'I feel silly but…yes the little girl would like it.' I played 'Happy Birthday' on the piano and we sang together. Cindy laughed afterwards. We talked about birthdays and how disappointing they'd been in the past. I felt like doing more to celebrate with her. I pulled out 'Happy Birthday' from 'Getting My Act Together and Taking It on the Road'. She had never heard of the show or the song and I was eager to share it with her. When we finished singing she smiled but didn't say anything. She started talking about other birthdays. I realized I really like this song but it probably wasn't the right song for her. When there was a pause in the conversation I asked her how she felt about singing the birthday songs. She hesitated then said, 'The first one was enough…it felt really satisfying'. I replied, 'The other one wasn't your kind of song, lyrically maybe, but not musically'. She nodded in agreement. I wondered if I sang the song to meet my own need. She asked me if it was a favourite song of mine and I said 'yes'. We both laughed. In that moment of shared truth and laughter it felt as if we grew closer.

Songs from the client

Sometimes clients want to sing alone and be listened to. They may simply want to share something meaningful to them. However, if this becomes a pattern it needs to be examined further. I have worked with several clients who always prefer to sing and play alone and seem to want me to be simply a responsive, appreciative audience. The clients I am referring to have deep narcissistic wounds related to not being seen, heard and appreciated as a child. Usually they are not developmentally capable of relating authentically to another and protect their fragile egos by creating a kind of musical wall or a wall of words that insulates but also isolates them from genuine contact with others. These clients require a great deal of empathy and carefully attuned listening in order to feel safe and understood. Once a positive transference is established with the therapist, the clients can be gently encouraged to interact with the therapist in the music and verbally and allow for more of a flow between the two of them. As the relationship deepens the music will become more of a co-creative process.

There are also clients who would prefer to sing or play alone at times but are reluctant or unable to tell me. I have found these clients often fit the description of the compliant, adaptive personality that Alice Miller (1981) refers to.

Case example: Sue

> Sue is a music therapy student whose primary instrument is the voice. During one session I asked her if she would like to use the music to explore her feelings about her upcoming graduation. She readily agreed. I asked her what she'd like to do and she said, 'Sing and play the piano.' I asked her if she wanted to sing a song or improvise and she said she had a song in mind. I then asked if she'd like to sing alone, have me sing with her or have me accompany her on another instrument. She said, 'I'd like us to sing it together.'
>
> I remember feeling uncomfortable during the song. I felt the singing lacked emotion and I felt a lack of connection between Sue and myself. I

remember having an intuitive sense during the session that Sue really wanted to sing the song by herself and have me listen to her but perhaps felt uncomfortable saying that. I had this same feeling on two other occasions when vocally improvising with Sue.

As mentioned above, some clients often feel reluctant to say they would prefer to play or sing alone especially if they sense the therapist wants to participate or that there is an expectation that they should sing and play together. I have noticed this especially with music therapists who may be more comfortable using music as a way of caretaking. They could also be symbolically illustrating their core issue in the music; the need to please others at the expense of their own needs in order to be loved.

I sometimes felt that Sue was trying to take care of me, by anticipating what she thought I wanted and doing it. An example is when she read that I enjoy working with dreams and started bringing several dreams to therapy each week. Eventually she was ready to discuss this pattern. We were able to return to its source through free associative singing. Sue had a depressed mother who was emotionally unavailable and could fly into fits of rage. Sue's survival depended on being a 'good girl' without any needs or feelings that would burden her mother and on anticipating her mother's needs and trying to meet them. Sue gradually began to realize that she had set herself an impossible task that was doomed to failure and that her own feelings and needs were more important.

Safe Enough to Sing

Voice one: So much to tell you

Voice two: The words are hard to find

Voice three: There are no words to say it

Voice one: so good to breathe

Voice two: to accept

Voice three: just to be here

Voice one: The music slows me down so I can sense my body

Voice two: It turns something so ugly into something so beautiful

Voice three: I find my voice

Voice one: The singing holds me close

Voice two: I find my feelings and a place to put them

Voice three: I'm safe inside a blanket of sound

Voice one: can you hear me

Voice two: can you see me

Voice three: can you help me find my way

All three: can I trust you

Voice four: I hear a small child singing to her mother
                  I see a lonely little girl with only a tree for a friend
                  I sense the words you need to name the feelings

Voice one: my heart is opening

Voice two: I'm connecting to my body

Voice three: I'm coming out

All: So many songs

Voice four: songs of longing and loss
                  songs of anger and fear
                  songs of rain falling on parched arid land

All: abandoned songs found within

Voice four: songs of hope
                  songs of healing

All: songs of coming home…again

CHAPTER 13

The Therapeutic Process: Connection

In 2004 I completed a qualitative research study of my clinical work. The purpose of this study was to illuminate my clinical model of in-depth music psychotherapy with adults. The title of the dissertation, 'When Words Sing and Music Speaks', reflects the importance of the integration of music, primarily vocal music, and words in my model and the various ways this synthesis occurs. The participants for my study were chosen from my private practice in music psychotherapy. Ann, Cindy and Marie all fit the profile of the client population I work with. The recursive analysis of the data started to reveal emergent trends in the study. Significant themes emerged: statements of meaning that run through all or most of the pertinent data (Ely *et al.* 1991). Connection was the overarching theme of my research study and continues to be at the heart of my work.

A dependable connection with someone (the therapist) who is perceived as safe enough and good enough to provide a corrective emotional experience is essential if deep and lasting change is to occur. This good-enough mother-therapist companions the client through the unconscious to retrieve and reconnect to lost or hidden aspects of the self. The music, the sounds and the singing facilitate the client–therapist relationship and the client's relationship with his or her self. Likewise as trust is developed and the client–therapist relationship grows stronger, clients are able to take more risks and delve more deeply into their own interiority and this is reflected in the singing, the songs and the vocal improvisations. Lyrics and melodies emerge like waking dreams and provide access to feelings, images and sensations so that splits (mind–body, thinking and feeling, conscious and unconscious) can be healed and clients can gain access to more of themselves.

Six core categories emerged from the theme 'connection'. They are:

1. the therapist's need to connect

2. the client's need to connect to the therapist

3. making connections: the therapist's inner process

4. making connections: client's insights

5. disconnection and connection: feelings

6. disconnection and connection: parts of the self.

The therapist's need to connect

The importance of 'connection' in vocal psychotherapy is not surprising, but the many and various ways it appears are. First, there is my need to connect with myself and others, which relates to the theme of therapist as wounded healer. I now realize one of my unconscious motivations for choosing this profession was to intensify my own healing process. In order to be an effective vocal psychotherapist, clinicians have to experience and learn how to connect to their own feelings and inner life so they can speak and sing with their own unique voices and recognize the sounds of authenticity in their clients' voices. One also has to gain the capacity to connect feelings to words and words to feelings. After all, how can we help our clients do this if we cannot do this ourselves? When we are embodied and present and have a consistent and coherent sense of identity, it is easier to maintain connections with others.

The intense, intimate connections I have experienced in vocal psychotherapy sessions is something I know I have craved. This degree of soul searching and truth telling does not occur frequently in the every day world. I have learned and benefited from these experiences and from the therapy and supervision necessary to be of service to my clients, and I have been able to take what I have learned into my personal life.

I know I have a desire to connect or make contact with others that seems related to my personal history. My parents were difficult to relate to. I never felt a real connection to my mother (or I don't remember having one). She was inaccessible for the most part. My father was somewhat more available.

We connected primarily through music. He played the piano and I sang with him. We also connected through humour and the arts, especially movies. Still, he was difficult to reach most of the time so my connections with friends became extremely important to me. Of course, initially I unconsciously chose friends who had some of my parents' personality traits or boyfriends who were somewhat impenetrable, but I was persistent in my desire to get through their invisible walls.

My personal experiences of feeling connected and disconnected inform and influence my clinical decisions and effect my ability to empathize with my clients. All of the following quotations are taken from my session notes and transcripts of vocal psychotherapy sessions.

> What bothered me about the session was that I said I could 'just' listen – as if it isn't enough to listen or that I'd probably prefer to participate. Is this countertransference? It's something to think about. Would I feel this way with every client? I don't think so – or at all times. Sometimes I feel fine listening and some very wounded clients need to sing and play alone and be witnessed. I know this is important. My hunch is that I wanted to sing because I felt thwarted in my efforts to connect to her.

> This is an important word for me (connection). When we connected in the toning I felt empathy for her. I know how she feels – to be cut off and disconnected.

> The session felt good to me – what does that mean? I felt we connected. I played the xylophone sound on the keyboard and we sang. It was interesting that it was non-verbal – she usually sings words. She sang on vowels and ended on 'la'. I noticed how carefully I listened and how concentrated I was on really meeting her.

I enjoy my work the most when I feel connected and emotionally present and the music facilitates this connection to self and other.

> There is a flow to the work when it's going well. This seems related to intimacy. There is strength of contact and a sense of my total presence especially in the music and the singing in particular – an immersion in the creative process. Does singing help me connect to myself and to her?

> She joins me and sings, 'It's OK to be afraid'. She sings in unison with me. She stops crying. I can identify and empathize easily with fear. It feels good

to sing this. I feel connected to her. I feel connected to myself. I think this is probably also healing for me. It feels good to hear 'It's OK to be afraid'.

The role of the therapist, the therapeutic relationship and the therapeutic process are not discrete categories. They intersect and overlap. My desire to connect to myself and others is linked to my stance as a wounded healer-therapist and my belief in the mutuality of the therapeutic relationship, both of which effect my clinical approach.

The client's need to connect to the therapist

The client's need or desire to forge a connection with the therapist as a transference object or as a significant person is not usually directly expressed in the earlier stages of therapy. Initially, this desire is likely to be revealed more subtly in the client's musical communication, in the subtext of the conversation, in body language, facial expression, behaviour, and the countertransference. The client is usually unconscious of this need until it is brought to conscious awareness and then there is often ambivalence about having needs for closeness and connection with the therapist.

The more disappointing and damaging past relationships with significant others have been, the more unmet needs the client is likely to have. An accumulation of unmet dependency needs can make intimacy feel threatening or impossible. Clients tend to blame themselves for the deprivation they experienced. They often feel ashamed of being 'too much' and both yearn for and fear close relationships. There is a need/fear dilemma. They need connection yet they fear getting close to someone and being rejected when their true feelings and needs are exposed.

Clients need to connect with the therapist; they need to be seen, listened to, understood and truly known. They need to sing, laugh and cry with someone safe and supportive. These interactions lead to increased self-esteem, a more complete and realistic sense of self and an ability to maintain an intimate connection to themselves and others.

Ann leaned forward and stared into my eyes. I felt as if she wanted something from me, probably to be finally seen for herself and not as an extension of her parents. As we talked and laughed together I felt we were making more contact than we had before. A connection was developing.

Marie expressed her needs for connection through sound, movement, music and words.

Marie started to move. She made a punching motion. I made the same movement. I suggested she add sound. She said 'uh' every time she punched. I did the same. We were perfectly in sync. I felt a chill run through my shoulders, and a twinge of sadness. I wondered if I was standing at a comfortable distance from her. I asked and she said she wanted to move closer to me. She began to cry and put her hands over her eyes.

I asked Marie what she experienced during the singing. She said, 'It felt hypnotic but not empty like before…full… I felt contained and safe; I felt connected to you and that made it totally different… I was anchored. You were playing the music and the music led me; it laid down a path.'

Cindy's body language and physical sensations revealed both the fear and the pleasure of increased intimacy with me:

Cindy turned on the piano bench to face me. Now we were directly facing each other. I asked how that felt and she responded, 'I feel relief and a ticklish feeling.' The feeling became pleasure and a fear of pleasure.

Ann was able to interact more with me and our growing connection was evident in the music of our conversation:

I can identify with what Ann is saying…it feels like she's leaving more breathing room, feeling room, room to interact a little more with me. Our conversation feels like music. Our melodies are overlapping and punctuated with phrases like 'yeah, yeah, right' on both our parts. The rhythm picks up and holds steady. We are in a groove. I feel present and engaged. It strikes me as funny that we're talking about her fear of intimacy.

After singing together, Cindy expressed a need to connect with me on a physical level:

Cindy is singing about her fears of changing and growing up. Her 'little girl' is afraid she won't be able to do what is required of her. The improvisation builds to a climax and ends with Cindy calling out to her mother. She says she'd never called out for her mother before, in therapy or otherwise. As she is leaving she says she wants to give me a hug. I ask her, 'Do you need a hug?' She laughs and says, 'Maybe… I never ask for hugs, I usually give them.' I hug her and she smiles shyly.

Clients need to connect to the therapist in order to get their needs met. These needs are met through the therapist's ability to attune to the uniqueness of each client and listen and respond empathically in the sounds, in the singing, in the words, through body language and physical contact. Clients' needs are also met through the therapist's capacity to provide them with a consistent, emotionally present companion who can help them contain, digest and make sense of their feelings. As their needs are met, clients come to trust and rely on the therapist and a partnership is forged between the therapist and the part of the client that is willing to work toward individuation.

Making connections: The therapist's inner process

As I listen to my clients' music, words and silence and observe their body language and actions, I make connections. These connections can occur in the form of thoughts, feelings, memories, sensations, images or intuitive flashes. I form hypotheses about the client's issues and then determine how best to intervene. At times the connections I make lead to interpretations. Some of these connections are between past and present, conscious and unconscious, parts of the self and projections, music and feeling states, music and personal associations, music and parts of the self, and music and relatedness.

An example of a connection I made in the singing, that led to an insight about an unconscious aspect of Ann, occurred when she sang about her discord with a close friend. Ann's improvised lyrics and music were about how different she was from her friend and that maybe this difference created the distance between them. I sang with her as she described her friend as dramatic, open, earthy and sexual. I made a connection (but did not share it) between these qualities and Ann's 'shadow' aspect – the unacknowledged, unconscious, disowned parts of Ann's personality that she seemed to be both attracted to and repelled by. This insight proved valuable in making further interventions with the intention of enabling Ann to begin to acknowledge and experience these aspects of herself.

When Marie and I sang together, I made a connection between Marie's music and her psychic state (and probable diagnosis) as this example illustrates:

Marie and I sang about her invisible wings. The music we created had a dreamy, hypnotic quality to it. I made a connection between this music and her lack of embodiment and difficulty staying grounded in reality. Her voice also sounded light and airy. At one moment near the end I sensed her absence and wondered if she was present or in her own world. When we processed the music I asked her where she went and she said she didn't know. I suspect Marie suffers from a dissociative personality disorder.

In the next example I made a connection between Cindy's behaviour and the behaviour of a former client who had post-traumatic stress disorder. This association led me to initiate a different and more effective intervention.

> I made an association between Cindy's behaviour (wanting to force herself to scream) and another client I used to work with. This former client was also traumatized and liked to scream but in the end I don't think it was always therapeutic or productive. When Cindy said it was 'like giving birth…pushing' my antenna went up. Her desire to 'push out a scream' made me think about (connect with) theories of trauma I have been studying that refer to the traumatized client's tendency and pull to retraumatize herself.

Ann's music evoked an image and a feeling in me that led to a musical intervention connecting her to her unconscious feelings:

> The chords Ann chose (minor sevenths) and the sound of her singing voice (soft and plaintive) affected me. I began to feel sad. I had an image of a little girl who was given an impossible task, a task she could not help but fail. I wondered if she was also feeling sad and if I was picking up her feelings. I decided to use my countertransference to move the process along so I sang 'I feel sad'. Ann responded and sang 'and so alone'.

I realized there was a connection between Ann's reluctance to make music and her fear of feelings associated with the young part of herself. This realization prompted my musical intervention:

> We were talking about her fear of having needs and being perceived as needy. I said, 'Do you have an image of a time in your life when you were aware that you were needy and it was scary to feel that way?' I was thinking about an incident she mentioned when she was five years old. Ann said she didn't have a particular memory but she thought she felt this way a lot when she was younger – 'five or six comes to mind'. I ask, 'Do you think you could give a voice to that part of yourself and play or sing it?' I sense she is avoiding the music, that there is a definite connection between resisting the music and her fear of the feelings associated with being a child and having her needs judged. At one point I say, 'The five-year-old is still alive. Can we give her space so she can get her needs met in the present and grow up?' I

am encouraging Ann to acknowledge and connect with this young part of herself to see that she has value and doesn't deserve to be abandoned because she has unmet needs.

Making connections: Client's insights

Just as I make connections between my clients' past and present, their singing and their affect, their visual and sound images and the underlying unconscious meaning of these images, so do the clients. They often have insights into their own process especially after engaging in sounds and movements, toning, singing songs or vocally improvising.

What constitutes an insight? In everyday usage we use the word insight to connote clear and immediate understanding of one's own problems or a situation.

> In psychoanalytic treatment, it may occur as a sudden flash of recognition and understanding, called the 'aha' experience, whereby the determining factors and connections of an idea or bit of behaviour, or more global aspects of one's way of thinking and feeling, are seen in perspective. (Moore and Fine 1990, p.99)

Usually, however, insight comes gradually as a result of self-examination and observation. A genuine insight can be viewed as a creative act in that it changes what existed before and creates a new awareness expanding a person's self-knowledge and/or knowledge of others (May 1975; Singer 1970).

Freud's (1913) concept of insight was synonymous with intellectual understanding. Today most therapists regard insight as experiential as well as intellectual and realize that cognitive awareness alone does not lead to therapeutic change (Jacobi 1965; Kalsched 1996; Neubauer 1979).

Amir (1993) identified moments of insight that occurred to clients during music therapy sessions. Her qualitative study found that clients experienced insights in 'four inner realms: intellectual, physical, spiritual, and emotional' (p.90). Gaining insight and awareness into oneself and others is a crucial part of the growth process and is one of the goals of vocal psychotherapy.

The theme 'Making Connections: Client's Insights' appeared throughout my research study. Through recursively examining my data, I identified four ways in which insights occurred for the clients as a result of the vocal psychotherapy process:

1. through projection onto the instruments and the voice and qualities of the elements of the music such as melody, harmony, rhythm, dynamics and timbre

2. through transferential feelings in response to singing with the therapist

3. through symbols and images that emerged or were explored in more depth in vocal/musical improvisations

4. through the intentional use of free associative and psychodramatic singing to evoke past experiences.

Projections onto the instruments, the music and the voice helped clients identify and gain insight into parts of themselves:

> Cindy was playing the drum... She sped up the tempo and played louder. She began to make loud, percussive vocal sounds. I felt like she was hitting someone. Then she stopped abruptly and said, 'It's like my father's voice...he could be so judgemental of me, especially about my looks. So now I criticize myself, I'm so hard on myself, not as bad as I used to be though.'

> I comment on the quiet, slow, repetitive quality of the melody Ann was singing. I ask her what she was feeling when singing this music. She smiles and says, 'Young...like the part of me that doesn't have words yet.' I ask her if she's aware that this lullaby motif is a recurrent theme in her vocal impro-visations. She says, 'Yes...the music feels very small, I feel like I'm getting closer to the sadness in this music... I think it's connected to the sad, hungry part of me...hmmm – I have been eating a lot lately. I think I soothe myself with food when I feel this way.' I ask her to say more about 'this way'. 'Hmm, sort of empty, sad I guess...needing something or someone to fill me.'

Transferential feelings that emerged in musical interactions gave birth to insights in the following two examples from category 2:

> Marie wanted us to play the black keys on the piano and sing together. She wanted my help creating a 'musical portrait' of her mother. She began by playing and singing a simple melody in the upper register of the keyboard. I played chords to support her melody and vocally harmonized with her. Several times we sang the same note and she held it. Gradually her hands

descended down the keys until our hands were very close together. At one point we almost played the same note. Even though we were physically close, I felt a distance between us. When we processed the music, Marie said, 'It felt odd…I could see my mother, I was picturing the last time she was here visiting, she, it's confusing.' I asked her about the music. 'As I came closer to you I felt further away, I think that's what it is. My mother seems to be coming toward me but she's really pulling away. It's a mixed message!'

Cindy and I are sitting quietly together. We just improvised a capella for quite a while. Our voices blend well and we have similar taste in music so it is fun and easy to improvise with her. We sit for another moment in silence and then she begins to process the musical experience. She says, 'At times I went to a very emotional place – really sung from my gut and then a few times I went into my head and started analysing what we were doing… I have difficulty with the middle.' At first I wasn't sure what she meant but as she continued talking I understood. When she goes into her 'emotional place', it is a private world which sounds like a self-soothing kind of state. 'I realized while we were singing that it's hard to stay in my feelings and look at you – to stay connected to myself and you at the same time. I think that is the middle.' Cindy's insight led to a discussion of working to be separate yet related, something she never experienced in her family. 'If I didn't merge with my mother, I felt abandoned by her…it was basically all or nothing.'

In the next example, the symbol of the snowman that emerged in the music led Cindy to an important insight about herself (category 3):

'I should be happy but I'm feeling sad.' Cindy tells me about all the good things happening in her life right now. 'Maybe it's just unfamiliar.' We talk about the difficulty of transition and change. She says her body feels 'frozen'. We decide to make up a song together. It turns into a song about a snowman. The music is medium tempo, in B flat major. It has ninths in the melody and some dissonance. It feels sad to me. At the end of the song the snowman melts when the sun comes out. Cindy cries for several moments then blows her nose and says, 'I think I'm melting, thawing out… I'm letting good stuff in so I guess I'm feeling so much pain because I never had it until now.'

Ann finds relief when she returns to her past in an intentional musical re-creation (category 4):

Our discussion of her early feelings of inadequacy bring up a memory of when Ann had to carry a huge plate of food to the dinner table. It was Christmas and a large family gathering. Ann was six or seven. 'I told my mother it was too heavy for me but she didn't listen.' We decided to work with free associative singing. We improvised words and melodies over two minor chords (E minor 7, A minor 7). We were going back in time to that Christmas. Ann seemed anxious but wanted to work on this issue. I set a time limit of 15 minutes to help her feel safer and contained and to leave time for closure. 'I can feel the weight,' she sang at one point. 'It's too heavy for me… I'm afraid of dropping it. I'm much too small to carry this!' I repeated her words and melody. She continued to sing and then began to cry and said, 'I dropped it. Everyone is looking at me… How could you… Why did you make me carry that? I told you but you didn't listen.' During the verbal processing Ann became angry. She realized her mother never listened to her and that what I had said to her in a previous session was true. She always had too much responsibility for someone her age so she never felt adequate for the task.

In the next example, all four categories are represented. Marie projects what feels like an archetypal image of the Great Mother or the Self onto the drums. She works with images that emerge from the music and movement. She has positive transferential feelings to me in the music. And there is an intentional musical re-creation of her past that becomes a developmental journey.

Marie wants to work with the image from her dream – a small child crawling along a dark corridor. I wonder if this is the same child who has been hiding and slowly making herself known to us. I ask Marie if she'd like to sing, play instruments, dance or combine modalities. She wants me to play the drum and maybe sing and watch her dance. She wants a steady, continuous rhythm. I do as she asks. I play the conga drum. She begins on the floor huddled up with her eyes closed. Very slowly, she starts to open up and explore the space. She crawls and looks around with curiosity, her eyes wide open. I chant softly while I drum. Her dance feels like a kind of birth or rebirth and I want my music to reflect this. By the end of the dance she is standing tall with her arms open wide. She says, 'I had no idea what I would do… I felt like I was emerging from a dark, quiet place into the light. The music grounded me and called me to stay in the room and not leave – not disappear. I realized that I needed to be called forth, invited out – I couldn't just come out by myself... The drums and your voice held and called me out and I needed you to witness so I would finally feel real.'

Disconnection and connection: Feelings

The majority of my musical interventions are motivated by moments of disconnection in the client and between the client and myself. Sometimes words are not connected to feelings, sometimes emotions have no connection to meaning, sometimes the conscious mind has little or no relationship to the unconscious realm and sometimes clients simply lack a connection to their real selves.

My awareness of these instances of disconnection come primarily from my countertransferential feelings: sensing the client's lack of feeling or inauthenticity of feeling, feeling bored by their words or music, feeling confused and unable to focus, feeling a sense of emptiness or a lack of energy, and sensing moments when the clients 'leave' (dissociate) and are no longer present and in the room with me. When appropriate, I will check out my feelings and hunches with the clients. Sometimes clients are aware of their inability to connect with their feelings and with themselves and volunteer this information.

The following examples illustrate musical interventions geared towards enabling clients to connect to their feelings so that they can experience being more spontaneous, fully alive, authentic and effective. In the first example, Marie is disconnected from herself and from me. I had seen her in this kind of dissociated state before. Music usually helped her to connect to her feelings. Singing was especially effective in that it required Marie to breathe deeply. Breathing brought her into her body and put her in touch with her feelings.

> Marie complains about feeling numb. She doesn't talk much but she periodically looks at me as if searching for something. I feel a sense of emptiness – as if she is insulated inside herself and I cannot reach her. I ask her if she'd like to play or sing. She says, 'Oh, I brought that song in, the one I told you about. We could sing it.' We sing a medium tempo song about the desire to let go and live more freely. Afterwards she seems somewhat more present. I ask her if she'd like to sing it again and this time I slow down the tempo so that she might be able to feel the effect of the lyrics and the music more intensely. We begin by breathing together several times. By the middle of

the song, Marie is crying and I feel she is in the room with me and no longer dissociated.

Ann's music felt disconnected. I made a musical intervention that helped her to connect to the music and her feelings:

> Ann had a dream. She had to work late and called her boyfriend to tell him but there was too much static on the line and he couldn't hear her. I asked her if she would like to explore the dream musically and she said 'Yes…but I'm not sure what I want to play'. She began playing the steel drum then moved on to various percussion instruments. Her rhythms were erratic and the music did not flow. I began to play and sing a dissonant melody on the piano that felt right somehow. The melodic line seemed to pull the improvisation together and we got into a groove. When we processed the music, Ann said she felt panicky when she began playing. Her boyfriend is leaving town for a week and the last time he was away that long it was very difficult for her. She realized she is feeling anxious about the upcoming separation. We talk about a plan to make this separation more tolerable for her.

Cindy's words were not connected to her feelings. In the music, she was able to express her anger and feelings of empowerment and reconnect with her life energy:

> I asked Cindy how she felt when her mother kept criticizing her opinions and insinuating that her feelings made no sense. She shrugged and said she was used to it. She was tired of trying to get her mother to change. Her voice sounded flat and she seemed depressed. I wondered if she was sitting on her anger. Anger was a difficult feeling for her to express and she usually turned it against herself. I asked her if she'd be willing to explore her feelings in the music. She said 'yes' and came over to the piano. We began with free associative singing. She picked minor chords, D minor 7 to A minor 7. She sang about her mother and how tired she was of hoping for something to change between them. Gradually her voice grew louder and more energized. She complained that her mother always judged her and never saw who she really was. I was mainly harmonizing with her and mirroring her phrases. I picked up the tempo and added syncopation to the music when her voice grew stronger. A few moments later I sang, 'No more!' She repeated my lyrics and we sang this phrase together several times. She then sang, 'I've had enough!', but it was more of a yell. She banged the piano and the music became dissonant and much louder. We ended by singing 'leave me alone'

over and over again while our voices ascended the scale. Afterwards she said, 'I felt angry at first but it turned into energy, it was empowering – especially when our voices got high and strong.'

Disconnection and connection: Parts of the self

Healing involves reconnecting with lost or disowned aspects of the personality as well as differentiating feelings and dis-identifying or separating from qualities that do not belong to us; for example, realizing you are living out your parents' unlived life and not your own life. Music is invaluable in this healing process. It can open the doors to the unconscious and bring these part-personalities into awareness through images, feelings, sensations and sounds. We can then connect and interact with these parts of ourselves through primal sounds, songs and vocal improvisations. Through vocal and musical conversations we can eventually make peace and even make friends with these unknown relatives so the life force they contain can be used to enlarge and enrich the conscious personality and we can become more complete human beings.

The research revealed three categories that describe the process involved in enabling clients to connect with and eventually integrate parts of themselves that had been previously dissociated from consciousness. The categories are:

1. Awareness/Access

2. Understanding/Acceptance

3. Relating/Integrating.

The first category refers to the use of the music to gain access to the unfamiliar, unknown, aspect of the self that is ready to emerge into conscious awareness. It can emerge in a symbolic form, such as Marie's bird, or as a part-personality, such as Cindy's scared child. The client may already have an intellectual or emotional awareness of this self-aspect, but difficulty accessing it, or may not even be aware of its existence. In either case the musical intervention can provide the necessary bridge to the unconscious inner world where clients can meet lost parts of themselves. Vocal and instrumental improvisation is extremely effective in this undertaking as it can be regarded as free association in music (Austin 1996, 1998, 1999b, 2001; Streeter 1999), loosening boundaries and bypassing defences that keep the unconscious at a distance. Songs that are meaningful to the client may carry feelings related to specific parts of the self and can help the client become aware of and gain access to parts of the personality left out in the client's development (Rolla 1993).

In this example, Ann became aware (intellectually) of a part of herself she had ambivalent feelings about:

> Ann played and sang a song I had never heard before. It was very rhythmic and lively. She said it was a song sung by one of her favourite singers. She described the singer as very earthy and sensual, not the way Ann thought of herself. Afterwards we talked about these qualities she had ambivalence about – this sensual, free part of herself that felt very foreign to her. She said she could only connect to it sometimes in the music.

Marie gained access to a young child-part that was not ready to relate to her:

> Marie and I are playing the piano. I am playing chords in the key of C and she is playing the melody. She begins singing 'ah' up a third and back down again. I sing unison and then harmonize with her...she tells me she saw a small child again. The child was hiding in a cave because she felt ugly and ashamed and didn't want anyone to look at her. She needed to be cleaned up before she would come out but she wasn't ready yet.

Ann became aware of a critical part of herself and made a connection to its source:

> 'I feel like I can never do enough, no matter how hard I try something goes wrong.' I sense that this is Ann's harsh inner critic that needs depotentiating. I invite her to play or sing what she is feeling. She picks up the cowbell and hits it over and over again...it sounds so loud, so harsh and cold to me... I ask her if she can add words to the rhythm of the cowbell. Ann starts making judgemental comments about herself, then stops and says, 'I had a fleeting image of my mother looking very angry. She gets so critical of me. Sometimes I dread seeing or even talking to her on the phone... I guess, yes, it sounds kind of like her voice, that disapproving voice she has sometimes.'

The second category refers to the part of the therapeutic process when clients begin to understand and accept the newly emerging aspects of themselves. The music can help them understand the origins of these parts through the musical associations they make to significant people or early experiences in their lives (the previous example illustrated this). They can hear the truth in the music without the therapist's interpretation. The past can be called up and the 'scene of the crime' can be re-created through the sensual and aesthetic properties of music such as melody, harmony and rhythm. As clients begin to understand these previously unacknowledged or unaccepted parts and the reasons behind the rejections, they begin to experience compassion for themselves. Compassion leads to acceptance. The therapist's empathy, understanding and emotional availability in the music can provide a reparative experience.

The following examples illustrate moments in the music when clients have an experience of understanding and begin to accept more of themselves:

> I asked Marie if she could sing to or as the sick bird in her dream…during the singing she regressed to seven or eight years old, a time when she felt so depressed she wanted to die. She sang about stillness, not being able to reach out and feeling isolated. She said, 'The bird couldn't connect to the other birds so she gave up trying.'

> The singing turns into imaginal play. We are playing in the ocean, jumping over waves and getting knocked down. Cindy says her little girl is so happy. Then we are both singing as her little girl…we play tag, we run and skip, we ice skate and fall down laughing. When we process the experience Cindy says, 'I don't remember playing much as a child… I think I was very serious… I'd like to know this part of myself better, this fun part.'

Parts of the self can make themselves known through projections onto people, places and objects (including music and musical instruments) and through the symbols that emerge in dreams, songs, movies (our modern myths) and creative expression. They can also communicate with us through our bodies in the form of sensations and physical symptoms.

They can both emerge in the music and be worked with in the music. Acceptance increases as these part-personalities are interacted with. Over time, a relationship can be built with parts of the self that were hated and feared or simply unfamiliar and unknown. Clients can dialogue with these parts and come to know them through sounds or vocal improvisation, with or without words.

The examples that follow depict clients in the process of relating to and beginning to integrate parts of themselves:

> Marie said she felt tired and disoriented. I asked her if she felt like doing some breathing exercises that involved moving… I led her in an exercise. We

moved our arms and bodies up on the inhalation and down on the exhalation. She laughed and said, 'I feel like a bird.' I then suggested we add sound and take turns changing the movement and sound... Marie seemed to be enjoying herself. I was enjoying the flow and exchange of energy between us. We ended up stamping our feet and saying 'I won't'. When we finished, Marie laughed. She said 'I'm in the room now... More of me. I loved stamping and yelling, "I won't". We talked about how helpless and passive she felt growing up, how afraid she was of her father's anger and that she would have the same aggressive tendencies. Now she saw the value of using her anger to protect herself and make boundaries. She said this assertive aspect of herself was new and she wasn't used to it yet but it made her feel very hopeful and less depressed.

Cindy begins to cry. She says, 'I can see my little girl...she is scared and won't leave her room.' We continue to sing to her to comfort her and let her know she is not alone. I feel I am providing Cindy with a reparative experience through the music. Cindy and I continue singing to her little girl and letting her know she is safe now. Big Cindy and I can protect her now. When we stop singing Cindy says, 'She is ready to leave the house now and come out into the yard but she needs to stand by the tree.'

Ann once again picks the big spotted dog (stuffed animal) to represent the part of her that would like more attention. She decides to sing as the dog in a free associative improvisation. It seems the dog wants to be seen but is afraid of being judged. I sing, 'I want to be seen and appreciated.' Ann responds to these lyrics and repeats them. 'See how well I'm doing', she sings. We both sing, 'Look at me', several times. When we process the music Ann says it was frightening at first, like it's a bad thing to want attention. We talk about how she never got her needs met as a child, how she was seen as an extension of her parents. I tell her she needs attention for her real self, not just her accomplishments. I then remind her that I am going on vacation for two weeks. I ask her if she would like to take the dog home and keep him until I return. She smiles and says, 'Yes.'

Through the music and lyrics, clients can experience not only the destructive elements but also the creative aspects of various parts of the self. They can be fully present to feelings, memories and associations related to part-personalities and begin to heal the wounds that caused these aspects to split off in the first place. The therapist usually takes the lead in this process by modelling acceptance, compassion and by helping clients view devalued self-aspects from a non-judgemental vantage point.

Images that are painful become easier to relate to when they are put into a musical form. Writing a song or listening to an audiotape of an improvisation are examples of ways to simultaneously look at and work on a difficult issue, to create some distance in order to enable clients to dis-identify from an aspect of themselves they may be ashamed of. Realizing this part is not the whole of who they are often gives clients the courage to relate to it; then they may discover it has something of value to contribute to their developing sense of self, something that is worth integrating.

Reunion

Child
Secret sleeping in the snow
Frozen in time
Wrapped in a lullaby
Of longing and loss
Waiting for her to notice you are missing
Waiting for her to want you back
Waiting till she is strong enough to make the journey
Down the long winding corridors
Through the thick still night
She begins to remember where she hid you so long ago
Now with each breath
She comes a little closer
So close that somewhere between dream and wakefulness
You can hear her calling you
You can hear her calling you
Home.

Spiritual connection

Since the completion of my research study, I have continued to examine my work through my own perceptions and those of my clients as well as through transcripts of my audiotapes and case notes. Working with a larger array of clients has opened the door to previously unexplored material that is included in this book. One example is a seventh category under the theme of connection: The spiritual connection.

Sarah, a 48-year-old illustrator, described her experience of toning with me as follows:

> I felt anxious at first. Then I started to relax and let go of my fears. I was enjoying the sound of our voices coming together and then moving to different places. Then I had an odd sensation, like there was this white light flowing all through my body and an incredible feeling of peacefulness came over me. I felt like my heart was expanding and love was flowing from me, into me and all around me, like some greater being was holding me and somehow I knew everything would be all right.

Karen, mentioned earlier, now a 36-year-old architect, had been working with me for several years before she became comfortable enough to enjoy singing. In the following example she describes a powerful experience she had in a vocal improvisation:

> When we sang, I felt vulnerable, like I was a little child being comforted by a warm, soothing and invisible hand. It accepted all that I thought, felt and sang, and I felt I could surrender to it completely. Toward the end of the improvisation I saw in my mind's eye a place by the sea where I used to sit and watch the sun go down over the water in late summer evenings. I had a sensation of letting go of a pressure to keep up a brave façade. The serenity of that place filled me with a sense of consolation and I felt tears running down my cheeks. Everything was still in the image: the sea, the wind, the birds, the rosy colours and I was connected to it all. The chords that we were singing over made me feel warm and comfortable. After we stopped singing, I sat still for a while, feeling an inner serenity that was new to me. It didn't erase the upsetting experiences of my day but just made it possible for me to look at them peacefully, as if I now had the tools to accept them.

Joseph, a 32-year-old drama therapist, wrote this description of his experience of vocal psychotherapy as part of his termination process:

> I can talk circles around myself. Give me a topic and I can discuss it effortlessly off the top of my head. I am a smooth operator and sometimes even fool myself. But vocal psychotherapy helped me find a way around verbal defences. While there was time to talk and reflect, this was not the center of the experience. The center was the music. After Diane and I had introductory conversations that usually led to feelings about a particular issue, she would ask me to 'sing and/or play it.' Whereas talking often reflects what I think about an issue, music captured my feelings. I could not hide from my

feelings when I sang, played the chimes or the drums. At first it was not easy to sing in therapy. Although I loved music, I feared my voice and the tunes that might emerge. I was afraid it would make me too vulnerable and unprotected. I was afraid of being crushed. But I sang, and the little child that emerged was not crushed. He was held by the piano chords and Diane's voice and the safety of the room. The child felt free. In our sessions, I always felt the music led me, not the other way around. The music took me where I needed to go. One example of this occurred toward the end of my time in therapy. I brought in a picture of a tree that I had drawn and was surprised how much feeling it evoked. Diane began to play chords on the piano and I just allowed sounds and broken syllables to emerge. Gradually, phrases developed, like crawling toward the tree; looking for light; remembering the wind; where is this hole leading me; where am I now; I feel dirt in my fingers; crawling, pulling myself forward; I'm going deeper down; searching for the roots of a tree that would somehow lead me to the light. These images had great psychological and spiritual significance for me. They seemed to represent the basis of my work in therapy: delving deeper into the pain and obscurity in the search for new life.

Final Thoughts

The majority of the vocal interventions in this book are described as they occurred with individual clients but many of them can be adapted to group work. The theory behind vocal psychotherapy can be a lens through which to view many populations. For every person has within them their own undeniable voice waiting to be discovered, listened to and accepted. And once that voice is heard, its song can no longer be silenced.

Ideally, there would be an individual approach to therapy for every client. Although this is probably impossible, I think with an open mind and heart and a willingness to perceive the unique qualities of every person who walks through the door, something less grand but perhaps conceivable could be achieved. If therapists are willing to leave the comfort zone of diagnoses and tried and true interventions and take the leap of faith required to follow the flow of their own spontaneity, they might, together with their clients, be brave enough to embark on another kind of journey, a journey requiring no less than everything.

References

Alvarez, A. (1992) *Live Company*. New York: Routledge.

Amir, D. (1993) 'Moments of insight in the music therapy experience.' *Music Therapy 12*, 85–100.

Ansdell, G. (1995) *Music for Life: Aspects of Creative Music Therapy with Adult Clients*. London: Jessica Kingsley Publishers.

Austin, D. (1986) 'The healing symbol: sound, song and psychotherapy.' Unpublished masters thesis, New York University.

Austin, D. (1991) 'The musical mirror: music therapy for the narcissistically injured.' In K.E. Bruscia (ed.) *Case Studies in Music Therapy*. Phoenixville, PA: Barcelona, pp.291–307.

Austin, D. (1993) 'Projection of parts of the self onto music and musical instruments.' In G.M. Rolla (ed.) *Your Inner Music*. Wilmette, IL: Chiron.

Austin, D. (1996) 'The role of improvised music in psychodynamic music therapy with adults.' *Music Therapy 14*, 1, 29–43.

Austin, D. (1998) 'When the psyche sings: transference and countertransference in improvised singing with individual adults.' In K.E. Bruscia (ed.) *The Dynamics of Music Psychotherapy*. Gilsum, NH: Barcelona, pp.315–333.

Austin, D. (1999a) 'Many stories, many songs.' In J. Hibben (ed.) *Inside Music Therapy: Client Experience*. Gilsum, NH: Barcelona, pp.119–128.

Austin, D. (1999b) 'Vocal improvisation in analytically oriented music therapy with adults.' In T. Wigram and J. De Backer (eds) *Clinical Applications of Music Therapy in Psychiatry*. London: Jessica Kingsley Publishers, pp.141–157.

Austin, D. (2001) 'In search of the self: the use of vocal holding techniques with adults traumatized as children.' *Music Therapy Perspectives 19*, 1, 22–30.

Austin, D. (2002) 'The voice of trauma: a wounded healer's perspective.' In J.P. Sutton (ed.) *Music, Music Therapy and Trauma: International Perspectives*. London: Jessica Kingsley Publishers, pp.231–259.

Austin, D. (2004) *When Words Sing and Music Speaks: A Qualitative Study of In Depth Music Psychotherapy with Adults*. Ann Arbor, MI: UMI Number 3110989.

Austin, D. (2006) 'Songs of the self: vocal psychotherapy for adults traumatized as children.' In L.C. Cary (ed.) *Expressive/Creative Arts Methods for Trauma Survivors*. London: Jessica Kingsley Publishers.

Austin, D. and Dvorkin, J. (1993) 'Resistance in individual music therapy.' *The Arts in Psychotherapy 20*, 423–429.

Balint, M. (1968) *The Basic Fault*. London: Tavistock Publications.

Bannister, A. (2000) 'Prisoners of the family: psychodrama with abused children.' In F. Kellermann and M.K. Hudgins (eds) *Psychodrama with Trauma Survivors*. London: Jessica Kingsley Publishers, pp.97–113.

Blatner, A. (1988) *Foundations of Psychodrama: History, Theory and Practice*. New York: Springer Publications.

Bowlby, J. (1969) *Attachment, Volume 1*. New York: Basic Books.

Bowlby, J. (1993) *Attachment and Loss: Volume II, Separation*. New York: Basic Books.

Braddock, C.J. (1995) *Body Voices*. Berkeley, CA: Pagemill Press.

Bruscia, K. (1987) *Improvisational Models of Music Therapy*. Springfield, IL: Charles C. Thomas.

Bruscia, K.E. (1998) 'An introduction to music psychotherapy.' In K.E. Bruscia (ed.) *The Dynamics of Music Psychotherapy*. Gilsum, NH: Barcelona, pp.1–15.

Bruscia, K.E. (2001) 'A qualitative approach to analyzing client improvisations.' *Music Therapy Perspectives 19*, 1, 7–21.

Bugental, J.F.T. (1965) *The Search for Authenticity*. Toronto: Holt, Rinehart and Winston.

Campbell, D. (1989) *The Roar of Silence*. Wheaton, IL: The Theosophical Publishing House.

Carnes, P.J. (1997) *The Betrayal Bond*. Deerfield Beach, FL: Health Communications.

Claremont de Castillejo, I. (1973) *Knowing Woman: A Feminine Psychology*. New York: Harper & Row Publishers.

Clift, S.M. and Hancox, G. (2001) 'The perceived benefits of singing: findings from preliminary surveys of a university college choral society.' *Journal of the Royal Society of Health 121*, 4, 248–256.

Crowe, B.J. and Scovel, M. (1996) 'An overview of sound healing practices: implications for the profession of music therapy.' *Music Therapy Perspectives 14*, 1, 21–29.

Darnley-Smith, R. and Patey, H.M. (2003) *Music Therapy*. London: Sage Publications.

Davies, J.M. and Frawley, M.G. (1994) *Treating the Adult Survivor of Childhood Sexual Abuse*. New York: Basic Books.

Davis, M. and Wallbridge, D. (1981) *Boundary and Space: An Introduction to the Work of D.W. Winnicott.* New York: Brunner/Mazel.

Dayton, T. (1994) *The Drama Within: Psychodrama and Experiential Therapy.* Deerfield Beach, FL: Health Communications.

Dayton, T. (1997) *Heartwounds: The Impact of Unresolved Trauma and Grief on Relationships.* Deerfield Beach, FL: Health Communications.

Diaz de Chumaceiro, C.L. (1992) 'What song comes to mind? Induced song recall: transference–countertransference in dyadic music associations in treatment and supervision.' *The Arts in Psychotherapy 19,* 325–332.

Diaz de Chumaceiro, C.L. (1998) 'Unconsciously induced song recall: transference–countertransference implications.' In K.E. Bruscia (ed.) *The Dynamics of Music Psychotherapy.* Gilsum, NH: Barcelona Publishers, pp.335–363.

Dvorkin, J. (1991) 'Individual music therapy for an adolescent with borderline personality disorder: an object relations approach.' In K.E. Bruscia (ed.) *Case Studies in Music Therapy.* Phoenixville, PA: Barcelona Publishers, pp.251–268.

Dvorkin, J. (1998) 'Transference and countertransference in group improvisation therapy.' In K.E. Bruscia (ed.) *The Dynamics of Music Psychotherapy.* Gilsum, NH: Barcelona Publishers, pp.287–298.

Edinger, E. (1972) *Ego and Archetype.* New York: Penguin Books.

Eldredge, C.B. and Cole, G.W. (2008) 'Learning from work with individuals with a history of trauma.' In F.S. Anderson (ed.) *Bodies in Treatment.* New York: Analytic Press.

Ely, M., Anzul, M., Friedman, T., Garner, D. and McCormack-Steinmetz, A. (1991) *Doing Qualitative Research: Circles within Circles.* London: The Falmer Press.

Fairbairn, R. (1952) *Psychoanalytic Studies of the Personality.* London: Routledge & Kegan.

Ferenczi, S. (1988) *The Clinical Diary of Sandor Ferenczi.* Cambridge, MA: Harvard University Press.

Fraiberg, S., Adelson, E. and Shapiro, V. (1974) 'Ghosts in the nursery: a psychoanalytic approach to the problem of impaired infant–mother relationships.' *Journal of the American Academy of Child Psychiatry 14,* 3, 387–412.

Freud, S. (1910) *The Future Prospects of Psychoanalytic Therapy: Therapy and Technique.* New York: Collier.

Freud, S. (1912) 'Recommendation for physicians on the psychoanalytic method of treatment.' In *Therapy and Technique.* New York: Collier.

Freud, S. (1913) *On Beginning the Treatment.* London: The Hogarth Press.

Freud, S. (1938) *An Outline of Psychoanalysis.* New York: W.W. Norton & Company.

Frisch, A. (1990) 'Symbol and structure: music therapy for the adolescent psychiatric inpatient.' *Music Therapy 9,* 1, 16–34.

Gardner, H. (1994) *The Arts and Human Development.* New York: Basic Books.

Gardner, K. (1990) *Sounding the Inner Landscape.* Stonington, MA: Caduceus Publications.

Gass, R. and Brehony, K. (1999) *Chanting: Discovering Spirit in Sound.* New York: Broadway Books.

Gaynor, M.L. (1999) *Sounds of Healing: A Physician Reveals the Therapeutic Power of Sound, Voice, and Music.* New York: Broadway Books.

Gitelson, M. (1952) 'The emotional position of the analyst in the psychoanalytic situation.' *International Journal of Psychoanalysis 33,* 1–10.

Goldman, J. (1992) *Healing Sounds.* Rockport, MA: Element Books.

Gorkin, M. (1987) *The Uses of Countertransference.* Northvale, NJ: Jason Aronson.

Greenberg, J.R. and Mitchell, S.A. (1983) *Object Relations in Psychoanalytic Theory.* Cambridge, MA: Harvard University Press.

Greenson, R. (1967) *The Technique and Practice of Psychoanalysis.* Madison, CT: International Universities Press.

Groesbeck, C.J. (1975) 'The archetypal image of the wounded healer.' *Journal of Analytical Psychology 20,* 122–145.

Guggenbuhl-Craig, A. (1971) *Power in the Helping Professions.* Dallas, TX: Spring Publications.

Hamel, P.M. (1978) *Through Music to the Self.* Boulder, CO: Shambhala Publications.

Harkins, D. (2005) 'Healing with music.' *Caring Today.* Accessed on 25 November 2008 at www.caringtoday.com/deal-with/healing-with-music

Hartmann, H. (1952) *Essays on Ego Psychology.* New York: International University Press.

Hegeman, E. (1995) 'Transferential issues in the psychoanalytic treatment of incest survivors.' In J.L. Alpert (ed.) *Sexual Abuse Recalled: Treating Trauma in the Era of the Recovered Memory Debate.* Northvale, NJ: Jason Aronson.

Herman, J. (1992) *Trauma and Recovery: The Aftermath of Violence from Domestic Abuse to Political Terror.* New York: Basic Books.

Hudgins, M.K. and Kiesler, D.J. (1987) 'Individual experiential psychotherapy: an analogue validation of the intervention model of psychodramatic doubling.' *Psychotherapy 24,* 245–255.

Hunter, B.C. (1982) 'Singing as a therapeutic agent in the Etude 1891–1949' *Journal of Music Therapy 36,* 2, 125–143.

Jacobi, J. (1942) *The Psyhology of C.G. Jung.* London: Routledge & Kegan.

Jacobi, J. (1965) *The Way of Individuation.* New York: New American Library.

Johns Hopkins Medicine (2008) 'This is your brain on jazz: researchers use MRI to study spontaneity, creativity.' Press release. Accessed on 24 November 2008 at www.hopkinsmedicine.org/press_releases/2008/02_26_08.html

Jourdain, R. (1997) *Music, the Brain, and Ecstasy.* New York: Avon Books.

Jung, C.G. (1916) 'The psychology of the unconscious.' *The Collected Works of C.G. Jung, Volume 7.* Bollingen Series. Princeton, NJ: Princeton University Press.

Jung, C.G. (1929) 'Problems of modern psychotherapy.' *The Collected Works of C.G. Jung, Volume 16.* Bollingen Series. Princeton, NJ: Princeton University Press.

Jung, C.G. (1946) 'The psychology of the transference.' *The Collected Works of C.G. Jung, Volume 16.* Bollingen Series. Princeton, NJ: Princeton University Press.

Jung, C.G. (1951) 'Fundamental questions of psychotherapy.' *The Collected Works of C.G. Jung, Volume 16*. Bollingen Series. Princeton, NJ: Princeton University Press.

Jung, C.G. (1959) 'The archetypes and the collective unconscious.' *The Collected Works of C.G. Jung, Volume 9*. Bollingen Series. Princeton, NJ: Princeton University Press.

Jung, C.G. (1961) *Memories, Dreams, Reflections*. New York: Vintage Books.

Jung, C.G. (1968) 'Alchemical studies.' *The Collected Works of C.G. Jung, Volume 13*. Bollingen Series. Princeton, NJ: Princeton University Press.

Jung, C.G. (1969) 'The structure and dynamics of the psyche.' *The Collected Works of C.G. Jung, Volume 8*. Princeton, NJ: Princeton University Press.

Jung, C.G. (2000) *Carl Young: Wounded Healer of the Soul*. New York: Parabola Books.

Kalsched, D. (1996) *The Inner World of Trauma*. London: Routledge.

Kast, V. (1992) *The Dynamics of Symbols*. New York: Fromm International Publishing.

Kellerman, P.F. (2000) 'The therapeutic aspects of psychodrama with traumatized people.' In P.F. Kellerman and M.K. Hudgins (eds) *Psychodrama with Trauma Survivors*. London: Jessica Kingsley Publishers, pp.23–38.

Keyes, L. (1973) *Toning: The Creative Power of the Voice*. Marina del Ray, CA: DeVorss.

Klein, M. (1948) *On the Theory of Anxiety and Guilt*. New York: Delacorte Press.

Knoblauch, S.H. (2000) *The Musical Edge of Therapeutic Dialogue*. Hillsdale, NJ: The Analytic Press.

Kohut, H. (1977) *The Restoration of the Self*. New York: International Universities Press.

Krutz, G., Bongard, S., Rohrmann, S., Hodapp, V. and Grebe, D. (2004) 'Effects of choir singing or listening on secretory immunoglobulin A, cortisol and emotional state.' *Journal of Behavioral Medicine 27*, 6, 623–635.

Levine, P.A. (1997) *Waking the Tiger: Healing Trauma*. Berkeley, CA: North Atlantic Books.

Linklater, K. (1976) *Freeing the Natural Voice*. New York: Drama Book Specialists.

Little, M. (1951) 'Countertransference and the patient's response to it.' *International Journal of Psychoanalysis 32*, 32–40.

Little, M. (1981) *Transference Neurosis and Transference Psychosis*. New York: Aronson.

Lomas, P. (1987) *The Limits of Interpretation: What's Wrong with Psychoanalysis?* New York: Penguin.

Machtiger, H.G. (1992) 'Reflections on the transference/countertransference process with borderline patients.' In N. Schwartz-Salant and M. Stein (eds) *Transference/Countertransference*. Wilmette, IL: Chiron Publications, pp.119–145.

Maroda, K.J. (1991) *The Power of Countertransference*. Northvale, NJ: Jason Aronson Publishers.

Maslow, A.H. (1976) *The Further Reaches of Human Nature*. New York: Viking Press.

May, R. (1975) *The Courage to Create*. New York: W.W. Norton & Company.

McBroom, A. (1977) *The Rose*. New York: Warner-Tamerlane Pub.

McCann, I.L. and Pearlman, L.A. (1990a) 'Vicarious traumatization: a contextual model forr understanding the effects of trauma on helpers.' *Journal of Traumatic Stress 3*, 1, 131–149.

McCann, I.L. and Pearlman, L.A. (1990b) *Psychological Trauma and the Adult Survivor: Theory, Therapy and Transformation*. New York: Brunner/Mazel.

McGuire,W. and Hull, R.F.C. (1977) *C.G. Jung Speaking*. Princeton, NJ: Princeton University Press.

Miller, A. (1981) *The Drama of the Gifted Child*. New York: Basic Books.

Miller, A. (1987) *The Drama of Being a Child*. London: Virago Press.

Miller, A. (1997) *The Drama of the Gifted Child: The Search for the True Self*, revised edition. New York: Basic Books.

Minson, R. (1992) 'A sonic birth.' In D. Campbell (ed.) *Music and Miracles*. Wheaton, IL: Quest Books, pp.89–97.

Moore, B. and Fine, B. (1990) *Psychoanalytic Terms and Concepts*. New Haven, CT: Yale University Press.

Moreno, L. (1994) *Psychodrama*. McLean, VA: American Society for Group Psychotherapy and Psychodrama.

Moses, P.J. (1954) *The Voice of Neurosis*. New York: Grune & Stratton.

Murdock, M. (1990) *The Heroine's Journey*. Boston, MA: Shambhala Publications.

Nachmanovitch, S. (1990) *Free Play: Improvisation in Life and Art*. New York: Tarcher/Putnam Publishers.

Natterson, J.M. and Friedman, R.J. (1995) *A Primer of Clinical Intersubjectivity*. Northvale, NJ: Jason Aronson Publishers.

Neubauer, P.B. (1979) 'The role of insight in psychoanalysis.' *Journal of the American Psychoanalytic Association 27*, 29–40.

Neumann, E. (1955) *The Great Mother: An Analysis of the Archetype*. Princeton, NJ: Princeton University Press.

Neumann, E. (1973) *The Child*. New York: G.P. Putnam's Sons.

Newham, P. (1994) *The Singing Cure*. Boston, MA: Shambhala.

Newham, P. (1998) *Therapeutic Voicework: Principles and Practice for the Use of Singing as a Therapy*. London: Jessica Kingsley Publishers.

Nolan, P. (1998) 'Countertransference in clinical song-writing.' In K.E. Bruscia (ed.) *The Dynamics of Music Psychotherapy*. Gilsum, NH: Barcelona, pp.388–406.

Nordoff, P. and Robbins, C. (1977) *Creative Music Therapy*. New York: John Day Publishing.

Ogden, T.H. (1991) *Projective Identification and Psychotherapeutic Technique*. Northvale, NJ: Jason Aronson Publishers.

Ogden, T.H. (1994) 'The analytic third: working with intersubjective clinical facts.' *International Journal of Psychoanalysis 75*, 3–19.

Oxford University Press (OUP) (2002) *Shorter Oxford English Dictionary*. New York: Oxford University Press.

Pearlman, L.A. and Saakvitne, K.W. (1995) *Trauma and the Therapist*. New York: Norton.

Perera, S.B. (1932) *Descent to the Goddess: A Way of Initiation for Women*. Toronto: Inner City Books.

Priestley, M. (1975) *Music Therapy in Action*. St. Louis, MO: Magnamusic-Baton.

Priestley, M. (1994) *Essays on Analytical Music Therapy*. Phoenixville, PA: Barcelona Publishers.

Racker, H. (1968) *Transference and Countertransference*. New York: International Universities Press.

Reik, T. (1948) *Listening with the Third Ear*. New York: Farrar, Straus Publishers.

Reik, T. (1953) *The Haunting Melody: Psychoanalytic Experiences in Life and Music*. New York: Da Capo Press.

Reinhart, T. (1989) *Chiron and the Healing Journey*. London: Penguin Boks.

Rippere, V. and Williams, R. (1985) *Wounded Healer: Mental Health Workers' Experiences of Depression*. London: John Wiley and Sons.

Rolla, G.M. (1993) *Your Inner Music*. Wilmette, IL: Chiron Publications.

Rugenstein, L. (1992) 'Becoming a sound woman by reclaiming the power within.' In D. Campbell (ed.) *Music and Miracles*. Wheaton, IL: Quest Books, pp.208–215.

Schafer, R. (1983) *The Analytic Attitude*. New York: Basic Books.

Scheiby, B. (1998) 'The role of musical countertransference in analytical music therapy.' In K.E. Bruscia (ed.) *The Dynamics of Music Psychotherapy*. Gilsum, NH: Barcelona Publishers, pp.213–247.

Schwartz-Salant, N. (1989) *The Borderline Personality: Vision and Healing*. Wilmette, IL: Chiron Publications.

Searles, H.F. (1979) *Countertransference and Related Subjects*. New York: International Universities Press.

Sedgwick, D. (1994) *The Wounded Healer: Countertransference from a Jungian Perspective*. London: Routledge.

Singer, E. (1970) *Key Concepts in Psychotherapy*. New York: Basic Books.

Spolin, V. (1963) *Improvisation for the Theater*. Evanston, IL: Northwestern University Press.

Stein, M. (1992) 'Power, shamanism, and maieutics in the countertransference.' In Schwartz-Salant and Stein (eds) *Transference-Countertransference*. Wilmette, IL: Chiron Publications, pp.67–87.

Stern, D. (1977) *The First Relationship: Infant and Mother*. New York: Open Books.

Stewart, R.W. and Stewart, D. (2002) 'See me, hear me, play with me: working with the trauma of early abandonment and deprivation in psychodynamic music therapy.' In J.P. Sutton (ed.) *Music, Music Therapy and Trauma*. London: Jessica Kingsley Publishers, pp.133–152.

Stolorow, R.D., Brandchaft, B. and Atwood, G.E. (1987) *Psychoanalytic Treatment: An Intersubjective Approach*. Hillsdale, NJ: Analytic Press.

Storr, A. (1992) *Music and the Mind*. New York: The Free Press.

Streeter, E. (1999) 'Definition and use of the musical transference relationship.' In T. Wigram and J. DeBacker (eds) *Clinical Applications of Music Therapy in Psychiatry*. London: Jessica Kingsley Publishers, pp.84–101.

Taylor, D.B. (1997) *Biomedical Foundations of Music as Therapy*. Saint Louis, MO: MMB Music.

Terr, L. (1990) *Too Scared to Cry*. New York: Basic Books.

Tomatis, A. (1991) *The Conscious Ear: My Life of Transformation Through Listening*. New York: Station Hill Press.

Turry, A. (1998) 'Transference and countertransference in Nordoff–Robbins music therapy.' In K.E. Bruscia (ed.) *The Dynamics of Music Psychotherapy*. Gilsum, NH: Barcelona Publishers, pp.161–212.

Turry, A. (2001) 'Supervision in the Nordoff–Robbins music therapy training program.' In M. Forinash (ed.) *Music Therapy Supervision*. Gilsum, NH: Barcelona Publishers, pp.351–377.

Turry, A. (2006) *The Connection between Words and Music in Music Therapy Improvisation: An Examination of a Therapist's Method*. New York University: AAT3247771.

Tyson, F. (1981) *Psychiatric Music Therapy: Origins and Development*. New York: Fred Weidner & Son.

Ulanov, A. (1971) *The Feminine in Jungian Psychology and in Christian Theology*. Evanston, IL: Northwestern University Press.

van der Kolk, B. (ed.) (1987) *Psychological Trauma*. Washington, DC: American Psychiatric Press.

van der Kolk, B.A. (1989) 'The compulsion to repeat the trauma.' *Psychiatric Clinics of North America 12*, 389–411.

Warming, P. (1992) 'Psyche and sound: the use of music in Jungian analysis.' In D. Campbell (ed.) *Music and Miracles*. Wheaton, IL: Quest, pp.230–241.

Weinberger, N. (1996) 'Sing, Sing, Sing!' *Musica Research Notes III*, 2, 2–6.

Winnicott, D.W. (1965) *The Maturational Process and the Facilitating Environment*. London: Hogarth Press.

Winnicott, D.W. (1971) *Playing and Reality*. London: Routledge.

Woodman, M. (1982) *Addiction to Perfection*. Toronto: Inner City Books.

Woodman, M. (1985) *The Pregnant Virgin*. Toronto: Inner City Books.

Yalom, I.D. (1989) *Love's Executioner and Other Tales of Psychotherapy*. New York: Basic Books.

Yalom, I.D. (2002) *The Gift of Therapy*. New York: HarperCollins Publishers.

Subject Index

abandonment/abandonment complex
  and countertransference case example
    96, 103
  and countertransference disclosure 108
  and free associative singing case example
    167, 168
  and Jungian psychology case example
    47, 49
  and songs 179, 180–1, 186, 188
  and trauma theory 63, 65
abuse *see* child abuse; criticism; judgemental
    abuse; physical abuse; sexual abuse;
    verbal abuse
acting 12
  see also psychodramatic singing
adaptive/false self
  and countertransference 91
  and free associative singing 163
  and object relations theory 53, 57, 58
  and resistance in vocal psychotherapy
    125, 126
  and trauma theory 68–9
adolescents 182, 183
adult children
  intuitiveness 53–4, 92, 93
  play in trauma recovery 77, 78
  therapists 92–3
  unmet emotional needs 55, 59, 64, 67,
    84, 92, 93, 101–2, 142, 165–6,
    191, 196, 197–8, 199–200
Akiko 161
alter ego 70–2, 160, 173, 174
altered states of consciousness 31, 197
  see also dreams; possession; regression;
    therapeutic regression; trance
alternate nostril breathing exercise 26–7
anger
  in connection in vocal psychotherapy
    case examples 205–6, 209
  in countertransference case examples 90,
    102–3, 107, 108
  in intersubjectivity case example 84
  and music of the speaking voice 33–4
  personal history of author 81
  and songs 181
  in trauma theory case examples 72,
    74–5
  in vocal improvisation case examples
    140, 144–5
animals, and resourcing 167, 168
Ann
  connection in vocal psychotherapy case
    examples 196, 197, 198, 199–200,
    202–3, 205, 207, 209
  countertransference case examples 95–6,
    97, 98, 102–3, 107–8, 109
  free associative singing case example
    159
  trauma theory case example 67–72
  vocal holding techniques case examples
    147, 149, 150

voice case example 33–5
apologizing 101–2
archetypes 42, 43, 44, 45, 65, 158
  see also good-enough mother; great
    mother; mother archetypes; patient
    archetype; positive mother
    archetype; tree archetype; wounded
    client; wounded healer
assessment 114–17
associations, in songs 178–9, 180–1
attachment *see* attachment trauma; mother
    and child connection; positive
    attachment
attachment trauma 62–3, 64, 152
audiotape analysis, and music of the
    speaking voice 33–7
authentic client-therapist relationship 54–5,
    82, 83, 86, 105, 109–10

babbling 22, 148, 149
babies 21–3, 148, 149
beginning a practice
  assessment 114–17
  case examples 115, 117, 118–19
  layers of listening 119–21
  Between the Lines 121–2
  music and words 118–19
  personal history of author 113
  setting the stage 113–14
  warm-up 117
Between the Lines 121–2
blood pressure 21
bodily sensations, awareness of 30–1, 74,
    99, 108, 119, 120, 121, 157, 197
  see also disembodiment; embodiment
body-centred therapeutic approach 61, 62
body issues 20, 30–1
body language *see* non-verbal
    communication
body-mind connection 60–2, 98, 108, 132,
    160–1
body-mind split 47, 132, 160
bonding *see* mother and child connection
brain 21, 22, 137–8
breathing deeply
  and connection in vocal psychotherapy
    204–5, 208–9
  in countertransference 99, 108
  diving deep and surfacing in
    countertransference 99
  and emotional release 19
  and free associative singing 158, 159
  and grounding 168, 173
  and music of the speaking voice 34
  and psychodramatic singing 173
  and resourcing 165, 168, 175
  and singing 20
  and toning 134
  in trauma theory case examples 69, 72,
    74
  use as vocal intervention 132–3

and vocal holding techniques 151, 155,
    157
  in vocal improvisation case example 143
  in voice case example 32
  and voice reconnection 24–7
  and warm-up 117
breathing exercise 26–7
Brenda 171–2

case examples
  beginning a practice 115, 117, 118–19
  breathing deeply 132–3
  connection in vocal psychotherapy
    196–7, 198–200, 201–6, 207,
    208–9, 211–12
  countertransference 89–91, 95–6, 97,
    98, 99, 101–3, 104, 105–9
  free associative singing 159, 161,
    162–4, 167–70, 171–2, 173–5
  intersubjectivity 82–4, 85, 87
  objects relations theory 56–9
  parts of the self, archetypes and
    complexes in Jungian psychology
    44, 47–51
  psychodramatic singing 173–5, 176–7
  resistance in vocal psychotherapy 125,
    126, 128, 129–30
  resourcing 166, 167–70
  songs 180–1, 184, 186–8, 189–91
  toning 133–4
  trauma theory 64, 67–72, 74–8
  vocal holding techniques 146–8,
    149–51, 153–7
  vocal improvisation 140–5
  voice 31–2, 33–7
catharsis *see* emotional release
central nervous system 22
centring 26, 61, 99, 117
chakras 30
chanting 135–6, 140
child abuse 23, 24, 56, 58, 64–5, 84,
    142–5
  see also judgemental abuse; physical
    abuse; sexual abuse; verbal abuse
child development 21–3, 52–4, 148
  see also developmental arrests
children
  and lost voice 23–4
  responsibility 64, 68, 74, 92, 203
  unmet emotional needs 52, 53, 54, 58,
    64, 68, 71, 92, 154, 199–200
  see also adult children; child
    development; developmental arrests;
    gifted children; intuitive children;
    mother and child connection
chills
  and breathing deeply 132
  and connection in vocal psychotherapy
    197
  and countertransference 96, 107, 109
  and listening 121

and toning 30, 31
and vocal holding techniques case
example 154–5
choice 151, 168, 176
Cindy
connection in vocal psychotherapy case
examples 197, 199, 201, 202,
205–6, 209
countertransference case examples 90–1,
97, 98, 101–2, 108, 109
free associative singing case examples
159, 167–70
psychodramatic singing case example
173–5
resourcing case examples 167–70
songs case example 189–90
trauma theory: case example 74–8
vocal holding techniques case example
147–8, 150–1
vocal improvisation case examples 140,
150–1
voice case examples 17–19, 36–7
client–therapist relationship 79–80, 110,
114–15, 118–19, 146, 194–8
see also authentic client–therapist
relationship; collaboration;
intersubjectivity
clients
individual needs in vocal psychotherapy
159, 213
insights 73, 106, 128, 180, 181, 200–4
need to connect to therapists 196–8
responsibility 41, 59, 82
songs from 190–1
see also adult children; client–therapist
relationship; intersubjectivity
collaboration 81–3, 103
collective unconscious 41–2
complementary identification 88, 90
complexes 42–4, 66
see also abandonment/abandonment
complex; negative mother complex;
power complex
concordant identification 88–9, 91
connection in vocal psychotherapy
case examples 196–7, 198–200, 201–6,
207, 208–9, 211–12
client's insights 200–4
client's need to connect to therapist
196–8
and disconnection: feelings 204–6
and disconnection: parts of self 206–10
Reunion 210
spiritual connection 210–12
themes 193–4
therapist's inner process 198–200
therapist's need to connect 194–6
consciousness
and client's need to connect to therapist
196
and collaboration in music 103
and complexes 44
concept in Jungian psychology 42
diving deep and surfacing in
countertransference 96–7, 98
and layers of listening 120
and singing 45
and songs 188
and vocal improvisation 136, 137,
140–1
countertransference
case examples 89–91, 95–6, 97, 98, 99,
101–3, 104, 105–9
and connection in vocal psychotherapy
196, 199–200, 204–5
definitions and concepts 39–40, 88–9,
90–1
disclosure 105–10
diving deep and surfacing 96–100
e-countertransference 89, 91, 143–4
and free associative singing 158, 160,
163–4
and human instrument 91–2, 99–100
and intersubjectivity 83
Jungian psychology case examples 48,
51

and music of the speaking voice 33–5
and object relations theory 54, 57–9
and projective identification 54
and songs 183, 185, 187–8, 189
and therapist's hook 101–4
and trauma theory 63–4, 67
and vocal holding techniques 149, 157
and wise wound 92–6, 100
Courtney 171–2
creative arts therapy 55, 61
creativity 82, 136–8, 145, 147
criticism 58, 106, 115–16, 125, 144, 157
see also self-criticism
crying
and connection in vocal psychotherapy
205, 209
and connection with feelings 205
in countertransference case examples 96,
104
emotional release through singing 13,
19
in free associative singing case examples
168–9, 172
in intersubjectivity case example 84
in Jungian psychology case example 49,
50
and mother and child connection 21, 23
in object relations theory case example
57
in psychodramatic singing case examples
175, 177
and songs 178, 181, 187–8
in trauma theory case example 71, 75,
77
in vocal holding techniques case
examples 150
in vocal improvisation case example
143–4
and warm-up 117
culture 161

Deb 134
defence mechanisms 63, 65, 72
see also denial; dissociation; projective
identification; resistance in vocal
psychotherapy
denial 47
depression 17, 36–7
developmental arrests 147, 148, 152, 153
dis-identification 44–5, 98–9, 128, 144,
206, 210
disclosure 105–10
see also self-disclosure, of therapist
disconnection
and connection of feelings 204–6
and connection with part of the self
206–10
and countertransference case examples
102, 103, 106
personal history of author 194–6
and vocal holding techniques 152
disembodiment 35, 60, 69, 107, 162,
198–9
see also embodiment
dissociation
and breathing deeply 132–3
concept in Jungian psychology 42
and connection in vocal psychotherapy
198–9
and countertransference case example
102, 103
and disconnection and connection of
feelings 204–5
and disconnection and connection of
parts of the self 206–7
and free associative singing case example
162
and music of the speaking voice 35–6
and song case example 186, 188
and trauma 63
and vocal holding techniques 152–3,
155, 156
and vocal improvisation case example
142
diving deep and surfacing, in
countertransference 96–100

Donna 56–9
dopamine 21
'double' 70–2, 160, 173, 174
dreams
and connection in vocal psychotherapy
case example 203–4, 205, 208
and countertransference case example
96, 104
and improvisation case example 142–5
and intersubjectivity case example 82–3
and Jungian psychology 40, 42, 65
and songs case example 191
and trauma theory case example 74–8
and vocal holding techniques 152, 154,
155–6
and voice case example 17–19
drumming
and connection in vocal psychotherapy
201, 203–4, 205
in countertransference case examples 90,
91, 107
and diving deep and surfacing in
countertransference 99
and empowerment 136, 205
in object relations theory case example
57
in trauma theory case example 75–7
in vocal improvisation case examples
140, 144, 145

e-countertransference 89, 91, 143–4
ear 21, 22, 120
see also listening
early childhood trauma 60–2, 63
eating disorders 30–1
ego
and complexes 44, 45
concept in Jungian psychology 42
diving deep and surfacing in
countertransference 98–9
and free associative singing 165
and singing 45
and songs 191
and trauma theory 64, 65, 78
and vocal holding techniques 147
embodiment 36, 50, 60, 98, 133, 166, 194
see also disembodiment
Emily 23
emotional blocks 23–4
emotional release
and breathing deeply 19
and complexes 42–3
and rocking 19
and singing 12–13, 19, 20, 97–8
and songs 180–1
and toning 134
and trained musicians/vocalists 18–19,
36, 37
and trauma theory 66, 73
and vocal connections between mother
and child 22, 23
empathic failures 101–2, 147
empathy
and connection in vocal psychotherapy
195–6, 197–8
and countertransference 92, 93–4,
95–7, 100, 103–4
e-countertransference 89, 91, 143–4
and free associative singing 160
and intersubjectivity 83, 92
and object relations theory case example
58–9
and songs 184
and supervision of therapists 170
and trauma theory case example 68, 70,
72–3
and vocal holding techniques case
example 157
and wounded healers 92, 93–4, 95–6
see also empathic failures
empowerment
and chanting 135, 136
and choice 151, 168
and drumming 136, 205
and intersubjectivity 82
and resourcing 165, 166, 168, 186

empowerment *cont.*
  and singing 31, 47, 205–6
  and songs 181
  and vocal improvisation 140
empty chair 175–7
endorphins 21
energy blocks 20
energy levels 124
energy release
  and complexes 44, 45
  and connection in vocal psychotherapy
    205–6, 209
  and natural sound exercises 28
  and singing 20, 45, 97–8, 205–6
  and toning 29–30
  and vocal holding techniques 147
  and vocal improvisation case example
    140
  and voice case study 32
essence statements 160, 187
exercises, using natural sounds 28–9
exhalation 27, 133, 165, 209
eye contact 17, 22, 133, 143, 151

false/adaptive self *see* adaptive/false self
fathers, negative 90
fear
  and resistance in vocal psychotherapy
    125, 126, 127, 128–9
  and vocal improvisation case examples
    142, 143–4, 145
feelings
  in assessment 116
  disconnection and connection 204–6
  essence statements 160, 187
  and exhalation 27
  and free associative singing 160, 161,
    162, 163, 168–72
  and layers of listening 119, 120, 121
  and natural sound exercises 28–9
  point of entry 127, 143
  and singing 19, 20
  and songs 20, 178, 179, 180–1, 183,
    184, 185, 187–8
  and supervision of therapists 170,
    171–2
  and therapist's need to connect 194
  and toning 30, 31, 134
  and vocal holding techniques 146–7,
    153, 154–5
  and vocal improvisation case examples
    140–1, 142, 143–4, 145
femininity 50, 125, 130, 156
fetus 22
Fred 84, 85, 87
free association 141, 158
free associative singing
  adaptations 164–5
  case examples 159, 161, 162–4,
    167–70, 171–2, 173–5, 176–7
  client's insight 201, 203
  described 158–61
  empty chair 175–7
  and feelings 160, 161, 162, 163,
    168–70
  psychodramatic singing 173–7, 201,
    203–4
  resourcing 165–70
  in supervision 170–2
  and vocal holding techniques 153,
    158–9, 161, 165
Freudian psychology 39, 66, 88, 120, 141,
    158, 200

gaze 148
generational trauma 61–2
gifted children 52–4, 56–9, 68–72
good-enough mother 50, 51, 64, 77, 132,
    187–8
gratitude list 165
great mother 50, 51, 203
groaning 23, 27, 32, 75, 133
Groesbeck's therapeutic approach 41
grounding
  and breathing deeply 168, 173, 186
  and chanting 136

diving deep and surfacing in
  countertransference 99
  and music 117
  and resourcing 165, 168, 186
  and vocal holding techniques 150–1,
    156, 157
group cohesion 135
Guggenbuhl-Craig's therapeutic approach
    40–1

harmonization
  and client's insight 201
  in countertransference case example 98
  in free associative singing 162, 165,
    168–9, 171, 172
  in intersubjectivity case example 84
  and psychodramatic singing 175
  in trauma theory case examples 70,
    75–6
  and vocal holding techniques 149–50,
    156
  in vocal improvisation case examples
    140–1, 144
heart rate 20, 21, 134
Henry 125
honesty 84, 85, 105
  see also authentic client-therapist
    relationship; trust
human instrument 91–2, 99–100
humility 82

identification 88–9, 90, 91, 93–4, 95–6
  see also dis-identification; identity;
    projective identification
identity 160, 163, 194
imagery 27
immune system 21
individual needs of client in vocal
  psychotherapy 159, 213
individuation
  and connection in vocal psychotherapy
    198
  and countertransference 95
  in Jungian psychology 28, 38, 44–5,
    50–1
  and songs 178, 184
  of therapists 81
  and vocal holding techniques 149–51
  and vocal improvisation 138
induction 39, 89
information withholding 85
inhalation 27, 133, 209
inhibitions 20, 28, 56, 57
inner persecutor 65
inner soundtrack 184–8
insight
  of clients 73, 106, 128, 180, 181,
    200–4
  of therapists 19, 100, 102, 120,
    198–200
  see also self-knowledge; therapeutic
    regression
instruments *see* drumming; human
    instrument; musical instruments
intersubjectivity
  case examples 82–4, 85, 87
  described 80–2, 83, 84–6
  and empathy 83, 92
  personal history of author 79–81
  therapist's self-disclosure 85, 86–7
intimacy
  and client's need to connect to therapist
    196–8
  and countertransference 97
  and countertransference disclosure 105
  and intersubjectivity 82
  and music 92
  and resistance in vocal psychotherapy
    125–7
  and songs 179
  and therapist's need to connect 194
  and therapist's self-disclosure 86
  and toning 30, 31
  and trauma 63
  and vocal holding techniques 151
  and vocal improvisation 97–8

intuition 92, 95–6, 118–20, 160
intuitive children 52–4, 58, 92–3

jazz musicians 137–8
Jenna 87
Jill 117
Jon 134
Joseph 146–7, 211–12
judgemental abuse 43, 44
Julie 180–1
Jungian psychology
  and client-therapist relationship 80, 110
  concepts 39–40
  countertransference 39–40, 89
  and creativity 138
  and femininity 130
  and learning 91–2
  participation mystique 39–40, 49, 58,
    89, 97
  parts of the self, complexes and
    archetypes 38, 41–51
  case examples 44, 47–51
  Song in Three Parts, A 45–6
  see also archetypes; complexes; parts of
    the self
  personal history of author 12, 38–9
  shadow archetype 81, 125, 145, 198
  and trauma theory 66
  wounded healer 40–1
  see also wounded client; wounded healer

Karen 132–3, 211
Klein's psychological theories 54, 58, 89
knowledge 40, 88, 100, 136, 160–1, 166,
    200
  see also insight; learning; self-awareness;
    self-knowledge

language 161
  see also non-verbal communication;
    symbolic language; verbal
    processing; words
laughter 21, 23, 27, 35
Lauren 134
learning 83, 91–2, 170–2
Leslie 184
Levine's somatic experiencing therapeutic
  approach 61, 62
life histories 180
  see also personal history of author
listening 22, 33–7, 119–21, 153, 179–80,
    181–4
Liz 142–5, 186–8
loss 102, 103, 104–5, 179, 180–1, 188
  see also abandonment/abandonment
    complex; separation
lost voice 23–4, 107, 134–5
lullabies 50, 51, 78, 108, 161, 175, 188–9,
    201
Lynn 126–7, 128
lyrics 20, 83, 84, 104–5, 116
  see also songs

Marie
  beginning a practice case example
    118–19
  connection in vocal psychotherapy case
    examples 196–7, 198–9, 201–2,
    203–5, 207, 208–9
  countertransference case example 97,
    98, 104–5, 106–7, 108–9
  free associative singing case examples
    159
  intersubjectivity case example 87
  psychodramatic singing case example
    176–7
  vocal holding techniques case examples
    148, 149–50
  vocal improvisation case example 140–1
  voice case example 35–6
Mary 117
Meg 126, 189
memories *see* remembering
Michelle 162–4

Miller's psychological theories 52–3, 54–5, 92–3
mind 119, 120, 121
    see also mind-body connection; mind-body split; thinking; verbal processing
mind-body connection 60–2, 98, 108, 132, 160–1
mind-body split 47, 132, 160
mirroring
    defined 18
    and free associative singing 158, 160–1, 162, 163, 165, 169
    in Jungian psychology case example 50
    and mother and child connection 148
    and resourcing 166
    in song case example 187
    in trauma theory case examples 70, 76
    and vocal holding techniques 150, 156
    in vocal improvisation case examples 141, 144
moaning 27, 32, 75, 82, 133, 165
modelling 28, 29, 50, 109, 209–10
mother and child connection
    and attachment trauma 62–3
    and object relations theory 54, 56–9
    and songs 179
    and vocal holding techniques 148, 149, 150–1, 152
    and voice 21–3, 148, 149
mother archetypes 44, 50, 58, 130
    see also good-enough mother; great mother; positive mother archetype
mother tongue 161
mother transference 50–1, 58
movements 28–9, 125, 151
    see also psychodramatic singing; rocking
muscular activity 20
    see also movements
music
    and archetypes 45
    and client's insight 201
    and client's resistance in vocal psychotherapy 126–7
    and complexes 43
    and intimacy 92
    and layers of listening 119, 120–1
    and object relations theory 55
    personal history of author 11, 195
    and safe environments 80
    in the speaking voice 17, 23, 24, 32–7
    and spiritual connection 211–12
    and therapist's resistance 130
    and trauma recovery 63, 78
    in vocal psychotherapy practice 118–19
    and warm-up 117
    see also drumming; jazz musicians; lullabies; lyrics; music therapy; musical ability, criticism of; musical countertransference disclosure; musical history, in assessment; musical hook; musical improvisation; musical instruments; professional musicians/vocalists; singing; songs; voice
music therapy 19–21, 182, 183
musical ability, criticism of 115–16
musical countertransference disclosure 107–8
musical history, in assessment 115–17
musical hook 104–5
musical improvisation 116–17, 124, 137–8, 201
musical instruments 32, 114, 124, 141, 201, 203–4
    see also drumming; voice

name game 29
Nan 181
narcissism 129, 190
natural sounds 11–12, 19, 22, 27–9, 90, 120–1, 125, 133, 149
    see also crying; groaning; moaning; screaming; sighing; toning

needs see unmet emotional needs; individual needs of client in vocal psychotherapy
negative father transference 90
negative mother complex 44, 50, 144, 145
nervous system 20
neuromuscular activity 20
neutrality 79, 103, 105, 171
newborn babies 21–2
non-authoritarian style 82, 124
non-verbal communication 114–15, 119, 120, 196
    see also eye contact; gaze; movements; physical distancing; physical proximity; postural straightening; touch
numbness 56, 63, 69, 73, 102, 204
    see also disconnection; dissociation

object relations theory
    case example 56–9
    described 52–6
objects 167, 168, 176–7, 179–80, 189
opioids 21

Pam 30–1
parallel woundedness 103–4
parents
    trauma 61–2
    unmet emotional needs 52–3, 58, 71, 140, 147, 154, 191
    see also child abuse; mother archetypes; mother transference; negative father transference; negative mother complex
participation mystique 39–40, 49, 58, 89, 97
parts of the self
    archetypes and complexes, concepts 42–5
        see also archetypes; complexes
    concept 41–2
    disconnection and connection 206–10
    and psychodramatic singing 176–7
    and singing 45–6
    and trauma 65
    and vocal improvisation 140–1
    see also consciousness; ego; unconscious
passivity 102, 103, 209
patient archetype 40–1
people 167, 168, 175–6
perfectionism
    and countertransference case example 106
    and object relations theory 53, 56–7, 58
    and trauma theory 64, 67–8
    and vocal holding techniques case examples 147, 154, 157
personal experiences, and self-disclosure of therapist 87
personal history of author
    acting 12
    anger 81
    beginning a practice 113
    disconnection and need to connect 194–6
    as gifted child 52
    intersubjectivity 79–81
    Jungian analysis 12, 38–9
    music 11, 195
    natural sounds 11–12
    singing 11, 12, 154, 195
    songs 178–9, 182–4
    teaching singing 12–13
    trauma and body–mind connection 60–2
    Turtle Bay Music School music therapy programme 182, 183
    vocal psychotherapy 13, 181–4
    'washing the day off' 100
Peter 64, 165
pets, and resourcing 167, 168
Phyllis 128, 141, 176
physical abuse 43, 56, 58, 132–3
physical arrangement of room 113–14
physical distancing 97, 98–9

physical proximity 97, 148, 197, 198, 202
physical resistance 124
physical sensations see bodily sensations, awareness of
play 55, 56, 77, 78, 109, 152, 153
pleasure 21–2, 27, 30–1, 197
point of entry 127, 143
positive attachment 63
positive attribute affirmations 165
    see also resourcing
positive mother archetype 50, 51, 91, 152, 153, 169–70
possession 43
post-traumatic stress disorder (PTSD) 47–51, 61–2, 199
postural straightening 99, 104
power complex 43
professional musicians/vocalists 20, 28, 130, 137–8
    see also Ann; Cindy; Donna; Emily; Vicky
projective identification
    concept 42, 47, 54, 89, 91
    and connection in vocal psychotherapy 201
    in countertransference 90, 91, 97
    and object relations theory case example 58–9
    and psychodramatic singing 175–7
    and songs 179
psychic infection 39, 89, 90, 103
psychodramatic singing 173–7, 201, 203–4
psychological blocks 23
psychological growth 80–1, 110, 149–50
    see also intersubjectivity
psychological history, in assessment 115
psychosomatic illness 153–7

questioning 117
    see also assessment

re-enactment 49, 63, 65–7, 70–2, 73
    see also regression; retraumatization; therapeutic regression
reflection 148, 160
regression 49, 124–5, 126, 129, 149
    see also re-enactment; retraumatization; therapeutic regression
relationships 208–10
    see also authentic client-therapist relationship; client-therapist relationship; intersubjectivity; intimacy; mother and child connection
relaxation 27
religion 135, 167, 168
    see also spirituality
remembering 19, 20, 66–7, 70–2, 180
repeated singing of a song 179
repeated traumas 62
repetition see mirroring; re-enactment; repeated singing of a song; repeated traumas; repetition compulsion; retraumatization
repetition compulsion 66
resistance in vocal psychotherapy
    case examples 125, 126, 128, 129–30
    in the music 126–7
    and silence 85, 129–30
    to singing 124–6
    in song case example 186
    theories 123–4
    therapist's resistance 129–30
    and vocal improvisation 125, 126–7, 141, 143
    working through 127–9
resourcing 165–70, 175, 179, 186
responsibility
    children 64, 68, 74, 92, 203
    clients 41, 59, 82
    therapists 83, 101
retraumatization 49, 73, 75, 93, 108, 199
Reunion 210
risk-taking 56, 59, 82, 97–8, 106, 138
rocking 19, 48, 50, 147, 151, 152, 155–6, 187

room, physical arrangement 113–14

Safe Enough to Sing 191–2
safe environments
    beginning a practice 113–14
    and connection in vocal psychotherapy
        196
    and intersubjectivity 80
    and music 80
    and play 55, 56
    and resourcing 167, 168
    and songs 179
    and trauma recovery 62–3
    and vocal holding techniques 146, 148,
        151, 157
    and vocal improvisation 55, 56
Sandy 83–4, 134, 146
Sara 167
Sarah 211
screaming
    and connection between mother and
        child 21
    and countertransference 94
    and emotional release 12–13, 17, 18, 19
    as natural sound 27, 29
    personal history of the author 11–12
    and trauma 75, 199
    in vocal improvisation case examples
        143, 145
Sedgwick's therapeutic approach 41, 80
self
    diving deep and surfacing in
        countertransference 98–9
    and free associative singing 158, 160–1,
        163–4, 165
    and intersubjectivity 79
    and Jungian psychology 38
    and layers of listening 119–21
    and object relations theory 54
    and resistance in vocal psychotherapy
        125, 126
    and therapist's resistance 130
    and trauma theory 63, 64, 72, 77, 78
    and vocal connection between mother
        and child 23
    and vocal holding techniques 146–7,
        149
    and voice 21
    and voice case example 32
    see also adaptive/false self; parts of the
        self; true self
self-acceptance 129, 131, 161, 207–8, 210
self-awareness 81, 82, 91–2, 93, 160,
        206–7
    see also bodily sensations, awareness of
self-criticism
    of musical ability in assessment 115
    and parts of the self, archetypes and
        complexes 44, 207
    and resistance in vocal psychotherapy
        125
    self-awareness of 207
    and silence as abuse 84
    and trauma theory 64, 68
    and vocal holding techniques case
        example 154
self-destructive behaviour 64
self-disclosure, of therapist 85, 86–7, 109
self-esteem
    and authentic client-therapist
        relationship 55
    and connection in vocal psychotherapy
        196
    and free associative singing 161, 165
    and object relations theory case example
        59
    and therapist's resistance 130
    and trauma 64
self-examination 166, 200
self-expression 132, 137–8, 145, 147
    see also creativity
self-knowledge 86, 91–3, 185, 200
    see also insight
self-supervision 33–7
sensuality 30, 31
separation 149–51, 167, 179–80, 188, 205

    see also abandonment/abandonment
        complex; loss
sexual abuse 65, 75, 78, 108, 168
sexual energy blocks 20
shadow archetype 81, 125, 145, 198
sharing countertransference 105–10
sighing 23, 25, 27, 82, 165
sight 148
silence
    as abuse 84
    and connections in vocal psychotherapy
        198
    and countertransference case example
        107
    emotional blocks and lost voice 23–4,
        35, 107
    following vocal psychotherapy 19, 157,
        172, 184, 202
    and layers of listening 120
    and resistance in vocal psychotherapy
        85, 129–30
    and warm-up 117
singing
    ability in assessment 115–16
    child communication 22
    and client's insight 201
    and connection of feelings 204
    and emotional release 12–13, 17–19,
        19, 20, 97–8
    and empowerment 31, 47, 205–6
    and energy release 20, 45, 97–8, 205–6
    importance in music therapy 19–21
    personal history of author 11, 12, 154,
        195
    resistance in vocal psychotherapy 124–6
    and spiritual connection 211, 212
    and therapist's resistance 130
    see also free associative singing;
        professional musicians/vocalists;
        psychodramatic singing; songs;
        voice
single blow traumas 62
small talk 117
So-Jin 134–5
somatic countertransference disclosure 107,
        108–9
somatic experiencing therapeutic approach
        61, 62
Song in Three Parts, A 45–6
songs
    in assessment 116
    case examples 180–1, 184, 186–8,
        189–91
    from clients 190–1
    and feelings 20, 178, 179, 180–1, 183,
        184, 185, 187–8
    and free associative singing 161, 167
    inner soundtrack 184–8
    listening to 179–80, 181–4
    personal history of author 178–9,
        182–4
    Safe Enough to Sing 191–2
    significance 179–81
    Song in Three Parts, A 45–6
    from therapists 188–90
sounds, natural *see* natural sounds
speaking voice 17, 23, 24, 32–7
spirituality 135, 136, 137, 167, 210–12
splitting 47, 132, 160
spontaneity
    and intersubjectivity 82
    and natural sounds 133
    and object relations case example 58, 59
    and resistance in vocal psychotherapy
        125
    and risk-taking 113
    and songs 185, 189
    and vocal holding techniques 147, 153
    and vocal improvisation 55–6, 98, 137
stress release 21
Sue 134, 190–1
supervision 170–2
    see also self-supervision
Susan 47–51
Suzy 31–2
symbiosis 94–5, 104, 149

symbolic language 136, 141, 154
symbolism 178–9, 180–1, 201, 202,
        203–4

teaching singing, in personal history of
        author 12–13
tempo, and working through resistance 128
Terry 44
therapeutic regression
    and connection in vocal psychotherapy
        203–4, 208
    and free associative singing 163–4
    and intersubjectivity 80
    and Jungian psychology case example
        49
    and songs case example 187–8
    and vocal holding techniques 146–7,
        152, 153, 156–7
    and vocal psychotherapy in trauma
        recovery 66–7, 70–2, 75–8
therapist-client relationship *see*
        client-therapist relationship
therapists
    ability to play 55
    as adult children 92–3
    free associative singing in supervision
        170–2
    as good-enough mother 50, 51, 64, 77,
        132, 187–8
    individuation 81
    inner processes and making connections
        198–200
    insights 19, 100, 102, 120, 198–200
    intersubjectivity 79–86
    meeting the unmet emotional needs of
        adult child 55, 59, 67
    need to connect in vocal psychotherapy
        194–6
    neutrality 79, 103, 105, 171
    as positive mother 50, 51, 91, 152, 153,
        169–70
    psychological growth 80–1
    resistance 129–30
    responsibility 83, 101
    self-awareness 81, 82, 91–2, 93
    self-disclosure 85, 86–7, 109
    songs from 188–90
    vicarious traumatization 73
    as wounded healers 40–1, 92–6, 100,
        103–4, 194, 196
therapist's hook 58–9, 101–4
thinking 99, 134
    see also mind; verbal processing
toning
    in countertransference case examples
        108
    resistance in vocal psychotherapy 125
    and spiritual connection 211
    in trauma theory case example 75
    use as vocal intervention 133–4
    in vocal holding techniques case
        example 156–7
    in vocal improvisation case example 142
    and voice 29–31, 32, 134–5
touch 22, 197
    see also physical proximity
toys 167, 168, 176–7
trance 137, 147, 162–3, 176
transference
    client's insight 201–2, 203–4
    client's need to connect to therapist 196
    concept in Jungian psychology 39
    and free associative singing 158
    and Jungian psychology case example
        48, 50–1
    and object relations theory 54, 57
    and projective identification 54
    and songs 179, 183–4, 185
    and trauma theory 63–4, 67
    and vocal holding techniques 149
transitional objects 179–80, 189
trauma
    and complexes 42–3
    countertransference 63–4
    effects 62–6
    and energy blocks 20

and inhibitions 56
in musical history assessment 115–17
and object relations theory 54
parents 61–2
personal history of author 60–2
and psychic numbing 56, 63
and repeated singing of a song 179
and screaming 75, 199
singing and energy release 20
transference 63–4
types 60–3
and vocal holding techniques 147, 154, 155
and vocal improvisation 55–6
see also post-traumatic stress disorder (PTSD); trauma dreams; trauma recovery; trauma theory; trauma vortex
trauma dreams 154
trauma recovery 63, 66–7
trauma theory
case examples 64, 67–72, 74–8
effects of trauma 62–6
and empathy 68, 70, 72–3
trauma recovery 62–3, 66–7
trauma types 60–3
trauma vortex 43, 61
tree archetype 50–1, 168–70, 212
true self
and connection in vocal psychotherapy 208–9
and countertransference 91
and free associative singing 160, 164
and object relation theory 53, 55, 56, 59
and songs 188
and trauma theory 77
trust
and authentic client-therapist relationship 55
and connection in vocal psychotherapy 197
and countertransference disclosure 105
and intersubjectivity 80, 82, 83
and object relations theory case example 59
and resistance in vocal psychotherapy 127, 129
and therapist's self-disclosure 86
and trauma theory 63, 71
and vocal holding techniques 153
and vocal improvisation 138
and wounded healers 93–4
Turtle Bay Music School music therapy programme 182, 183

unconscious
and collaboration in music 103
and complexes 43, 44
concept in Jungian psychology 42
and connection in vocal psychotherapy 196, 199
disconnection and connection 206–7
diving deep and surfacing in countertransference 97, 98
and free associative singing 158, 160
and layers of listening 120
and songs 179, 184–5, 188
and therapist's need to connect 194
and vocal holding techniques 146–7, 152, 153, 154, 157
and vocal improvisation 136, 137, 140–1
see also countertransference; transference
understanding 129, 170, 207–8
unison singing
and client's insight 201–2
in countertransference case example 98
and free associative singing 159, 162, 165, 168–9, 171, 172
in intersubjectivity case example 83–4
in Jungian psychology case example 48
in object relations theory case example 58
and psychodramatic singing 175
in trauma theory case examples 70, 76

and vocal holding techniques 149, 150, 156
and vocal improvisation case examples 140–1, 144
in voice case examples 18–19, 32
unmet emotional needs
of adult children 55, 59, 64, 67, 84, 92, 93, 101–2, 142, 165–6, 191, 196, 197–8, 199–200
of children 52, 53, 54, 58, 64, 68, 71, 92, 154, 199–200
of parents 52–3, 58, 71, 140, 147, 154, 191
of therapists 92, 93

verbal abuse 43, 44, 56, 58, 132–3, 157
verbal countertransference disclosure 106–7
verbal processing 126, 129, 181, 203
see also mind; thinking; words
vibrations
diving deep and surfacing in countertransference 100
and fetus 22
and importance of singing 19
and toning 30, 31, 134
vicarious traumatization 73, 93
Vicky 153–7
vocal holding techniques
case examples 146–8, 149–51, 153–7
client types, appropriateness for 146–51
described 146–9
and free associative singing 153, 158–9, 161, 165
reasons for using 153
in song case example 186
stages 149–51
vocal improvisation
case examples 140–5
and client's insight 201–4
in countertransference case examples 90, 95–6, 97, 98, 99, 102, 107–8
diving deep and surfacing 97
and intersubjectivity 80, 82–4
and intimacy 97–8
in Jungian psychology case example 48–9
in object relations case example 57–9
and power complex 43
resistance in vocal psychotherapy 125, 126–7, 141, 143
and resistance in vocal psychotherapy 125, 126–7, 141
and safe environment 55
in song case example 186
and spiritual connection 211
and spontaneity 55–6, 98, 137
in trauma theory case examples 69–72, 74–7
use as a vocal intervention 136–8, 140–1
vocal holding techniques *see* vocal holding techniques
vocal interventions
chanting 135–6
natural sounds 27–9, 32, 90, 133
see also breathing deeply; toning; vocal improvisation
vocal psychotherapy
final thoughts 213
personal history of author *see* personal history of author
practice *see* beginning a practice; connection in vocal psychotherapy; free associative singing; resistance in vocal psychotherapy; songs; vocal holding techniques; vocal interventions
purpose 131–2
theory *see* countertransference; intersubjectivity; Jungian psychology; object relations theory; trauma theory; voice
voice
in assessment 115–16
case examples 17–19, 31–2, 33–7

connection between mother and child 21–3
lost voice 23–4, 35, 107, 134–5
and mother and child connection 21–3, 148, 149
music in the speaking voice 17, 23, 24, 32–7
natural sounds 27–9
as primary instrument in music therapy 19–21
reconnection: breathing deeply 24–7
and resistance in vocal psychotherapy 125
and therapist's resistance 130
and toning 135
see also natural sounds; singing; toning; vocal improvisation
Voices on Voice 138–40
vowel sounds *see* toning

warm-up 117
'washing the day off,' personal history of author 100
wise wound *see* wounded healer
words
and free associative singing 158, 160–1, 162, 163, 164
and layers of listening 119, 120–1
and vocal holding techniques 149
and vocal psychotherapy practice 118–19
see also language; lyrics; verbal processing
wounded client 94–5, 103–4
wounded healer 40–1, 92–6, 100, 103–4, 194, 196

yoga 30
Yuriko 166

Author Index

Adelson, E. 62
Alvarez, A. 36, 95, 106
Amir, D. 200
Ansdell, G. 82, 118
Atwood, G.E. 86
Austin, D. 23, 24, 25, 26, 28, 39, 41, 42,
    43, 63, 65, 80, 83, 85, 93, 103,
    125, 126, 129, 130, 136, 137, 141,
    143, 146, 147, 151, 155, 173, 184,
    187, 206

Balint, M. 67, 181
Blatner, A. 175, 176
Bowlby, J. 63, 148
Braddock, C.J. 25, 26
Brandchaft, B. 86
Brehony, K. 135
Bruscia, K.E. 124, 180
Bugental. J.F.T. 123–4

Campbell, D. 29, 135
Chumaceiro, C.L. Diaz de *see* Diaz de
    Chumaceiro, C.L.
Claremont de Castillejo, I. 98
Clift, S.M. 21
Cole, G.W. 62
Craig, A. Guggenbuhl- *see*
    Guggenbuhl-Craig, A.

Davies, J.M. 54, 63, 65, 66, 89, 105–6
Davis, M. 109
der Kolk, B.A. van *see* van der Kolk, B.A.
Diaz de Chumaceiro, C.L. 185
Dvorkin, J. 85, 125, 126, 129, 130, 143,
    179, 187

Edinger, E. 42, 66
Eldredge, C.B. 62
Ely, M. 193

Fairbairn, R. 64–6
Fine, B. 39, 54, 89, 123, 179, 200
Fraiberg, S. 62, 66
Frawley, M.G. 54, 63, 65, 66, 89, 105–6
Freud, S. 66, 88, 120, 158, 200
Friedman, R.J. 80, 82, 105, 109
Frisch, A. 183

Gardner, H. 149
Gardner, K. 26, 30
Gass, R. 135
Gaynor, M.L. 21, 25, 26, 30
Gitelson, M. 105
Goldman, J. 29, 30
Greenberg, J.R. 54
Greenson, R. 66, 83
Groesbeck, C.J. 41
Guggenbuhl-Craig, A. 40–1, 92, 93

Hamel, P.M. 30
Hancox, G. 21
Harkins, D. 21
Hartmann, H. 183
Herman, J. 60–1, 63, 66, 83, 86, 147, 186
Hudgins, M.K 160, 165, 173
Hull, R.F.C. 45

Jacobi, J. 28, 42, 200
John Hopkins Medicine 137–8
Jourdain, R. 20
Jung, C.G. 28, 39–40, 42–3, 58, 66, 80,
    81, 89, 91–2, 103, 110

Kalsched, D. 53, 62, 63, 65, 66, 80, 154,
    200
Kast, V. 42, 43, 51, 66
Keyes, L. 20, 29–30
Kiesler, D.J. 160, 165, 173
Klein, M. 54, 58, 89
Knoblauch, S.H. 32, 34
Kohut, H. 79, 80, 83
Kolk, B.A. Van der *see* van der Kolk, B.A.

Levine, P.A. 20, 43, 61, 165, 186
Linklater, K. 24
Little, M. 84, 105

Machtiger, H.G. 48, 67, 94–5
Maroda, K.J. 81, 83, 84, 95, 104, 105
Maslow, A.H. 138
McBroom, A. 104
McCann, I.L. 66, 73, 86
McGuire, W. 45
Miller, A. 22, 24, 52–4, 57, 68, 83, 84–5,
    92–3, 154, 190
Minson, R. 22, 23
Mitchell, S.A. 54
Moore, B. 39, 54, 89, 123, 179, 200
Moreno, L. 160, 173, 175
Moses, P.J. 22, 23, 25, 32
Murdock, M. 50

Nachmanovitch, S. 100, 137
Natterson, J.M. 80, 82, 105, 109
Neumann, E. 51
Newham, P. 20, 23, 26, 148
Nolan, P. 179, 185
Nordoff, P. 118

Ogden, T.H. 54, 80, 89
Oxford English Dictionary, Shorter (OUP) 135

Pearlman, L.A. 66, 73, 86, 92, 93, 105, 109
Perera, S.B. 97
Priestley, M. 33, 85, 89, 100, 124, 143,
    181

Racker, H. 39, 88–9
Reik, T. 32, 120, 185
Rippere, V. 93
Robbins, C. 118
Rolla, G.M. 184–5, 207
Rugenstein, L. 27

Saakvitne, K.W. 86, 92, 93, 105, 109
Scafer, R. 82
Schwartz-Salant, N. 89
Searles, H.F. 84, 92, 95
Sedgwick, D. 39, 40, 41, 58, 80, 92, 93,
    96, 103–4, 105
Shapiro, V. 62
Spolin, V. 55, 137
Stein, M. 103
Stolorow, R.D. 86
Streeter, E. 85, 141, 206

Taylor, D.B. 22
Terr, L. 62
Tomatis, A. 22, 148
Turry, A. 85, 137, 138, 141
Tyson, F. 181

van der Kolk, B.A. 61, 63, 66

Wallbridge, D. 109
Warming, P. 121
Williams, R. 93
Winnicott, D.W. 22, 53, 54, 55, 57, 64, 66,
    80, 83, 148, 179
Woodman, M. 20, 26, 66

Yalom, I.D. 83, 99, 109, 110

23340484R00126

Made in the USA
Middletown, DE
23 August 2015